ABA Section of
International Law
Your Gateway to International Practice

NAVIGATING EU PRIVACY AND DATA PROTECTION LAWS

W. GREGORY VOSS AND KATHERINE WOODCOCK

Cover design by Andrew Alcala/ABA Publishing.

The materials contained herein represent the opinions of the authors and/or the editors and should not be construed to be the action of either the American Bar Association or the Section of International Law unless adopted pursuant to the bylaws of the Association.

Nothing contained in this book is to be considered as the rendering of legal advice, either generally or in connection with any specific issue or case. Nor do these materials purport to explain or interpret any specific bond or policy, or any provisions thereof, issued by any particular insurance company, or to render insurance or other professional advice. Readers are responsible for obtaining advice from their own lawyer or other professional. This book and any forms and agreements herein are intended for educational and informational purposes only.

19 18 17 16 5 4 3 2 1

Library of Congress Cataloging-in-Publication Data is on file with the Library of Congress

Discounts are available for books ordered in bulk. Special consideration is given to state bars, CLE programs, and other bar-related organizations. Inquire at ABA Publishing, Book Publishing, American Bar Association, 321 N. Clark Street, Chicago, Illinois 60610.

www.ShopABA.org

Table of Contents

PREFACE

Privacy and data protection laws in Europe are distinct from privacy laws in the United States, both in their history and focus. Generally, Europe developed its body of laws in a broader sense, as omnibus legislation, and not on a sector-by-sector basis of legislation such as that in the United States.[1] This has been driven forward by the (mis)use of information during World War II, and in certain European countries (such as Germany, Spain, and France) sensitivity with respect to data protection runs high. One American scholar speaks of U.S.–Western Europe "significant privacy conflicts."[2] He describes a divide in which privacy in Western Europe is an aspect of dignity, and privacy in the United States is an aspect of personal liberty.[3]

The Organisation for Economic Co-operation and Development (OECD) Guidelines, discussed later, and European national laws developed in the 1970s spurred the proliferation of data protection laws in Europe. Despite the many differences in these rules, they exhibited substantial similarities.[4] The main legislative text on data protection in Europe is the Directive 95/46/EC on data protection (the Directive).[5] It sets out the basic principles of data protection and—as a European Union directive—requires that the various European Union Member States[6] (Member States) implement its rules into their national legal system, generally through the respective Member States' parliaments adopting national legislation. Under European Union primary law—in this case, Article 288 of the Treaty on the Functioning of the European Union (TFEU), as in force today—it is left up to the "national authorities" of the Member States to choose the "form and methods" of the implementation of directives.[7] Inevitably,

---

1. *See* Paul M. Schwartz, *The EU-U.S. Privacy Collision: A Turn to Institutions and Procedures*, 126 HARV. L. REV. 1966, 1974 (2013).

2. James Q. Whitman, *The Two Western Cultures of Privacy: Dignity versus Liberty*, 113 YALE L. J. 1151, 1155 (2004).

3. *Id.* at 1161.

4. For a concise and exhaustive global overview of data protection and privacy laws, *see* Hon. Michael Kirby, ch. 1: *Remarks on the 30th Anniversary of the OCED Privacy Guidelines, in* OECD, THIRTY YEARS AFTER THE OECD PRIVACY GUIDELINES, http://www.oecd.org/sti/interneteconomy/49710223.pdf.

5. Directive 95/46/EC of the European Parliament and of the Council of 24 Oct. 1995 on the protection of individuals with regard to the processing of personal data and on the free movement of such data, 1995 O.J. (L 281) 31 (Nov. 23, 1995), *available at* http://eur-lex.europa.eu/LexUriServ/LexUriServ.do?uri=CE LEX:31995L0046:en:HTML.

6. There are 28 member states. For the full list, see http://europa.eu/about-eu/countries/member-countries/index_en.htm.

7. *See* Consolidated Version of the Treaty on the Functioning of the European Union, art. 288, at 171–72, May 9, 2008, 2008 (C 115) 47, http://eur-lex.europa.eu/LexUriServ/LexUriServ.do?uri=OJ:C:2008:115:00 47:0199:EN:PDF.

this leads to a degree of variation in laws between countries. Similarly, the European Union's neighbors in the European Economic Area (EEA)[8] and Switzerland adopted similar legislation following the provisions of the Directive but again without achieving complete uniformity. For the purposes of this book, the term "EU" will be used, but it is important to know that the EEA contracting party nations and Switzerland are not EU Member States; however, they do share fundamental principles found in the Directive.

Today, the main challenges for global businesses and companies lie in compliance with the varying requirements under EU national law. Compliance is even more burdensome for companies that do not have dedicated privacy compliance personnel within their organizations and for companies without sufficient resources and time to ensure such compliance. This book aims to present the various concepts for EU privacy and data protection law in a comprehensible manner, providing analysis of the existing law and practical advice on how to approach data privacy compliance. This book does not seek to give detailed advice on every EU Member State's specific national legislation or to point out all the differences from one Member State to another; however, where this information is readily available or easy to communicate, it will be included.

Finally, it is important to highlight that the Directive is currently under review and many important points will change with the introduction of the new law. As currently proposed by the European Commission (Commission), the new law will take the form of an EU regulation[9]—the General Data Protection Regulation (GDPR)—which, unlike a directive, will be directly applicable in all Member States. As such, Member States will not need to pass their own national laws in order to give these laws in effect—instead, the provisions ofthe GDPR will have direct effect in the Member States. In proposing the GDPR, the Commission seeks to ease compliance burdens for businesses (e.g., notification obligations to the local authorities and the obligation to comply with different national laws) and bring a higher level of uniformity and comprehensive coverage to the EU's approach to data protection. With these goals in

---

8. The European Economic Area (EEA) is formed among the nations that are parties to the Agreement creating the EEA signed on May 2, 1992 (entered into force on Jan. 1, 1994), and is comprised of 27 of the 28 Member States of the European Union together with Iceland, Liechtenstein, and Norway (as of this writing, the procedure for finalizing the accession of Croatia was well underway, which when complete, would mean that the EEA includes all 28 current Member States). *See* this Agreement at 1994 O.J. (L 1) 3 (Jan. 3, 1994), http://eur-lex.europa.eu/LexUriServ/LexUriServ.do?uri=OJ:L:1994:001:0003:0522:EN:PDF. *See also* http://ec.europa.eu/world/agreements/prepareCreateTreatiesWorkspace/treatiesGeneralData.do?s tep=0&redirect=true&treatyId=1; *see also* http://eeas.europa.eu/eea.

9. Proposal for Regulation of the European Parliament and of the Council on the Protection of Individuals with regard to the Processing of Personal Data and on the Free Movement of such Data (General Data Protection Regulation) COM (2012) 11 final (Jan. 25, 2012), http://ec.europa.eu/justice/data-protection/document/review2012/com_2012_11_en.pdf. NB: References herein to the GDPR are to the version originally proposed by the European Commission, and not to any subsequent draft proposed by the European Parliament, the Council, or any of their respective committees.

mind, the GDPR will substantially change the EU framework on data protection and privacy and shift the substance of companies' compliance burdens. When important differences exist between the Directive and the GDPR, this will be indicated at the end of each relevant section in a separate box. Of course, the differences indicated are based on the Commission's draft proposed regulation from 2012 and do not necessarily reflect those in the final legislation. This information is provided to permit some insight into the eventual requirements of the GDPR, keeping in mind that the GDPR is still in the drafting phase and has not been adopted.

1

Introduction to EU Privacy and Data Protection

I. RELEVANT LEGISLATIVE INSTRUMENTS AND TREATIES

To properly understand EU privacy and data protection laws and requirements, it is important to understand the essential EU legislative instruments and relevant treaties. In the European Union, privacy and data protection are fundamental rights, meaning that they cannot be waived or contracted away. It is also important to note the difference between a right to privacy and a right to protection of one's data. These two concepts are closely linked both in their history and development of legislative instruments. Nevertheless, they are distinct concepts. This book will focus on data protection law and privacy law as applied to companies in the private sector operating or offering goods or services in Europe. This section will introduce the fundamental legal instruments and treaties, specifically the EU's enshrinement of privacy and data protection as a fundamental right, the Council of Europe's Convention 108 (Convention 108),[1] the OECD Guidelines on the Protection of Privacy and Transborder Flows of Personal Data (OECD Guidelines),[2] both in their original form and the version as amended on July 11, 2013 (Revised OECD Guidelines),[3] and finally the Directive.

A. Privacy and Data Protection as Fundamental Rights

The right to data protection is intimately associated with the right to privacy. The Council of Europe first adopted the European Convention on Human Rights[4]

---

1. Convention for the Protection of Individuals with regard to Automatic Processing of Personal Data, Jan. 28, 1981, ETS No. 108 [hereinafter Convention 108], as amended, full text and protocol *available at* http://www.conventions.coe.int/Treaty/en/Treaties/Html/108.htm.

2. *OECD Guidelines Governing the Protection of Privacy and Transborder Flows of Personal Data*, Sept. 23, 1980, C(80)58/FINAL [hereinafter *OECD Guidelines*], *available at* http://www.oecd.org/internet/ieconomy/oecdguidelinesontheprotectionofprivacyandtransborderflowsofpersonaldata.htm.

3. *OECD Guidelines*, as amended on July 11, 2013 by C(2013)79 [hereinafter *Revised OECD Guidelines*]; for full text, *see* http://www.oecd.org.sti/ieconomy/2013-oecd-privacy-guidelines.pdf.

4. European Convention for the Protection of Human Rights and Fundamental Freedoms, Nov. 4, 1950, as amended and supplemented (ECHR) [hereinafter ECHR], http://www.echr.coe.int/Documents/Convention_ENG.pdf.

(ECHR), which established a right to privacy. This right to privacy protects individuals against invasion of their personal life by public authorities unless it meets certain conditions specified in the law.[5] This was followed by the right to the protection of one's data, initially presented in Convention 108. This right was further enshrined within the European Union in the Charter of Fundamental Rights of the European Union (Charter), Article 8,[6] which provides:

Protection of personal data

1. Everyone has the right to the protection of personal data concerning him or her.
2. Such data must be processed fairly for specified purposes and on the basis of the consent of the person concerned or some other legitimate basis laid down by law. Everyone has the right of access to data which has been collected concerning him or her, and the right to have it rectified.
3. Compliance with these rules shall be subject to control by an independent authority.

The right to privacy as established in Article 7 of the Charter is a right to "respect for private and family life: everyone has the right to respect for his or her private and family life, home and communications."[7] The Charter became legally binding on all Member States on December 1, 2009, with the entry into force of the Treaty of Lisbon, which made the ECHR legally binding in the European Union as well.

B. Convention 108

Convention 108 was the first binding international treaty in the field of data protection. It has been adopted by the European Union, by many European countries, and increasingly by non-European jurisdictions[8] and is open to accession by international organizations.[9] It was drafted with the aim of developing "common core of substan-

---

5. ECHR, art. 8, provides: "Right to respect for private and family life. 1. Everyone has the right to respect for his private and family life, his home and his correspondence. 2. There shall be no interference by a public authority with the exercise of this right except such as is in accordance with the law and is necessary in a democratic society in the interest of national security, public safety or the economic well-being of the country, for the prevention of disorder or crime, for the protection of health or morals, or for the protection of the rights and freedoms of others."

6. Charter of Fundamental Rights of the European Union, Dec. 7, 2000, 2010 O.J. (C 83) 389 (Mar. 30, 2010), art. 6, at 393, http://eurlex.europa.eu/LexUriServ/LexUriServ.do?uri=OJ:C:2010:083:0389:0403:EN:PDF.

7. *Id.* art. 7, at 393.

8. For example, Uruguay, which is not a member of the Council of Europe, has ratified the Convention 108. For a full list of signatories and the status of ratification, *see* http://conventions.coe.int/Treaty/Commun/ChercheSig.asp?NT=108&CM=1&DF=&CL=ENG.

9. *See* modernized version of Convention 108, art. 23, http://www.coe.int/t/dghl/standardsetting/dataprotection/TPD_documents/TPD%282012%2904Rev4_E_Convention%20108%20modernised%20version.pdf.

tive law" in order to unify data protection principles in the law of the Council of Europe's members.[10] Specifically, Convention 108 seeks to secure individual fundamental freedoms and rights in privacy and in the automatic processing of personal data, drawing on Article 8 of the ECHR. The inclusion of these freedoms and rights creates a level of uniformity between Convention 108 signatory states, particularly in light of cross-border data flows.

Convention 108 applies to the ratifying countries and its scope extends to automated personal data files and the automatic processing of personal data—both in the private and the public sector.[11] It establishes minimum standards for the protection of individuals that arises from collecting and using their personal data. Convention 108 targets automated files, as they have greater computing power and speed to perform a wider variety of transactions, as opposed to manual or paper files. Further, recognizing the flow of data across borders, the Council of Europe proposed an Additional Protocol obligating members to establish supervisory authorities to oversee data protection.[12]

In 2012, Convention 108 underwent a modernization, maintaining its original core principles, but being revised to account for new challenges arising from the use of new technologies (Modernization Text). It also seeks to strengthen the follow-up mechanism for multilateral cooperation by expanding the tasks of the Consultative Committee (renamed the Convention Committee under the Modernization Text) and the powers and independence of supervisory authorities.[13] The Modernization Text will come into force between three and four months (depending on the date of ratification) after five members of the Council of Europe have signed and ratified the text, and it will enter into force for members also between three and four months (depending on the date of deposit) after depositing the final instrument.[14]

C. OECD Guidelines

On September 23, 1980, shortly before the publication of Convention 108, the OECD Guidelines were adopted. In light of the new technological developments and the ability to quickly transmit data (internationally), the OECD developed the OECD Guidelines (and later, the Revised OECD Guidelines) to help harmonize national legislation on privacy and data flows. The Revised OECD Guidelines aim

---

10. *See* Explanatory Report to the Convention 108, art. 23. Full text *available at* http://conventions.coe. int/Treaty/EN/Reports/HTML/108.htm.

11. Convention 108, art. 3.1.

12. Additional Protocol to Convention 108 regarding Supervisory Authorities and Transborder Data Flows (ETS No. 181) (Nov. 8, 2001), *available at* http://conventions.coe.int/Treaty/EN/Treaties/Html/181.htm.

13. Consultative Committee of the Convention for the Protection of Individuals with regard to Automatic Processing of Personal Data, *Final Document on the Modernisation of Convention 108*, Dec. 18, 2012, TPD(2012)04 rev2, http://www.coe.int/t/dghl/standardsetting/dataprotection/TPD_documents/TPD%282012%2904Rev4_E_Convention%20108%20modernised%20version.pdf.

14. *Id.* art. 22, at 11.

to protect the privacy of individuals while at the same time taking into account the possibilities that varying restrictions and national legislation could restrain the free flow of personal data and disrupt important economic activity. The Revised OECD Guidelines lay out core principles forming the basis of modern global data protection and privacy legislation: collection limitation, data quality, purpose specification, use limitation, security safeguards, openness, individual participation, and accountability.[15]

D. EU Directive

Borrowing concepts from the Convention 108 and the OECD Guidelines, the European Union drafted and negotiated the Directive, which was finally adopted in 1995. Other complementary legal instruments on data protection and privacy are in place within the European Union. One such instrument is the e-Privacy Directive,[16] which establishes the protection of privacy within the electronic communications sector. There is also the Framework Decision on the protection of personal data in the framework of police and judicial cooperation in criminal matters,[17] which is beyond the scope of this book. As mentioned, the Directive is currently undergoing a revision. This was first announced by the Commission in November of 2010.[18] Subsequently, a public consultation was held on the issue, which culminated in the proposed draft General Data Protection Regulation (GDPR).[19] This text was then reviewed in detail by the Parliament's Committee on Civil Liberties, Justice and Home Affairs ("LIBE Committee") and its draft amendments were formally adopted by the Parliament on March 12, 2014.[20] The EU Council finally established

---

15. *Revised OECD Guidelines*, paras. 7–14, at 14–15.

16. Directive 2002/58/EC of the European Parliament and of the Council of 12 July 2002, concerning the processing of personal data and the protection of privacy in the electronic communications sector (Directive on privacy and electronic communications), 2002 O.J. (L 201) 37, (July 31, 2002) [hereinafter e-Privacy Directive], as amended by Directive 2009/136/EC of the European Parliament and of the Council of 25 November 2009 amending Directive 2002/22/EC on universal service and users' rights relating to electronic communications networks and services, Directive 2002/58/EC concerning the processing of personal data and the protection of privacy in the electronic communications sector, and Regulation (EC) No 2006/2004 on cooperation between national authorities responsible for the enforcement of consumer protection laws, 2009 O.J. (L 337) 11.

17. Council Framework Decision 2008/977/JHW of 27 November 2008 on the protection of personal data processed in the framework of police and judicial cooperation in criminal matters, 2008 O.J. (L 350) 60, Dec. 30, 2008), http://eur-lex.europa.eu/LexUriServ/LexUriServ.do?uri=OJ:L:2008:350:0060:0071:EN :PDF.

18. Communication, European Comm'n, *A Comprehensive Approach on Personal Data Protection in the European Union*, Nov. 4, 2010, COM (2010) 609 final, http://ec.europa.eu/health/data_collection/docs/com_2010_0609_en.pdf.

19. *See* Proposal for Regulation of the European Parliament and of the Council on the Protection of Individuals with regard to the Processing of Personal Data and on the Free Movement of such Data (General Data Protection Regulation) COM (2012) 11 final (Jan. 25, 2012), http://ec.europa.eu/justice/data-protection/document/review2012/com_2012_11_en.pdf.

20. *See* Progress on EU Data Protection Reform Now Irreversible following European Paliament Vote (March 12, 2014), http://europa.eu/rapid/press-release_MEMO-14-186_en.htm.

its common position on all points of the GDPR on June 15, 2015, which allowed the beginning of a "trilogue" between the EU Council, the Parliament and the Commission on the GDPR text.[21] More on the GDPR progress is outlined at the end of this book in Chapter 8.

II. KEY TERMS AND DEFINITIONS

Terms from the Directive are defined in ways that require further guidance to understand the legislation, its application, and the rights and obligations arising under it. Much of such guidance is provided through opinions and recommendations of the European Union's Article 29 Data Protection Working Party (the Working Party), an independent advisory panel created under Article 29 of the Directive. By issuing advice and guidance through its opinions and recommendations, the Working Party seeks to harmonize EU privacy laws between Member States.[22] The Working Party is composed of, inter alia, representatives of the data protection authorities of each of the Member States. Working Party guidance, which may take the form of opinions or working documents, may also be referred to by practitioners to anticipate Member State application of the Directive to new issues, such as those raised by data processing for new uses or using new technologies. Nevertheless, it is important to keep in mind that the Working Party's guidance is merely a recommendation and is not binding (although it could be persuasive).

This section develops a few of the relevant key terms and their definitions, which are referred to throughout this text and are crucial to understanding EU privacy jargon.

A. Personal Data

The Directive defines "personal data" as:

> [A]ny information related to an identified or identifiable natural person ("data subject"); an identifiable person is one who can be identified, directly or indirectly, in particular by reference to an identification number or to one or more factors specific to his physical, physiological, mental, economic, cultural or social identity.[23]

---

21. Press Release, Eur. Comm'n, Commission Proposal on New Data Protection Rules to Boost EU Digital Single Market Supported by Justice Ministers (June 15, 2015), http://europa.eu/rapid/press-release_IP-15-5176_en.htm. For a comprehensive overview of the GDPR's legislative developments, *see* http://www.huntonregulationtracker.com/legislativescrutiny/.

22. *See Article 29 Working Party*, European Comm'n, *available at* http://ec.europa.eu/justice/data-protection/article-29/index_en.htm.

23. Directive 95/46/EC of the European Parliament and of the Council of 24 Oct. 1995 on the protection of individuals with regard to the processing of personal data and on the free movement of such data [hereinafter Directive], 1995 O.J. (L 281) 31 (Nov. 23, 1995), art. 2(a), at 38.

A clear understanding of this definition is crucial as it establishes the perimeter of application of the Directive. Acknowledging the uncertainty surrounding this definition, the Working Party issued an opinion on the definition in 2007 (WP 136).[24] WP 136 highlights that the definition of personal data is intended to be broad, aimed at protecting individuals' right to privacy. It divides the definition into four "blocks": "any information," "relating to," "an identified or identifiable," and "natural person."[25] We will take up each of these blocks individually to better understand when data or information qualifies as personal data.

1. "Any Information"

The broad term "any information" is analyzed by its nature, content, and format.

With respect to its nature, it is meant to cover both "objective" and "subjective" information (whether the information is "information, opinions or assessments") about an individual. An example of objective information could include the "presence of a certain substance in one's blood"; and an example of subjective information could be information on the creditworthiness of a borrower.[26] There is no requirement that the information be true or factual to qualify under this block.

In terms of content, this covers "data providing any sort of information." This could include information about a person's private or family life, his or her work life or economic and social behavior, as well as "sensitive data" about that person. An example given by the Working Party is information about drug prescriptions (whether with respect to an individual prescription or as a pattern of prescription history), which can constitute personal data about a patient (perhaps revealing sensitive information about the person's health) or about a doctor (showing work behavior).[27]

Finally, the format in which the information is found may take any form. WP 136 includes information on paper, in computer memory, in digital code, on videotape, and in textual, numerical, graphical, acoustic, or photographic forms. Examples given include audiotapes of voices recorded during telephone banking (one can think of the countless times one has heard "this call may be recorded for quality control purposes"), recognizable images of individuals on videotape for surveillance, and even a child's drawing to the extent that it may indicate his or her psychiatric health or parents' behavior.

This block also includes biometric data, such as "fingerprints, retinal patterns, facial structure, voices . . . hand geometry, vein patterns," as well as behavioral characteristics such as keystrokes or handwritten signatures. This data can be classified as both content and as a link between certain information and a specific individual.[28]

---

24. Working Party, *Opinion 4/2007 on the Concept of Personal Data* (WP 136) (June 20, 2007), http://ec.europa.eu/justice/policies/privacy/docs/wpdocs/2007/wp136_en.pdf.
25. *Id.* at 4–6.
26. *Id.* at 6.
27. *Id.* at 6–7.
28. *Id.* at 7–8.

2. "Relating to"

In order to relate to a person, data must include one of the following elements: "content," *or* "purpose" *or* "result."[29] We will take each of these alternative elements in order.

Information satisfies the content element test if it is about a particular individual, as determined on a case-by-case basis. For example, smart passports with RFID chips would contain information about the person whose passport it is.

The purpose element is fulfilled if the information is used, or is likely to be used, taking into consideration the facts of the case, "with the purpose to evaluate, treat in a certain way or influence the status or behavior of an individual." One example of a case with a purpose element is a telephone call log that could be used to evaluate the behavior of the employee whose phone it is, or even the person on the receiving end of the line.[30]

The result element is present when the use of information is likely, under the circumstances, "to have an <u>impact</u> on a certain person's rights and interests." The Working Party uses the example in WP 136 in which a taxi company utilizes GPS data to optimize the use of its fleet. Although the data is related to the cars (and not linked to a particular person), the company could also use this information to track the car's driver (e.g., by treating its drivers differently through monitoring compliance with speed limits). This monitoring is not necessarily the purpose of the information processed, but nonetheless it can be associated with a particular person—in the current example, the car's driver.[31]

3. "An Identified or Identifiable"

A natural person may be identified, either directly or indirectly, by one of several "identifiers" mentioned in the definition of personal data above: "identification number or to one or more factors specific to his physical, physiological, mental, economic, cultural or social identity." If not identified, the person is "identifiable" when it is possible to distinguish him or her from other members of a group through the information, even when the controllers of the data choose not to identify him or her.

A person may be identified directly by name or indirectly through a telephone number, a car license plate number, a social security or passport number, etc., as these numbers—or identifiers—are specific to individuals. He or she may also be indirectly identified by narrowing down a profile to get to an individual—for example, using information such as an address, age, or occupation.[32] Furthermore, a person may be

---

29. *Id.* at 10.
30. *Id.*
31. *Id.* at 11.
32. *Id.* at 12–13.

identified other than through the use of a name—for example, through the use of a unique identifier on the web (for example, through web traffic analysis tools).[33]

Somewhat controversially, the Working Party considers that IP addresses—even dynamic ones—are data related to an identifiable natural person (through the use of Internet Access Provider or LAN manager logbooks, for example).[34]

4. "Natural Persons"

The term natural persons refers to human beings and, in principle, to *living* human beings.

In principle, the data of legal persons (such as corporations) in most Member States do not fall within this definition. Nonetheless, if the information relates to a corporation that bears the name of a natural person, or to a small business with a natural person as its owner, or to an e-mail address held by a natural person at the corporation, then these types of information may indirectly relate to a natural person.[35] Moreover, a few important jurisdictions do include data of legal persons in their definition of personal data, including Austria, Italy, Lichtenstein, and Switzerland.[36] This means that the rules on processing personal data also extend, in principle, to data of companies in these jurisdictions.[37]

Information on deceased persons may indirectly offer information on living ones, so an analysis with respect to the data of the dead should be carried out on a case-by-case basis (when relevant).

What exactly constitutes personal data should also be reviewed under the applicable Member State's legislation and case law; however a good rule of thumb is that it is very broadly interpreted.

---

33. *Id.* at 14.

34. Working Party, *Working Document Privacy on the Internet—An Integrated EU Approach to On-line Data Protection* (WP 37) (Nov. 21, 2000), http://ec.europa.eu/justice/policies/privacy/docs/wpdocs/2000/wp37en.pdf, at 21.

35. WP 136, *supra* note 22, at 21–24.

36. The Swiss Federal Data Protection and Information Commissioner has issued an overview of different countries' treatment of data protection with a view to determining adequacy in the cross-border transfer of personal data (more on adequacy is discussed in Chapter 3 Section C.1). This document indicates which jurisdictions also treat data of legal entities as personal data. *See Etat de la protection des données dans le monde* [The State of Data Protection in the World], June 2, 2014, *available at* http://www.edoeb.admin.ch/datenschutz/00626/00753/index.html?download=NHzLpZeg7t,lnp6I0NTU042l2Z6ln1ae2IZn4Z2qZpnO2Yuq2Z6gpJCDdXt3fmym162epYbg2c_JjKbNoKSn6A--&lang=fr

37. Douwe Korff, *EC Study on Implementation of Data Processing Directive: Comparative Summary of National Laws*, Sept. 2002, at 15, *available at* http://194.242.234.211/documents/10160/10704/Stato+di+attuazione+della+Direttiva+95-46-CE (referenced on http://www.garanteprivacy.it website; last visited on Mar. 11, 2015). *See generally* Douwe Korff, *Study on the Protection of the Rights and Interests of Legal Persons with regard to the Processing of Personal Data relating to such Persons*, Study Contract ETD/97/B-5-9500178, European Commission, Brussels, Oct. 1998, http://ec.europa.eu/justice/data-protection/document/studies/files/20000202_rights_interests_legal_en.pdf.

B. Data Subject

The Directive does not specifically define "data subject," contenting itself to make the reference to "an identified or identifiable natural person" in the definition of "personal data"[38] (see Section II.A).

In essence, the data subject is a natural person (or "individual") to whom personal data relates. It is the individual who is identified or is identifiable by personal data.

C. Processing of Personal Data

The Directive defines "processing" as:

[A]ny operation or set of operations which is performed upon personal data, whether or not by automatic means, such as collection, recording, organization, storage, adaptation or alteration, retrieval, consultations, use, disclosure by transmission, dissemination or otherwise making available, alignment or combination, blocking, erasure or destruction.[39]

This broad definition is seemingly clear and covers almost any action taken on or relating to personal data — "from the collection to the erasure."[40] This is a crucial definition as "processing" is at the heart of EU data protection jargon and the determination of applicable law (see Chapter 2 Section I). Hence the wide applicability, taking the approach that it is "better to ensure that individuals are protected."[41]

D. Personal Data Filing System

A "personal data filing system" or "filing system" is defined as "any structured set of personal data which are accessible according to specific criteria, whether centralized, decentralized or dispersed on a functional or geographical basis."[42]

The Directive limits the scope of its application by providing an exemption for certain types of processing. Article 3(1) provides that the processing by nonautomatic means is covered only if the data "form part of a filing system or are intended to form part of a filing system." This aims to include only so-called structured filing systems, which are nonautomated (paper) files "structured so as to facilitate access and searches for data on individuals."[43]

---

38. Directive, art. 2 (a), at 38.
39. Directive, art. 2 (b), at 38.
40. *See Commission Explanatory Memorandum to the Amended Proposal*, COM (92) 422 final-SYN 287, Oct. 15, 1992, at 10.
41. *Id.*
42. Directive, art. 2(c), at 38.
43. *See Commission Explanatory Memorandum to the Amended Proposal*, *supra* note 36, at 10.

The definition of "filing system" and its sparse use in the Directive[44] has led to divergence in Member State laws and—correspondingly—a certain level of confusion. To create clarity around the processing and coverage of the Directive and any applicable national laws, there are three basic forms of processing: (1) wholly automated processing, (2) partially automated processing, and (3) manual processing.

Partially automated processing involves some level of automation occurring during the processing. This could be the case for a company archiving system. Say, for example, employee files are stored only in paper form. But if the company gives each of these files a number and includes this in an electronic spreadsheet together with the numbering or location of the corresponding files, then this would be partially automated processing.

Some Member States have chosen to include all forms of processing, including manual processing, in the scope of their national laws (e.g., Latvia and Estonia).

E. Controller and Processor

The Directive defines "controller" as:

> [T]he natural or legal person, public authority, agency or any other body which alone or jointly with others determines the purposes and means of the processing of personal data; where the purposes and means of processing personal data are determined by national or Community laws or regulations, the controller or the specific criteria for his nomination may be designated by national or Community law.[45]

The Directive defines "processor" as:

> [A] natural or legal person, public authority, agency or any other body which processes personal data on behalf of the controller.[46]

The Working Party recognized in its Opinion 1/2010 (WP 169) that there are difficulties in applying this definition of controller and that of "processor" (see Section II.E.2) in a "complex environment," particularly when changes in technology and the various actors no longer reflect the historical context in which the Directive and its definitions were drafted. The definitions and distinctions between

---

44. Other than the recitals, definition, and the limitation of the Directive's scope in art. 3(1), the only other reference to filing systems is in art. 32, guiding Member States on what to do if their national provisions do include manual filing systems.
45. *Id.* art. 2(d), at 38.
46. Directive, art. 2(e), at 38.

controller and processor are crucial in determining the parties responsible for compliance with data protection law and the means for data subjects to exercise their rights.[47] Thus, the distribution of responsibility and—more importantly—of liability is at the heart of these two definitions.

The concepts of controller and processor are borrowed from older computing models based on the concept that one party is the owner or in control of the data and this party generally processes the data by itself on its own hardware. When the controller does not process the data itself, then the external party would be considered a processor who processes personal data on behalf of the controller. One can picture a company sending magnetic tapes to a physical center to be 'processed' on hardware or equipment that was not commonly available to most companies. The Directive still qualifies data processing based on this convention.

Due to modern technological interactions, such as the Internet, VPN, and cloud technology, these roles are increasingly blurred, and the definition of controller or processor varies based on the factual circumstances at any one moment.

1. Controller

Whether one is a controller is a factual qualification, applying regardless of how the role is formally classified in a contract, for example. It should be determined by a review of the facts, regardless of whether or not the entity was legally able or formally appointed to act as controller. Furthermore, the determination of who is a controller is autonomous and should primarily be interpreted based on data protection law.[48] Thus, the responsibility will not be changed by concepts from other areas of law, for example, the holder of IP rights or the responsible entity under e-com. The practical application of the controller/processor distinction is presented in Chapter 2 Section III.

Again, the Working Party analyzes the definition of "controller" by dividing it into three main "building blocks":

1. Personal element: "the natural or legal person, public authority, agency or any other body."
2. Possibility of pluralistic control: "which alone or jointly with others."
3. Essential distinguishing elements: "determines the purposes and means of the processing of personal data."

We will detail these elements, starting first, as the Working Party does, with the last of the three.[49]

---

47. Working Party, *Opinion 1/2010 on the Concepts of "Controller" and "Processor"* (WP 169) (Feb. 16, 2010) [hereinafter WP 169], http://ec.europa.eu/justice/policies/privacy/docs/wpdocs/2010/wp169_en.pdf.
48. *Id*. at 8–9.
49. *Id*. at 7–8.

a. "Determines the purposes and means of the processing of personal data"

Turning first to the key elements that distinguish a controller, we look at the term "determines," which relates to the concept of control. The party that is considered the controller is one that "has chosen to process personal data for its own purposes."

The Working Party elucidates three possible categories of control when determining whether an entity is a controller. The first is when control arises from "explicit legal competence"; this can be either a direct appointment—when the controller is designated as such by national or EU law—or an indirect establishment of a party as a controller. Direct classifications of controllers in the law are infrequent; more often the law indirectly establishes a controller. This occurs when the law "establishes a task or imposes a duty on someone to collect and process certain data," such as when, in connection with their duties, a public authority is appointed by national law as being responsible for processing certain personal data. This is also the case when an entity is entrusted with a public task and must carry out the processing of personal data in order to do it (e.g., the social security administration), or when there is a legal obligation for an entity to provide or keep certain data. In these cases, the public authority (in the first case), or the entity (in the latter two cases), will be the controller.[50]

The second category is where control derives from implicit competence; where "common legal provisions or established legal practice" naturally result in control of the personal data processing, the party in control is the controller. Here, existing conventional roles allude to a particular responsibility. Examples cited in WP 169 include the employer that controls the processing of its employee's data or a publisher with respect to data on its subscribers.[51] An interesting distinction is the use of telecommunications services for the transmission of messages such as e-mail. Here, the sender generally is considered the controller for the personal data contained in the message, while the operator is the controller of other services, such as processing related to invoicing data.[52]

Finally, control may be determined based on the facts and surrounding circumstances. Often this may be drawn from examining contractual relationships and the assigned roles and responsibilities of the parties. Contracts may be silent on who is a controller; nevertheless they could include "sufficient elements to assign the responsibility of controller to party that apparently exercises a dominant role in this respect." Furthermore, "[t]he fact itself that somebody determines how personal data are processed may entail the qualification" of controller—whether outside of the scope of the

---

50. *Id.* at 10.
51. *Id.*
52. *Id.* at 11.

contract or explicitly excluded by the contract.[53] Aside from contractual associations, other criteria are also useful, including "degree of actual control exercised by a party," the outward impression projected toward data subjects, and their reasonable expectations based on this projection.[54]

Next, when determining whether a party is considered a controller, one must look to whether it determines the *purposes* and *means* — or the why and the how — of processing. The Working Party makes clear that an entity may be considered the controller based on its determining the purposes alone — for example, an entity making a decision that personal data of customers will be processed for invoicing and for marketing purposes. Determining means (both technical and organizational) results in a similar conclusion only when the decision "concerns the essential elements of the means."[55] This not only pertains to the technical means of processing, but also *how* the personal data is processed, such as which data will be processed, the duration of processing, and the granting of access to the data.[56] Against this, the Working Party explains that there are circumstances where a party is acting as a controller but leaves the technical means (what software to use) to be determined by the processor. An example of a controller determined under this test is a company that instructs different companies to carry out various data processing services for it, such as mail marketing campaigns and payroll, with clear-cut and defined instructions while limiting the discretion of the service providers in the processing. In this example, the controller decides "what marketing material to send out and to whom, and who to pay, what amounts, by what date etc," and would be the only party that could use the data processed.[57]

Finally, WP 169 highlights that if a contractor in such a situation would process the personal data of another for its own benefit (to generate value-added services), it could be qualified as a controller or joint controller for this processing activity and would be similarly subject to data protection laws as a controller.[58]

---

53. The Working Party refers to the case against the Society for Worldwide Interbank Financial Telecommunication (SWIFT), a Belgian entity subject to administrative subpoenas from the U.S. Treasury's Office of Foreign Assets Control (OFAC) to provide personal data stored on its U.S. servers to OFAC for counterterrorism. Here, SWIFT took a decision to provide personal data that was initially processed by banks and financial institutions for commercial purposes to OFAC. It was determined that since this disclosure and transfer was for SWIFT"s own purposes, it was a de facto controller — regardless of what was designated in the contract. *See* Belgian Privacy Commission's Decision of 9 Dec. 2008, *Control and Recommendation Procedure Initiated with Respect to the Company SWIFT SCR*, unofficial English translation, http://www.privacycommission.be/sites/privacycommission/files/documents/swift_decision_en_09_12_2008.pdf, and *see generally* Working Party, *Opinion 10/2006 on the Processing of Personal Data by the Society for Worldwide Interbank Financial Telecommunication (SWFIT)* (WP 128) (Nov. 22, 2006), http://ec.europa.eu/justice/policies/privacy/docs/wpdocs/2006/wp128_en.pdf.
54. WP 169, *supra* note 43, at 12.
55. *Id.* at 14.
56. *Id.*
57. *Id.* at 13.
58. *Id.* at 14.

b. "Natural person, legal person or any legal body"

This part of the definition is what the Working Party calls the "personal side"—detailing who can be a controller. If a legal person such as a company, or a body, is involved, the company or body itself should preferably be considered the controller, rather than a specific natural person within such organization. Generally speaking, such specific persons act on behalf of the legal person. However, in the case where they act "outside the scope and the possible control of the legal person's activities," they could potentially be considered the controller and would be liable for this out-of-scope processing.[59]

c. "Alone or jointly with others"

Joint or co-controllers for the processing may exist, as different actors can be involved in various processing operations or sets of operations taking place at the same time or in different phases. In order to determine whether joint control exists, an evaluation under Section II.E.1.a of whether more than one party determines the purposes and means of the processing should be made. This determination does not have to be equally shared and can take different forms, but entities should be "sharing purposes or means in a common set of operations" in order to be considered joint controllers, and not just separate controllers engaging in a transfer of data (so-called co-controllers). Again, WP 169 highlights the necessity in complex processing environments of assigning roles and responsibilities ensuring a logical and functional approach.[60] This allocation requires a pragmatic approach.

WP 169 also contains a couple of illustrations that point out the differences between being merely separate controllers involved in separate data processing of personal data, and acting as joint controllers. In the first, a travel agency transfers its customers' personal data to an airline and a hotel chain for them to each act as controllers for their specific processing—checking availability within their organizations (whether for seats or rooms). The travel agency processes the ticketing and vouchers.[61] In a second example, the travel agency, hotel chain, and the airline act together to set up a common Internet platform, agreeing on purposes and the essential elements of the means together. Thus, in this case they would be joint controllers.[62]

Finally, WP 169 notes that complex processing environments are becoming more prevalent with cloud-based software and the transition to outsourcing not only of simple tasks but even entire departments within companies. In these complex scenarios, the focus should be on the clear allocation of the roles and responsibilities to ensure compliance with data protection laws and to avoid the reduction of protection

---

59. *Id.* at 15–16.
60. *Id.* at 17–19.
61. *Id.* at 19.
62. *Id.* at 20.

or the creation of loopholes when parties do not ensure rights and obligations arising from the Directive.[63]

These distinctions will have an impact on data protection obligations under the Directive, as we shall see later.[64]

2. Processor

As the processor processes the personal data "on behalf of the controller," it is the controller that decides whether there should be a separate processor (and if not, the controller acts in both roles). WP 169 underscores two key conditions for an entity to be considered a processor: first, the processor must be someone legally independent from the controller; second, the processor processes data, as we have seen, on behalf of the controller.[65] This relationship will be set out in a contract or other legally binding act,[66] and the processor will act only under the instructions of the controller.[67]

As we saw in Section II.E.1.a above, the controller is the one who determines the purposes of the processing and the essential means used, and it merely delegates to the processor the carrying out of the processing on behalf of the controller. This is always the case in outsourcing roles related to processing of personal data including payroll services, recruitment, and so on when using cloud-based software. Attention, however, as a processor may acquire the status of (joint) controller if it exceeds its mandate and plays "a relevant role in determining the purposes or the essential means of processing."[68] This can arise if a processor transfers personal data outside of the European Union without the consent, approval, or instructions of the controller. It is possible, that there can be a "certain degree of discretion" on how to execute a controller's instructions, "allowing the processor to choose the most suitable technical and organizational means."[69] In summary, a determination of whether or not an entity is a processor should be made on a case-by-case basis, for each set of data or operations.[70]

As was the case for controllers (see Section II.E.1.c), there may be a multiplicity of processors for the processing of the same personal data, all following the instructions of the same controller, and it is important that the allocation of data protection responsibilities is clear.[71]

---

63. *Id.* at 22.
64. *See* chapter 3.
65. WP 169, *supra* note 43, at 25.
66. Directive, art. 17(3), at 43.
67. *Id.* art. 16, at 43.
68. WP 169, *supra* note 45, at 25.
69. *Id.* at 27.
70. *Id.* at 25.
71. *Id.* at 27.

Applicable Law under the GDPR

The GDPR changes certain definitions used in the Directive. Perhaps the most significant change is a reorganization of the definition of "data subject," which affects the way the definition of "personal data" is presented.

Under the GDPR, "data subject" has become a separate defined term—no longer contained within the definition of "personal data":

> "Data subject" means an identified natural person or a natural person who can be identified, directly or indirectly, **by means reasonably likely to be used by the controller or by any other natural or legal person**, in particular by reference to an identification number, **location data, online identifier** or to one or more factors specific to the physical, psychological, genetic, mental, economic, cultural or social identity of that person. (emphasis added)[72]

The GDPR adds the language indicated in bold above to the existing definition. While basing itself upon existing essential elements, it has the effect of clarifying the definition by further specifying for identification of a natural person by new technologies (use of "location data" and "online identifiers"). The definition also elaborates on a more general possibility—including persons identifiable by "means reasonably likely to be used by the controller."[73] This concept incorporates Recital 26 of the Directive, which can be appreciated in light of the state-of-the-art technology used in the future by controllers. At the same time, this leaves the door open for any possible means used by the controller to identify individuals—serving as a catchall.

By segmenting the definition of data subject, the GDPR changes the meaning of "personal data" to:

> [a]ny information relating to a data subject. In effect, this shifts the focus from what will qualify as "personal data," a question often currently questioned when assessing if EU data protection law will apply, to whether a data subject can be identified from the information at hand.

III. GENERAL PRINCIPLES OF PRIVACY

EU privacy principles draw inspiration from provisions of other data protection and privacy texts, such as Convention 108 and the OECD Guidelines. The principles serve as a focal point when making comparisons to other countries' privacy provisions, including when assessing whether a country provides adequate protections (for the purposes of transfers—see Chapter 3 Section III). An important point on the privacy principles is that they are to be approached holistically, meaning that they are to be applied broadly and in combination with one another; not individually, without regard to the other principles or provisions. The principles can be found generally

---

72. General Data Protection Regulation, *supra* note 19, art. 4(1), at 41.
73. *Id.*

in Chapter II of the Directive (General Rules on the Lawfulness of the Processing of Personal Data, containing Articles 5 through 21), although they are not clearly presented or consistently referred to in Working Party documentation or scholarly articles. For example, sometimes there are six principles; other times there are seven or even eight.[74] Here, an attempt is made to present them in a clear manner, combining terminology from various references.

A. Purpose Limitation (Finality) Principle

Personal data must be collected for specific, explicitly defined and legitimate purposes and processed lawfully and in a proper and careful manner. By limiting how an individual's data is collected and used, the purpose limitation principle is a key component of data protection. This principle sits among the other provisions on data quality in Article 6 of the Directive.[75] It specifies that "personal data must be . . . collected for specified, explicit and legitimate purposes and not further processed in a way incompatible with those purposes."[76] The principle is composed of two elements — purpose specification and compatible use. These elements lay the groundwork for "transparency, legal certainty and predictability"[77] by placing limitations on the use of data subjects' personal data by controllers and ensuring that the use is within the expectations of data subjects.[78]

Purpose specification means that personal data must be collected for specified, explicit, and legitimate purposes. This requirement is a precondition for other data quality requirements specified under Article 6, as the defined purpose(s) will set the bar for what data should be collected, how long it should be retained, and the other safeguards (such as information security).[79]

---

74. For example, Paul M. Schwartz cites eight principles, referring to them as "fair information principles" (or FIPs). He cites the eight FIPs as: "(1) limits on data collection, also termed data minimization; (2) the data quality principle; . . . (3) notice, access and correction rights for the individual; . . . (4) a processing of personal data made only pursuant to a legal basis; (5) regulatory oversight by an independent data protection authority; (6) enforcement mechanisms, including restrictions on data exports to countries that lack sufficient privacy protection; (7) limits on automated decision making; and (8) additional protection for sensitive data [citation omitted]." *See* Paul M. Schwartz, *The EU-U.S. Privacy Collision: A Turn to Institutions and Procedures*, 126 Harv. L. Rev. 1966, 1976 (2013). These have been distilled slightly differently by the European Union Agency for Fundamental Rights and the Council of Europe — European Court of Human Rights: (1) the principle of lawful processing; (2) the principle of purpose specification and limitation; (3) relevancy of data; (4) accuracy of data; (5) limited retention of data; (6) exemption for scientific research and statistics; (7) the principle of fair processing; and (8) the principle of accountability. *See* Eur. Agency for Fundamental Rts. and Council — Eur. Ct. H.R., *Handbook on European Data Protection Law*, 2014, sec. 3, at 63–79, *available at* http://fra.europa.eu/en/publication/2014/handbook-european-data-protection-law.
75. Working Party, *Opinion 03/2013 on Purpose Limitation* (WP 203) (Apr. 2, 2013), http://ec.europa.eu/justice/data-protection/article-29/documentation/opinion-recommendation/files/2013/wp203_en.pdf. The purpose limitation principle is articulated in the Directive, art. 6(1)(b), at 40.
76. Directive, art. 6(b), at 40.
77. WP 203, *supra* note 73, at 11.
78. *Id.*
79. *Id.* at 11–12.

The compatible use requirement stipulates that personal data is not "further processed in a way incompatible"[80] with the specified purposes. The Working Party's Opinion 03/2013 (WP 203) clarifies that this requirement does *not* focus on the originally specified purpose and the subsequently defined purposes; but rather it looks to the first processing operation (the collection of data) and then subsequent processing operations (storage and further processing). Processing activities that take place following the collection of data are considered further processing and must meet the compatible use requirement. To meet the requirement, the processing activities must undergo an assessment in one of two ways:

1. A *formal assessment* compares the originally specified purposes, together with any other formal uses, to determine whether the further processing activities are covered.
2. Alternatively, a *substantive assessment* can be made, looking beyond the formal statements, to how the purposes are understood in fact, taking into consideration all of the surrounding circumstances to identify whether the new and original purposes were included in substance.[81]

B. Data Quality and Legitimacy

Article 6 of the Directive outlines the data quality requirements that a controller must meet when processing personal data. The purpose limitation principle (as outlined previously) is also included in the provisions on data quality within the Directive. Article 7 lays out the criteria, or legal bases, for which data may be legitimately (legally) processed; these are the so-called legitimate bases for processing. Again, these provisions must be approached and applied holistically. For the purposes of coherency, first the legal bases for processing will be discussed (Article 7) followed by the provisions on data quality (Article 6).

1. Legal Basis for Processing (Legitimacy)

In principle, personal data may be processed only if based on one of the criteria listed in Article 7. However, these bases can vary depending on the jurisdiction's implementation of the Directive. Thus, personal data must be processed based on one of the legal bases provided in the applicable national law of the EU Member State. The fundamental bases from the Directive are:

a. The data subject has given his or her unambiguous consent.
b. The processing is necessary for the performance of a contract that the data subject is a party to *or* to take precontractual steps at the data subject's request.

---

80. *Id*. at 12.
81. *Id*. at 21.

   c. The processing is necessary for the controller in order to comply with a legal obligation.

   d. The processing is necessary to protect the data subject's vital interests.

   e. The processing is necessary for the performance of a task in the public interest or when the controller (or third party to whom the data is disclosed) is exercising official authority.

   f. The processing is necessary for the controller's legitimate interest or by a third party to whom the data is disclosed except when these interests are outweighed by the data subject's fundamental rights and freedoms.

These legal bases are analyzed in detail in Chapter 2 Section IV.

2. Data Quality

In addition to the rule on purpose limitation, personal data must be:

   a. Processed fairly and lawfully;

   b. Adequate, relevant, and not excessive to the purposes;

   c. Accurate and, if relevant, up to date;

   d. Not kept in an identifiable format for longer than necessary for the purpose for which the data was collected or subsequently processed.

a. Fair and Lawful Processing

Lawful processing requires that processing of personal data must be done in compliance with the law, including data protection laws (i.e., the provisions of the Directive, including satisfying one of the criteria in Article 7) and any other legal requirements that may apply.[82]

> For example: WP 48 outlines where an employer owes a general duty of confidence to its workers or where a specific law prohibits discrimination in hiring.[83] There could also be a general duty of confidentiality from a lawyer towards his or her client or a specific prohibition of selling customer lists to third parties.

Fair processing requires that the processing take place in a manner that is not unfair to the data subject. This is an additional element of proportionality.

b. Proportionality Principle

Personal data must be proportional—*adequate, relevant, and not excessive*—to the purposes for which it was collected or further processed. The principle of proportionality is another key principle; when considering any type of processing (collection,

---

82. Working Party, *Opinion 8/2001 on the Processing of Personal Data in the Employment Context* (WP 48) (Sept. 13, 2001), at 18, http://ec.europa.eu/justice/data-protection/article-29/documentation/opinion-recommendation/files/2001/wp48_en.pdf.

83. *Id.*

storage, transfer, or deletion), a company should consider whether the activity is proportional to the purposes or objective for which the information is collected. Generally, controllers should try to ensure that the processing is the least intrusive form of processing when trying to achieve the purpose(s). This quality is very important when considering personal data of customers or employees, as one must consider the risks involved, the quantity of data, and relevant purposes or objectives.[84]

c. Accuracy and Retention of Data

Personal data must be accurate and, when relevant, must be kept up to date. Controllers must take every reasonable step to ensure that the data is accurate and complete, in light of the purpose for which they are collecting or further processing the data. It must also be kept up to date to ensure that the controller is not processing data that is no longer correct. This is important for certain types of data sets when the personal data at hand can be historical and is subject to changes or alterations over time (such as data subject addresses, credit history, etc.).

Furthermore, data must be kept in a format that allows identification of data subjects for no longer than necessary for the purpose for which the data was collected or further processed. This signifies that personal data must be de-identified or anonymized when the identification of the data subject is no longer necessary to achieve the purposes. More information on anonymization will be elaborated upon in Chapter 7 Section IV.C.

C. Individual Rights of Data Subjects (Transparency Principle)

Transparency takes into account both the information (notice) requirements laid out in Articles 10 and 11 and the data subject's right of access and rectification in Article 12 (together, Chapter II, Sections IV (Information to Be Given to the Data Subject) and V (The Data Subject's Right of Access to Data) of the Directive.

1. Information (Notice) Requirement

Data subjects have the right to be informed about (1) the identity of the controller (or its representative), (2) the intended purposes of processing, and (3) any additional information about the specific circumstances of processing to ensure fairness. This typically includes recipients or categories of recipients, whether providing the information is required or voluntary (and the possible consequences of not responding), and the existence of the right to access and correct personal data.[85]

For the timing of the notice, data subjects should receive the information at the time of collection or, at the latest, prior to processing. There are separate notice requirements for when the data is not collected from the data subjects themselves (such as when data is acquired through a third party). It is important to note that each EU member state has its own notice requirements and that these provisions are

---

84. *Id.* at 21.
85. Directive, art. 10, at 41.

not consistent—aside from the basic requirements of identity of the controller and providing the purposes of processing. Therefore, due to the wide variances in notice requirements, drafting information notices presents an exercise of adjustment.

Generally speaking most notices should include the following elements:

1. Identity of the controller of the personal data;
2. Purposes of the processing;
3. Recipients or categories of recipients of the data;
4. Information on transfers of data to other countries; and
5. Individuals' rights.

2. Access, Correction, and Deletion

Individuals have certain rights with respect to their data, including the right to access information held in their personal data file at "reasonable intervals and without excessive delay or expense."[86] The Directive specifies that data subjects have the right to:

a. Know whether their personal data is being processed and information on the purposes of processing, data categories, and recipients or the category of recipients to whom the personal data is disclosed.
b. Receive "in an intelligible form" the data being processed and "any available information . . . [on its] source."[87]

Access rights of individuals vary between Member States, therefore the form and exact information disclosed about the personal data held by the controller will vary. Access content can be very different based on the circumstances, for example, an individual with a simple online account can include basic information like user name, contact details, and contact preferences. On the other hand, an access request for a social media platform or to an employer will be substantively different. One commonality is that when personal data of other data subjects are included in a file (such as a personnel file) or database, access to the personal data of the requestor is limited, so as to also protect the rights of third-party data subjects. This often arises in access requests to personnel files that include evaluations, comments, or personal opinions of colleagues and line management of an employee. There are situations in which personal data of these individuals will not and should not be disclosed. As an alternative, a description of the document or data category can be provided without compromising the rights of the third party individuals. Again, it is important to look to local law when dealing with an access request—particularly when certain information included in the personnel file should not be disclosed.

---

86. Directive, art. 12(a), at 42.
87. *Id.*

Individuals also have the right to update or rectify their personal data when it is incomplete or inaccurate and to delete or block data "which does not comply with the [Directive's] provisions . . . , in particular because of the incomplete or inaccurate nature of the data.[88] These rights are granted in the Directive "as appropriate" and can be conditioned or limited depending on the circumstances. Recently, many organizations are encouraging a shift in control, so that the ability to update personal data is in the hands of the data subjects themselves (this is also spurred on by technological developments, e.g., Software as a Service, or SaaS). This permits companies to set up databases or rely on software when certain data fields (e.g., emergency contact information, home addresses, and telephone numbers) are updated or entered by the data subjects directly (e.g., in an Intranet directory). In such cases, it is of course important to remember the principles of proportionality and fairness: controllers should not be collecting more information than necessary to achieve the purposes of processing. Thus, although it may be tempting to broaden certain information to be entered by the data subjects, companies need to ensure that they are getting only the information necessary (and not other information that, although it may be useful to have, is not really necessary). Moreover, the individual right to blocking of processing and deletion of personal data held by controllers is not absolute. These rights are conditioned and may be invoked based on legitimate grounds. As an example, a former employee cannot request the deletion of his or her personnel file upon departure; as the employer is required to retain and further process information, for tax, social security purposes or to allow the employer to defend itself for instance in the context of litigation.

3. Remedies and Liabilities

Individuals are, in principle, granted the right to a judicial remedy and compensation for breaches of EU data protection law. Article 22 of the Directive states that Member States must provide for "the right of every person to a judicial remedy for any breach of the rights guaranteed him by the national law applicable to the processing in question."[89] Article 23 lays out the provisions for compensation:

a. Member States shall provide that any person who has suffered damage as a result of an unlawful processing operation or of any act incompatible with the national provisions adopted pursuant to this Directive is entitled to receive compensation from the controller for the damage suffered.

b. The controller may be exempted from this liability, in whole or in part, if he proves that he is not responsible for the event giving rise to the damage.

---

88.   Directive, art. 12(b), at 42.
89.   *Id.* art. 22, at 45. Recital 55 states "national legislation must provide for a judicial remedy; whereas any damage which a person may suffer as a result of unlawful processing must be compensated for by the controller, who may be exempted from liability if he proves that he is not responsible for the damage." *Id.* recital 55, at 36.

These provisions are not without shortcomings, as oftentimes the corresponding measures under national law do not have a sufficient mechanism to ensure adequate enforcement or compensation.[90] Furthermore, the types of damages and the level of exculpatory provisions vary.[91]

D. Security Principle

Processing of personal data must be confidential and protected by appropriate technical and organizational measures. Article 17 spells out the security requirements: "controller[s] must implement appropriate technical and organizational measures to protect personal data against accidental or unlawful destruction, loss, alteration, disclosure or access."[92]

Furthermore, processing must be confidential. This requirement is outlined in Article 16: "any person acting under the authority of the controller or of the processor . . . who has access to personal data must not process them except on instructions from the controller, unless he is required to do so by law."[93] In practice this means that all processing—both by controller and processors (and their respective employees, independent contractors, and subcontractors)—must be done confidentially.

These security principles are enshrined for both controllers and processors. Of course, ultimate liability under current EU data protection rules remains with controllers. Therefore, when a controller outsources processing, it must choose a processor (third-party processor service provider) that provides "sufficient guarantees [for] . . . technical security measures and organization measures governing the processing to be carried out" and it must ensure compliance with the same.[94]

All outsourced processing (i.e., all processing carried out by processors) must be administered by a *written* ("or in another equivalent form") contract or legally binding undertaking that binds the processors to the controller and stipulates at least: (1) that the processor will process only under the instructions of the controller, and (2) the information security provisions of the Member States where the processor is established are binding upon the processor.[95]

---

90. For example, in Belgium, an individual would complain to the DPA, who would then look into the matter and refer the complaint to the public prosecutor. Then, the public prosecutor decides whether to file a criminal complaint.

91. Douwe Korff, *EC Study on Implementation of Data Processing Directive: Comparative Summary of National Laws*, Sept. 2002, at 179–81, *available at* http://www.garanteprivacy.it/web/guest/home/docweb/-/docweb-display/docweb/455584 (click on "Stato di attuazione della Direttiva 95-46-CE"; last visited on Feb. 25, 2015).

92. Directive, art. 17, at 43.

93. Directive, art. 16, at 43.

94. Directive, art. 17(2), at 43.

95. Directive, art. 17, at 43.

E. Restrictions on Transfers

Cross-border transfers or transfers to third-party recipients must ensure that the personal data is similarly protected—providing an adequate level of protection for the data. Any transfers must be in line with the provisions of Article 26(1) of the Directive. For transfers within the European Union and European Economic Area (EEA), these transfers are not treated as cross-border exchanges, as they fall under the principle of the freedom of movement of services and goods within the community. The rules on transfers of personal data are elaborated upon in Chapter 3 Section III.

F. Restrictions on Special Categories of Data (Sensitive Data)

Under the Directive, the processing of sensitive personal data is generally prohibited. Sensitive personal data is defined as personal data that reveals racial or ethnic origin, political opinions, religious or philosophical beliefs, trade-union membership, and data concerning health or sex life.[96] Furthermore, national laws vary and may include broader data categories, such as criminal convictions, biometric information, national identity or social security numbers, and so on. When such categories are processed, additional safeguards should be put in place, such as the data subject's consent and higher security protections.[97]

G. Restrictions on Automated Individual Decision Making

Article 15 of the Directive lays outs "the right to every person not to be subject to a decision which produces legal effects concerning him or significantly affects him and which is based solely on automated processing of data intended to evaluate certain personal aspects relating to him, such as his performance at work, creditworthiness, reliability, conduct, etc."[98] If such decision making is permitted, then individuals have the right to be informed about the logic behind such decisions and the measures taken to safeguard their interests.

H. Direct Marketing Provisions

When personal data is transferred or used for direct marketing, individuals should be provided the opportunity to opt out or revoke their consent for the use of their personal data for such purposes.

For more information about direct electronic marketing, see Chapter 6 Section I.

---

96. Directive, art. 8(1), at 40.
97. Working Party, *Working Document on Transfers of Personal Data to Third Countries: Applying Articles 25 and 26 of the EU Data Protection Directive* (WP 12) (July 24, 1998), at 7, http://ec.europa.eu/justice/policies/privacy/docs/wpdocs/1998/wp12_en.pdf.
98. Directive, art. 15, at 43.

2

What Do EU Data Protection Rules Mean in Practice

Among the most important questions for multinational companies to have answered is whether their activities are subject to EU data protection rules and, if so, which EU Member State's national law they should follow. The rules of applicable data protection law are enumerated in Article 4 of the Directive. These applicable law rules are drafted in a broad manner to ensure expansive protection. Furthermore, applicable data protection law is distinct from the jurisdiction of a court, which means, for example, that one can apply Dutch data protection law while sitting in a court in Spain. An understanding of the concepts of controller and processor is crucial for applying the data protection laws in EU Member States. These definitions establish which national law should apply, who is accountable for compliance with data protection requirements, what information security requirements should be applied, and how data subjects can apply their individual rights, among other requirements.[1] Finally, companies will need to know whether they have a proper legal basis for processing the personal data, which is to say that their activities with respect to personal data are in compliance with relevant laws. This chapter will look in turn at each of these practical concerns for companies.

One clear exclusion from the scope of the Directive is stipulated in Article 3(2), which provides that the Directive does not apply to the processing of personal data "by a natural person in the course of a purely personal or household activity."[2] Thus, processing in the context of domestic or personal activities (e.g., creating and maintaining spreadsheets with addresses and telephone numbers for a private individual to use in a nonprofessional context) is not subject to the data protection rules. What level qualifies as household or personal activity varies slightly from one Member State to another, especially when it comes to personal or independent (self-employed) commercial activities. One can see that in Spain, doctors and certain independent professions are subject to the data protection rules (e.g., requiring

---

1. Working Party, *Opinion 1/2010 on the Concepts of "Controller" and "Processor,"* at 2 (WP 169) (Feb. 16, 2010) [hereinafter WP 169], http://ec.europa.eu/justice/policies/privacy/docs/wpdocs/2010/wp169_en.pdf.
2. *Id.* at 39.

registration with the DPA), whereas in other countries, such independent commercial activities fall outside the scope of such national laws. The Court of Justice of the European Union (ECJ) has found that this household use exemption would not apply when an individual publishes personal data about others on the Internet. In such a case, EU data protection law would apply:

> The act of referring, on an internet page, to various persons and identifying them by name or by other means, for instance by giving their telephone number or information regarding their working conditions and hobbies, constitutes the processing of personal data wholly or partly by automatic means within the meaning of Article 3(1) of [the Directive].[3]

I. APPLICABILITY OF THE DIRECTIVE–DOES THE DIRECTIVE APPLY TO MY COMPANY OR ACTIVITIES?

EU data protection laws apply to the *processing* of personal data. Processing is very broadly defined as any operation performed on personal data including collection, storage, access, transfers, and deletion. Essentially, processing is any activity related to personal data or utilizing personal data (the definition of what constitutes personal data, as well as other definitions such as that of controller, are further explored in Chapter 1 Section II). The Directive—and the various corresponding Member State national data protection laws—is applicable when a controller processes personal data in the specific EU territory. The law will also apply where an entity, even if not established in the country, processes data on equipment that is physically located in a specific Member State (unless the equipment is used only for transit through the territory).[4] It is also applicable where EU Member State national law applies via public international law. Personal data that is processed by a company in a certain country or by a foreign entity using equipment (such as computers, a server, storage, etc.) located in the European Union will be subject to Member State national data protection laws.

Generally, the application of the Directive's provision on applicable law—Article 4—raises many questions of interpretation.[5] Correspondingly, Member States'

---

3. *See* Case C-101/01, Bodil Lindqvist (Nov. 6, 2003), holding para. 1, *available at* http://curia.europa.eu/juris/showPdf.jsf?text=&docid=48382&pageIndex=0&doclang=en&mode=lst&dir=&occ=first&part=1&cid=30128. In addition, the ECJ also recently ruled that the use of a home CCTV system for home security did not fit within the household use exemption, where the CCTV system also monitored a public space, such as a street. See Case C-212/13, František Ryneš v. Úřad pro ochranu osobních údajů (Dec. 11, 2014), http://curia.europa.eu/juris/celex.jsf?celex=62013CJ0212&lang1=en&type=TXT&ancre=.

4. Directive 95/46/EC of the European Parliament and of the Council of 24 Oct. 1995 on the protection of individuals with regard to the processing of personal data and on the free movement of such data [hereinafter Directive], 1995 O.J. (L 281) 31 (Nov. 23, 1995), art. 4, at 39.

5. Douwe Korff, *EC Study on Implementation of Data Processing Directive: Comparative Summary of National Laws*, Sept. 2002, at 179–81, *available at* http://194.242.234.211/documents/10160/10704/Stato+di+attuazione+della+Direttiva+95-46-CE (referenced on http://www.garanteprivacy.it website; last visited on Mar. 11, 2015).

national laws on application of the law vary widely, and companies and organizations struggle to understand the applicable law provisions. This chapter will first present a contextual note on the applicable law rules, followed by the rules on applicable law for controllers with EU establishments and then for controllers in Third Countries. This section will end by looking at some practical scenarios that provide guidance about which EU national law will be applicable.

(For practical suggestions on this point, see "Practical Tips" near the end of this section.)

A. Note on the Legislative Intent and Historical Context of the Applicability Provisions

The legislative intent for the applicable law provision was to ensure uniform application of privacy laws throughout the European Union via a harmonized system while, at the same time, preventing the possibility of avoidance of EU data protection law by EU entities relocating their data processing activities to countries outside the European Union (Third Countries). This is confirmed by the preparatory works of the Directive, in which the Commission commented:

> This article lays down the connecting factors which determine which national law is applicable to processing within the scope of the Directive, in order to avoid two possibilities: that the data subject might find himself outside any system of protection and particularly that the law might be circumvented in order to achieve this and that the same processing operation might be governed by the laws of more than one country.[6]

Furthermore, when Article 4 was drafted, it was not with a mind to the applicability of the Directive (and Member State national data protection law) on the Internet — or scenarios in which data processing activities are delocalized between data centers. Thus, the Directive and many of its underlying concepts date from a time when data resided in only one physical location at a time. In a time when data was stored primarily on personally held physical media, such as diskettes, transfers involved a basic process of physically passing data to an external party, where it would then be housed in another physical location. As a result, there remains ambiguity on the exact scope and meaning of this article. In 2010, the Working Party issued an opinion on the scope and application of the provision (WP 179),[7] seeking to clarify some long-standing questions and provide some legal certainty on the matter. There still remains ambiguity in

---

6. *Commission Explanatory Memorandum to the Amended Proposal*, COM (92) 422 final-SYN 287, Oct. 15, 1992, at 13.

7. Working Party, *Opinion 8/2010 on Applicable Law* (WP 179) (Dec. 16, 2010) [hereinafter WP 179], http://ec.europa.eu/justice/policies/privacy/docs/wpdocs/2010/wp179_en.pdf.

complex processing (e.g., cloud computing and Internet-based processing) scenarios due to the complexity of the provision.[8]

B. Does the Directive Apply to Me?

Generally, the Directive is applicable as soon as processing occurs on equipment located in the European Union or when personal data is collected through automated or other means in the European Union.[9] When determining whether data protection law applies, the first criteria to examine are the location of the establishment of the controller and the location of the equipment being used (if the controller is a non-EU entity). The nationality or residence of data subjects and the physical location of the data do not influence whether EU data protection law applies.[10]

As mentioned above, the provisions on the applicability of the Directive aim to ensure that the whole of the European Union is covered, while at the same time ensuring that companies do not utilize entities outside of the European Union to avoid application of the law or to create loopholes in its application. Additionally, the Directive is meant to ensure that only one Member State national law will be applicable to the individual (data subject) and that multiple Member State national laws will not be applicable to a single processing operation.[11]

1. Controllers with EU/European Economic Area (EEA) Establishment(s)—Article 4(1)(a)

Under Article 4(1)(a), a Member State's national law will apply when

> [t]he processing is carried out in the context of the activities of an establishment of the controller on the territory of the Member State; when the same controller is established on the territory of several Member States, he must take the necessary measures to ensure that each of these establishments complies with the obligations laid down by the national law applicable.[12]

This provides that EU Member State national data protection law will apply to the processing of personal data carried out in the context of the activities of an establishment of a responsible party located in an EU Member State. Thus, personal data controlled by a company located in an EU Member State is subject to the Directive.

---

8. *Id.* at 5.
9. This can be inferred from the opinion of the Working Party with respect to the processing of personal data on the Internet; *see generally* http://ec.europa.eu/justice_home/fsj/privacy/docs/wpdocs/2002/wp56_en.pdf.
10. WP 179, *supra* note 7, at 8.
11. *See Commission Explanatory Memorandum to the Amended Proposal, supra* note 6, at 13, and WP 179, *supra* note 7, at 9.
12. Directive, art. 4(1)(a), at 39.

a. Establishment

WP 179 highlights that for determining whether an "establishment" of a controller is involved depends on "whether the organization . . . conducts the effective and real exercise of activities."[13] It does not have to be an organization with legal personality; the controller must have both "human and technical resources necessary" for the accomplishment of certain services through "stable arrangements." WP 179 mentions that a "server or computer is not likely to qualify as an establishment as it is simply a technical facility or instrument for processing of information." Further, the legal form of the office or establishment is not controlling, as a single-person office could also qualify if it was "actively involved in the activities in the context of which the processing of personal data takes place."[14]

b. Processing in the Context of Activities

The applicability of Member State national data protection law is associated with the processing of personal data. Thus it is important to look at where processing is taking place within the "context of activities." This does not focus on the location of the data but instead looks to where an establishment of a controller is involved in activities related to data processing.[15] Therefore, when determining whether the law is applicable, one needs to consider the "degree of involvement of the establishment(s)"[16] in the processing to determine the role of each actor. A secondary element is to look at the "nature of the activities of the establishments" to determine whether or not data processing is taking place. The definition of the term "processing" plays an important role, as the applicable law will apply to the organization that is processing the personal data for its own activities. Finally, WP 179 emphasizes that the aim is to grant effective protection in a clear and practical manner; thus it is important that this analysis is focused on the factual circumstances of processing (and not on what would be most convenient for a company).

2. Non-EU/EEA Controllers Processing Data in the EU/EEA—Article 4(1)(c)

Article 4(1)(c) provides that EU data protection law also applies where

> [t]he controller is not established on Community territory and, for purposes of processing personal data makes use of equipment, automated or otherwise, situated on the territory of the said Member State, unless such equipment is used only for purposes of transit through the territory of the Community.[17]

The Directive specifies that controllers located outside of the European Union are subject to the Directive if they make use of equipment, automated or otherwise,

---

13. WP 179, *supra* note 7, at 29.
14. *Id.* at 13.
15. *Id.*
16. *Id.* at 14.
17. Directive, art. 4(1)(c), at 39.

situated on EU territory. In such case, a representative must be designated that is established in the territory of that relevant Member State.[18]

This provision comes into effect only if Article 4(1)(a) does not apply, meaning that the controller does not have any entity in the EEA/EU for the purposes of the processing activities in question. This does not mean that the controller does not have any other establishments in the European Union; it means merely that these entities are not involved in the processing activities in question (i.e., when the processing is not in the context of such an establishment).[19]

a. Use of Equipment Situated on EU Territory

The essential element here is whether there is a use of equipment situated on an EU territory. There must be some form of activity by the controller, and the controller must have the clear intention to process the data.[20] The controller does not need to own or control the equipment.

It is also possible to have both Article 4(1)(a) and 4(1)(c) apply if a company has "diverse activities [which] could trigger the application of both . . . if it used equipment and had establishments in different contexts."[21] In such circumstances, different laws would apply to different activities depending on the role of the controllers and the processing activities taking place.

b. "In Transit" Exemption

There is an exemption from the application when data is only stored in transit through the EU territory (e.g., postal services or telecommunications networks). This exemption is extremely narrow[22] and, in practice, is not relevant for most companies. This leaves some ambiguity with respect to the use of EU-based processors by controllers in Third Countries. WP 179 clarifies that in instances when a Third Country controller uses processors or service providers in the European Union, then EU data protection rules would apply in these instances, even if the controller has no other connection to the European Union. The Working Party acknowledges that this is commercially a disadvantage and earmarks this provision for clarification in future legislation[23] (see the box titled "Applicable Law under the GDPR" near the end of this section).

---

18.   This requirement is contained in Article 4(2) of the Directive, which provides that in situations where Article 4 applies, "the controller must designate a representative established in the territory of that Member State, without prejudice to legal actions which could be initiated against the controller himself."

19.   WP 179, *supra* note 7, at 20.

20.   *Id.*; *see also* Working Party, *Working Document on Determining the International Application of EU Data Protection Law to Personal Data Processing on the Internet by Non-EU Based Web Sites* (WP 56) (May 30, 2003), at 9, http://ec.europa.eu/justice/policies/privacy/docs/wpdocs/2002/wp56_en.pdf.

21.   WP 179, *supra* note 7, at 19.

22.   *Id.* at 23.

23.   *Id.* at 24.

c. Appointment of a Representative

If a controller does not have a presence in the European Union, Article 4(1)(c) requires that the controller appoint a representative in the territory whose law is applicable. There is a serious lack of uniformity with respect to the Member State implementation of this provision and in many Member States there are no specific rules on this provision. Most companies choose to appoint either a local entity (in cases in which the Third Country parent is a controller) or a law firm or other private company as such a local representative. The appointment of a representative may give rise to liability or exposure of the representatives in some Member States. For example, some Member State national laws provide for fines for the representatives. Therefore, any arrangements for appointing the representatives should be carefully contemplated to ensure that the relevant responsibilities and sanctions (either civil or criminal) are sufficiently taken into account.

3. Other Circumstances in Which EU Data Protection Law Applies

There is an additional circumstance when a controller is not established within the European Union but EU data protection law would apply; it is when Member State national law applies by means of public international law.

This provision is aimed at specific situations, for example, those involving embassies, ships, and so on, to ensure that the individuals working at an EU embassy abroad would be covered by the Member State national data protection law of their EU government employer (as if they were on their home territory). Conversely, a non-EU embassy would not be subject to an EU host state's national data protection law, as this is determined by international agreement.[24]

PRACTICAL TIPS

In practice, it is safe to assume the applicability of the Directive if personal data is collected through automated or other means in the European Union.[25] Non-EU based entities struggle with the appointment of a representative within the relevant Member State(s). Often, companies appoint an affiliate or company/partner with which they conduct business. From a liability perspective, this raises concerns, and, increasingly, EU-based companies hesitate to perform such a function and, when they do perform it, they tend to ensure that any liability arising from the controller's EU obligations will be covered by the controller.

---

24. WP 179, *supra* note 7, at 18 and 29.
25. In practice, it must be assumed that the applicability of the Directive will always be triggered if personal data is *collected* through automated or other means in the European Union. No formal position has been taken, however, by the Working Party with respect to the mere *importation and processing* of personal data on EU territory (through the retention of an EU-based data center) and the re-exportation of such data.

4. The Multiple Controllers

If companies have multiple establishments, the application of data protection law will depend on the activities of each entity. Additionally, establishments do not necessarily have legal personality and the concept of establishment is rather flexible and—more importantly—is not defined. Thus, it could be that a branch or representative office in a certain jurisdiction could still be a controller. The determining factor is the "effective and real exercise of activities in the context of which personal data are processed."[26] Thus, the presence of a server or computer within a country would not qualify necessarily as an establishment, as this is merely the technical means.[27] If broad sets of operations on personal data occur at the same time, or in a very close period in time, and within multiple EU jurisdictions, it is important to have the global pictures of processing. In such instances, the notion of "context of activities"—and not the location of data—is a decisive factor in identifying the applicable law. Where complex and broad EU processing activities occur, emphasis should be on the controller's establishment that is actively involved in the data processing activities. In practice, it is possible that this scenario could result in one Member State's data protection law having application to all of a controller's processing within the European Union.[28]

The Working Party emphasizes that applicable law is not to be confused with jurisdiction for resolution of disputes (or choice of forum), as the application of data protection law will oftentimes not correlate to jurisdiction.[29] When looking at the activities of entities, the Working Party focuses on the following factors:

a. The degree of involvement of the establishment in the activities—that is, who is doing what? If an entity is processing data in the context of its own activities, then its Member State national law would apply. If it is processing information on behalf of another entity established within the European Union, then that Member State's law would apply.
b. The nature of the activities of the establishments.
c. The objective of "effective protection" under the Directive. Is the data subject properly, fairly, and sufficiently covered?[30]

As the Directive was drafted based on older computing scenarios (i.e., when information was stored in the same place where it was utilized), the issue of whether the law applies or not becomes increasingly convoluted when dealing with data storage, backups, software as a service (SaaS), and cloud-computing scenarios.

---

26. WP 179, *supra* note 7, at 11.
27. *Id.*
28. WP 179, *supra* note 7, at 13.
29. *Id.* at 10.
30. *Id.* at 14.

Thus, it can be the case that information relating to a non-EU citizen is processed by a service provider on EU territory, and therefore EU law would be applicable—even if none of the data relates to individuals in the European Union. This form of territorial spillover makes EU-based software and storage companies very unappealing to non-EU based companies, as, for example, no U.S. company would want to risk application of EU law merely based on a business choice to use an EU company. From an economic and competitive perspective, this is not good for EU businesses, as they are placed at a regulatory disadvantage when it comes to compliance. The GDPR takes this concern into account (see the box titled "Applicable Law under the GDPR").

II. IF THE DIRECTIVE APPLIES, WHICH MEMBER STATE'S NATIONAL LAW WILL BE APPLICABLE?

Most data protection authorities (DPAs) choose to follow the interpretation that provides the maximum protection for data subjects, therefore applying their Member State national laws broadly. By deferring to a broad application of such national laws, this creates possible jurisdictional overlap with other Member States or the extraterritorial application of their laws. In practice, regardless of the language of the Directive and its legislative history, all disputes will be determined by a national court or DPA in accordance with its own Member State national law. Thus, it is important to focus on the application of EU law from the Member State that will be applying it, in order to ascertain a concrete and functional analysis.

When assessing which national law is applicable, it is important to focus on the activities of the different establishments. Oftentimes a Third Country parent company (for example, the United States) will host a human resources database for all of its subsidiaries outside the European Union. This does not necessarily mean that the parent company is collecting and processing an EU entity's employee information for its own purposes. This scenario may be possible; however, the first assumption should always be that within the employment context the entity that employs the relevant individuals is processing their information for its *own* activities. There are instances in which a Third Country parent company could be actively involved in its subsidiary's human resources processing activities and may qualify as a co-controller. On the other hand, it is possible that a Third Country parent collects customer information and is solely in charge of collecting and processing customer information for marketing purposes. In such instances, the parent could qualify as a controller by itself, assuming that the local entity in the European Union does not decide on the purposes and means of processing and that it is not involved in the marketing of products.

Additionally, WP 179 highlights that different applicable laws can be applicable at different stages of processing. Meaning that, depending on the circumstances, the identity of the applicable data protection laws may shift based on such activities. It is also possible to have multiple entities carrying out processing; however, if all of the processing is "to serve a single purpose" this could result in a single Member State national law being applied.

In addition, EU/EEA data protection law will apply "by the location of an establishment of the controller in that Member State, and other Member States' laws could be triggered by the location of other establishments of that controller in those Member States."[31] This means that no single Member State national law will apply to all of a multinational enterprise's activities within the European Union. In a two important cases, the ECJ ruled that Article 4(1)(a) requires that the processing that takes place 'in the context of the activities' of the establishment and what it means to be qualify as an establishment.[32]

Other Member States' laws can be triggered by the location of other establishments of that controller in the relevant Member State. In its opinion, the Working Party highlighted the conflicting issues within the provision and issued recommendations for future clarifications. These have been taken into account in the draft GDPR.

PRACTICAL TIPS

Another issue that companies with large footprints in the European Union face is the question of which Member State national law applies. Often, multinational enterprises store data in one country (at a data center), which all of the group companies in the European Union entities utilize for their information technology (IT) and storage needs. Companies are then confronted with the issue of which Member State national laws they should be following vis-à-vis their personal data processing. A lot of confusion remains around this issue; however, it is best to assume that the Member State national laws of the entity that collects the data (even if ultimately for the parent or a sister company) should be the relevant law. If a subsidiary in the Netherlands collects employee and customer information, which is then stored on the parent company's servers in the United Kingdom, it is best to assume that Dutch law would be applicable to the processing by the sister company and that the UK parent, through the use of its servers and data center, is merely operating as a processor.

---

31. *Id.* at 29.
32. Cases C131/12, Google Spain v Agencia Española de Protección de Datos (AEPD) para. 52, May 13, 2014, *available at* http://curia.europa.eu/juris/document/document.jsf?text=&docid=153853&pageIndex =0&doclang=EN&mode=req&dir=&occ=first&part=1&cid=91349, and C230/14 Weltimmo s. r. o. v. Nemzeti Adatvédelmi és Információszabadság Hatóság, para. 41, Oct. 1, 2015, *available at* http://curia. europa.eu/juris/document/document.jsf?docid=168944&mode=req&pageIndex=1&dir=&occ=first&part =1&text=&doclang=EN&cid=89655, respectively. In Weltimmo, the Court notes "Article 4(1)(a) of Directive 95/46 must be interpreted as permitting the application of the law on the protection of personal data of a Member State other than the Member State in which the controller with respect to the processing of those data is registered, in so far as that controller exercises, through stable arrangements in the territory of that Member State, a real and effective activity — even a minimal one — in the context of which that processing is carried out..." *Id.*

Applicable Law under the GDPR

Under the GDPR, the provisions of applicable law have been split into provisions on material scope and territorial scope. The Commission's initial draft provides that in terms of material scope:

> This Regulation applies to the processing of personal data wholly or partly by automated means, and to the processing other than by automated means of personal data which form part of a filing system or are intended to form part of a filing system.[33]

Specifically excluded are processing activities (1) "which [fall] outside the scope of Union law, in particular concerning national security," (2) of EU institutions (covered by a Regulation on the matter), (3) by Member States in the context of foreign and security policy (i.e., activities under Chapter 2 of the Treaty on the European Union), (4) that are personal or constitute household activities by a private person "without any gainful interest," (5) authorities for the prevention, detection, and investigation of crimes (this is also separately covered by the draft Criminal Justice Data Protection Directive[34] on the matter).[35]

Thus, it is directed at all manual and automated filing systems to maintain a broad scope of possible processing activities. It also specifically excludes activities relating to national security, EU Institutions, activities by Member States with the scope of the processing on common foreign and security policy by the European Union, and activities by natural persons and cooperation authorities for criminal matters.

The territorial scope is broadened under the GDPR and "applies to the processing of personal data in the context of the activities of an establishment of a controller or a processor in the [European Union]."[36] Thus, processors are now expressly included in the scope of application of data protection law. Additionally, to ensure broad coverage for EU data subjects, the GDPR specifies that it applies to the processing of personal data of data subjects residing in the Union by a controller not established in the Union, where the processing activities are related to:

(a) The offering of goods or services to such data subjects in the Union; or

(b) the monitoring of their behavior.[37]

The provision regarding the application due to public international law remains more or less the same.

The GDPR applies to establishments of a controller or processor within the European Union and to non-EU controllers that offer goods or services to EU data subjects or monitor their behavior. The provision maintains the application of EU law within the context of public international law.

---

33. Proposal for Regulation of the European Parliament and of the Council on the Protection of Individuals with regard to the Processing of Personal Data and on the Free Movement of such Data (General Data Protection Regulation) COM (2012) 11 final (Jan. 25, 2012) [hereinafter GDPR], art. 2(1), at 40.

34. Proposal for a Directive of the European Parliament and of the Council on the Protection of Individuals with Regard to the Processing of Personal Data by Competent Authorities for the Purposes of Prevention, Investigation, Detection or Prosecution of Criminal Offenses or the Execution of Criminal Penalties, and the Free Movement of Such Data, COM (2012) 10 final (Jan. 25, 2012), http://eurlex.europa.eu/LexUriServ/LexUriServ.do?uri=COM:2012:0010:FIN:EN:PDF.

35. GDPR, art. 2(2), at 40.

36. GDPR, art. 3(1), at 41.

37. GDPR, art. 3(2), at 41.

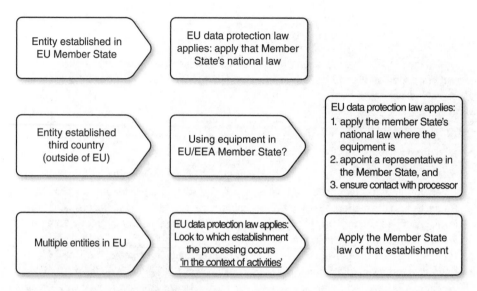

Figure 2.1: Does the Directive Apply?

III. AM I A CONTROLLER OR A PROCESSOR?

As mentioned, the distinction under the Directive between controller and processor is a pivotal one for the determination of the national law applicable to the processing and the responsibility for data protection law compliance, among other reasons. Many (but not all) of the responsibilities under the Directive fall on controllers, not processors.

As we have seen, a controller determines the purpose and means of the processing, regardless of how this is classified by contract (see Chapter 1 Section II.E). Nonetheless, from various examples it can be distilled that the subcontractor who supplies services of the processing of personal data is generally a processor, working for its client—a controller. The processor conducts its processing activities on behalf of its client—the controller.

Thus, a company collecting its customers' personal data and determining the purpose of such collection and further processing would be the controller, and the service provider who processes the data for the company—whether this is in terms of storing the data in the cloud, using the data in a call center, or analyzing the data—would generally be a processor. The processor acts on behalf of, and upon the instructions of, the controller. The processor accesses the data *for the purpose of processing*, but does not *establish the purposes* for the processing.

Furthermore, the processor is a subcontractor that carries out processing under a "contract or legal act binding the processor to the controller and stipulating in particular that:—the processor shall act only on instructions from the controller."[38]

---

38. Directive, art. 17(3), at 43.

From Working Party examples and guidance, one may extract certain qualities of a controller and a processor:

Controller	Processor
Gives instructions	Receives and follows instructions
Determines purposes of processing	Does not determine purposes of processing
Has great discretion regarding the processing	Has limited discretion regarding the processing
Is the *client* in the processing service relationship	Is the *service provider* in the processing service relationship
Contracts for another party–the processor–to act on its behalf	Acts on behalf of another party–the controller
Determines the essential means of the processing	Does *not* determine the essential means of the processing
If it processes personal data, it does so for its own purposes	Does not process personal data for its own purposes–only for those of the controller

Some examples drawn from Working Party guidance make clear the distinction between controller and processor, and they will assist in determining the status of your client or your employer:

I am a controller when:

- *In a direct mailing campaign*, I give "clear instructions" to service providers as to the materials to be sent, and other purposes and means of the campaign (payments, addressees of the campaign, etc.) and they are bound to follow them, where the service providers have limited discretion, and where only I am entitled to use the processed data. (WP 169, Example 2)[39]
- *In a cloud-computing service relationship*, I am the client and I determine the "ultimate purpose of the processing," and decide to outsource and delegate processing.[40]
- *I am a social network service provider*, and I provide the means for processing the personal data of data subjects and provide the "basic" account management services (e.g., registration). I also determine the marketing use of the personal data.[41]
- *I am a social network application provider*, and my applications, which are selected by the data subjects, run in addition to ones from the social network service provider.[42]

---

39. WP 169, *supra* note 1, at 13.
40. *See* Working Party, *Opinion 05/2012 on the Cloud Computing* (WP 196) (July 1, 2012) [hereinafter WP 196], at 17, http://ec.europa.eu/justice/data-protection/article-29/documentation/opinion-recommendation/files/2012/wp196_en.pdf.
41. *See* Working Party, *Opinion 5/2009 on Online Social Networking* (WP 163) (June 12, 2009), at 5, http://ec.europa.eu/justice/policies/privacy/docs/wpdocs/2009/wp163_en.pdf.
42. *Id.*

- *I am a search engine provider* that processes the personal data of data subjects, including IP addresses or cookies with unique user IDs.[43]

I am a processor when:
- *In a direct mailing campaign*, I receive "clear instructions" from my client as to the materials to be sent, and other purposes and means of the campaign (payments, addressees of the campaign, etc.), where I have limited discretion in the processing, and where I am not entitled to use the processed data. Such is the case even when I may choose certain means such as software used in the process, and where I may offer advice. (WP 169, Example 2)[44]
- *I am an Internet service provider (ISP)*, and I provide hosting services for customers for their website hosting, and I do *not* further process the data contained on their websites for my own purposes. (WP 169, Example 16)[45]
- *In a cloud-computing service relationship*, I am the cloud provider—an "entity that provides cloud computing services" and that "supplies the means and the platform, acting on behalf of the cloud client."[46]

An example of when an entity is designated as a processor but in fact is acting as a controller would be when a marketing company provides advertisements and direct marketing to certain companies. To the extent that the marketing company uses one of its customer's databases for marketing another customer's marketing, it would be acting as a controller—it has added an additional purpose to the processing.[47]

With respect to certain data processing there may exist *joint data controllers*, and a processor may at other times be a separate controller. This may be the case, for example, when a cloud provider, in addition to processing personal data on behalf of its client, "processes data for its own purposes."[48] This may also arise in other situations in which data is transferred to multiple controllers with each processing the personal data for its own purposes.

- An example is when a travel agency, hotel company, and airline set up an Internet platform for travel management. "They agree on important elements of the means to be used, such as which data will be stored, how reservations will be allocated and confirmed and who can have access." Thus, each will act as a joint controller vis-à-vis the customers whose personal data is included in the platform.[49]

---

43. *See* Working Party, *Opinion 1/2008 on Data Protection Issues Related to Search Engines* (WP 148) (Apr. 4, 2008) [hereinafter WP 148], at 9, http://ec.europa.eu/justice/policies/privacy/docs/wpdocs/2008/wp148_en.pdf.
44. WP 169, *supra* note 1, at 13.
45. *Id.* at 25.
46. WP 196, *supra* note 39, at 8.
47. *Id.* at 14.
48. WP 196, *supra* note 39, at 8.
49. *Id.* at 20.

This is distinguished from situations in which different actors are processing the same data in sequential order.

- One example is when a company processes salary data of its employees and it must send this information to the tax authorities under law. Although each processes the same data, they do so for different purposes and means. Thus, each will act as a separate sole controller.[50]

In addition, there may be *subprocessors* with ostensibly the same obligations as the processor itself and subject to the controller's instructions.[51] This might be the case in a cloud-computing context, for example, when the cloud service provider—a processor—subcontracts out for server storage of personal data and other processing operations.

IV. DO I HAVE A SUFFICIENT LEGAL BASIS FOR PROCESSING?

In order to process personal data in the European Union, there must be a sufficient legal basis for processing—that is, the processing must be *legitimate*. The alternative criteria for the establishment of legitimacy are set out in Article 7 of the Directive,[52] and general principles regarding data quality are set out in its Article 6.[53]

As noted, personal data must be processed lawfully (Article 6(a)) and in a proper and careful manner and collected for specific, explicitly defined and legitimate purposes (Article 6(b)).[54] In addition, personal data must be processed based on one of the legal bases provided in the national laws of Member States implementing the Directive. It is important to note that a transfer of personal data, whether within the EEA or outside of it, qualifies as processing. As such, prior to transfer one will also need to rely on a legitimate basis for such transfer (see Chapter 3 Sections III and IV for more on transfers outside of the European Union and transfers to third parties, respectively). In practice, one of the following legal bases will likely be relevant:

(1) Unambiguous consent of the data subject has been obtained (Article 7(a));
(2) Processing is necessary for the performance of a contract to which the data subject is a party (e.g., a labor agreement or a consumer agreement) or for actions to be carried out at the request of the data subject and which are *necessary*

---

50. *Id.*
51. WP 196, *supra* note 39, at 9.
52. Directive, art. 7, at 40.
53. *Id.*, art. 6, at 40.
54. For example, a legitimate purpose for the processing of employee data could be payroll administration, performance management, and/or coordination of work-related travel. An unlawful purpose would be to sell employees' information to third parties who would use such information for marketing purposes.

for the conclusion of a contract (e.g., granting and administering benefits to employees) (Article 7(b));

(3) Processing is *necessary* to comply with a legal obligation to which the controller is subject (Article 7(c)); or

(4) Processing is *necessary* to uphold the legitimate interests of the controller or of a third party to whom the data are supplied (Article 7(f)).

Note that the grounds for processing-related bases in items 2, 3, and 4 apply a test based on *necessity*—if the processing is not necessary, the test is not met and the relevant ground does not legitimize the processing. In this context, it should be noted that the concept of necessity has "its own independent meaning" in EU law, in the interest of legal harmonization between the Member States, and it "must be interpreted in a manner which fully reflects the objective of [the Directive], as laid down in Article 1(1) thereof."[55] That objective involves the protection of fundamental rights and freedoms of individuals "and in particular their right to privacy with respect to the processing of personal data."[56] Also, several of the bases listed here may relate to a given fact situation. An example from Working Party guidance illustrates this:

Example: buying a car

The data controller may be entitled to process personal data according to different purposes and on the basis of different grounds:

- Data necessary to buy the car: Article 7(b) [basis 2],

- To process the car's papers: Article 7(c) [basis 3],

- For client management services (e.g., to have the car serviced in different affiliate companies within the EU): Article 7(f) [basis 4],

- To transfer the data to third parties for their own marketing activities: Article 7(a) [basis 1].[57]

---

55. Case C-524/06, Heinz Huber v Bundesrepublik Deutschland, para. 52, at 13, Dec. 16, 2008, *available at* http://eur-lex.europa.eu/legal-content/EN/TXT/HTML/?uri=CELEX:62006CJ0524&qid=140154349 3120&from=EN. For a further discussion of this point, *see* Working Party, *Opinion 06/2014 on the Notion of Legitimate Interests of the Data Controller under Article 7 of Directive 95/46/EC* (WP 217) (Apr. 9, 2014) [hereinafter WP 217], at 11, http://ec.europa.eu/justice/data-protection/article-29/documentation/opinion-recommendation/files/2014/wp217_en.pdf.

56. Directive, art. 1(1), at 38.

57. *See* Working Party, *Opinion 15/2011 on the Definition of Consent* (WP 187) (July 13, 2011) [hereinafter WP 187], at 8, http://ec.europa.eu/justice/data-protection/article-29/documentation/opinion-recommendation/files/2011/wp187_en.pdf.

To further clarify these concepts, a short discussion of each of these grounds follows.

A. Unambiguous Consent of the Data Subject

The unambiguous consent should generally be an expression of the data subject's intent to allow processing (which should be entirely clear, or "unambiguous"), and there should be some affirmative action taken by the data subject (e.g., providing a writing, making an oral statement, or engaging in behavior—such as clicking on a website button or checking an originally unchecked box) in order to provide such consent. The data subject should have been properly informed about the use of his or her personal data (including the purposes of the processing) and about his or her rights, and the data subject should have freely given his or her specific consent for the processing. Proper evidence of such consent should be carefully stored and retained.[58]

Processing of sensitive personal data is generally prohibited, although several exceptions apply. Sensitive personal data is personal data revealing racial or ethnic origin, political opinions, religious or philosophical beliefs, trade-union membership, and data concerning one's health or sex life.[59] However, some national laws provide for specific exemptions from the general prohibition, and the Directive provides that "explicit" consent (e.g., actively opting in) may be a basis for processing when the relevant Member State does not preclude this.[60]

B. Processing is Necessary for the Performance of a Contract or for Actions to be Carried Out at the Request of the Data Subject that are Necessary for the Conclusion of a Contract

The legal basis related to a contract provides in part that processing may be made when required in order to perform a contract to which the data subject is a party. An example of when this basis may be used is when a search engine provider may use personal data that a data subject provides in order to register for a certain service (e.g., a user account).[61] Another example is when siblings submit hair samples for DNA testing to confirm that they truly are siblings. The laboratory has a "sufficiently legal basis" for the processing

---

58. *Id.* at 11–25. For a short discussion of WP 187, *see* W. Gregory Voss, Katherine Woodcock, et al., *Privacy, E-Commerce, and Data Security*, 46 INT'L LAW. 97 (2012), at 99–100; *see also* W. Gregory Voss, *Survey of Recent European Union Privacy Developments*, 68 BUS. LAW. 205 (2012), at 207–208.

59. *Id.* art. 8(1), at 40.

60. *Id.* art. 8(2)(a), at 40. For a discussion of this provision, and, more generally, of requirements to be met for processing, *see* Gregory Shaffer, *Globalization and Social Protection: The Impact of EU and International Rules in the Ratcheting Up of U.S. Privacy Standards*, 25 YALE J. INT'L L. 1, 15 (2000).

61. WP 148, *supra* note 42, at 17.

of biometric data here under Article 7(b) of the Directive.[62] The Working Party cautions, however, that this provision "must be interpreted strictly and does not cover situations in which the processing is not genuinely necessary for the performance of a contract, but rather unilaterally imposed on the data subject by the controller," such as when profiling of a website user's tastes and lifestyle is done based on clicks and purchases on the website, for which the profiling has not been contracted. In addition, "electronic monitoring of employee internet, email or telephone use, or video-surveillance of employees more clearly constitute processing that is likely to go beyond what is necessary for the performance of an employment contract."[63]

Steps taken during the precontractual period may fit under this basis, subject to their having been requested by the data subject, such as when he or she accepts an offer for a product, in which case "processing for these purposes, such as keeping address details and information on what has been requested, for a limited period of time, will be appropriate under this legal ground." On the other hand, background checks by insurers and credit reference requests, when not requested by the data subject, would not fit under this basis.[64]

C. Processing is Necessary to Comply with a Legal Obligation to Which the Controller is Subject

One fact situation that fits within the legal basis for processing is when fingerprints and biometric identifiers are used in passports or visas.[65] Another example is when employers must report salary information to tax authorities, when such obligation is imposed by the law of the European Union or one of its Member States. This would not be the case when an obligation is imposed, for example, by a U.S. law with extraterritorial effect, such as Sarbanes-Oxley.[66]

In another situation, the Working Party highlights that law enforcement authorities may request personal data of search engine users in order to fight crime and that complying with such a request should not be confused with *complying with a legal obligation*.[67] In such a case, one should instead determine whether the processing is necessary to uphold the legitimate interests of a third party.

---

62. *See* Working Party, *Opinion 3/2012 on the Developments in Biometric Technologies* (WP 193) (Apr. 27, 2012) [hereinafter WP 193], at 11, http://ec.europa.eu/justice/data-protection/article-29/documentation/opinion-recommendation/files/2012/wp193_en.pdf.

63. WP 217, *supra* note 54, at 16–17.

64. *Id.* at 18.

65. WP 193, *supra* note 61, at 12.

66. WP 217, *supra* note 54, at 19.

67. WP 148, *supra* note 42, at 18.

D. Processing is Necessary to Uphold the Legitimate Interests of the Controller or of a Third Party to Whom the Data are Supplied

In its Opinion on the Notion of Legitimate Interests of the Data Controller under Article 7 of [the Directive] (WP 217), the Working Party highlights that this basis "has its own natural field of relevance" and that its use, "in the right circumstances and subject to adequate safeguards, may also help prevent misuse of, and over-reliance on, other legal grounds."[68] This legal basis, referred to in item 4, is a limited one. Indeed, Article 7(f) expressly provides that it does not apply "where such interests are over-ridden by the interests for fundamental rights and freedoms of the data subject which require protection under Article 1(1)," such as the right to privacy.[69] A case-by-case balancing of the two interests must be done to apply this limitation. The Working Party states that

[i]n order to be relevant under Article 7(f), a "legitimate interest" must therefore:

- be lawful (i.e., in accordance with applicable EU and national law);

- be sufficiently clearly articulated to allow the balancing test to be carried out against the interests and fundamental rights of the data subject (i.e., sufficiently specific);

- represent a real and present interest (i.e., not be speculative).[70]

Notwithstanding this balancing requirement, one scholar has referred to this basis as "relatively flexible for non-sensitive information used for ordinary servicing of clients." (citation omitted)[71]

An example of when this basis may apply is when a company engaging in dangerous research (e.g., research on dangerous viruses or bacteria) secures laboratory entrance based on use of biometrics such as fingerprints or eye scans, which is considered very intrusive processing. The company has a legitimate interest in restricting access to the laboratory to relevant trustworthy persons, and this overrides privacy concerns.[72]

In the case of search engines, system security or fraud prevention may be grounds for processing in order to uphold their legitimate interests; however, the Working Party cautions that data stored for these purposes must be "subject to strict purpose

---

68. WP 217, *supra* note 54, at 9.
69. Directive, art. 7(f), at 40.
70. WP 217, *supra* note 54, at 25. For guidance on how to carry out this balancing test, *see id.*, at 55–56.
71. *See* Gregory Shaffer, *supra* note 59, at 14.
72. WP 193, *supra* note 61, at 13.

limitation"—that is, it must be limited to that purpose only, it must not exceed the data that is necessary for such purpose, and it must have a retention period limited to what is strictly necessary.[73]

E. Summary

When the Directive does apply, one of the grounds for legitimate processing contained in Member State implementing legislation must be present to process personal data. This means that the data subject has given his or her unambiguous consent to the processing, after having received proper information, through some affirmative action. Alternatively, it means that other bases for legitimacy exist, such as those relating to what is necessary for the performance of a contract to which the data subject is a party, or in order to comply with a legal obligation of the controller, or to uphold the latter's legitimate interests. The specific provisions of applicable Member State law should be verified to ensure that a national legitimate basis exists prior to proceeding with the processing.

Applicable Law under the GDPR

Similar data quality requirements (moved to Article 5 of the GDPR) and legitimate grounds for processing (moved to Article 6 of the GDPR) apply under the GDPR.

However, the GDPR does make several changes:

- It adds a requirement that the data be processed ":n a transparent manner." (Article 5(a))
- It expands on the concept of data not being "excessive" by referring to the data being "limited to the minimum necessary in relation to the purposes for which they are processed; they shall be processed only if, and as long as, the purposes could not be fulfilled by processing information that does not involve personal data" instead. (Article 5(c))
- It adds a time requirement for the erasure or rectification of inaccurate personal data—"without delay." (Article 5(d))
- It makes it clearer that compliance with the GDPR is the *responsibility and the liability* of the controller and it adds that the controller must also "*demonstrate* for each processing operation the compliance with the provisions" of the GDPR. (Article 5(f)) (emphasis added)
- Finally, it requires that consent be given "for one or more *specific purposes*." (Article 6.1(a), underscoring the fact that consent must be specific) (emphasis added)

---

73. WP 148, *supra* note 42, at 18.

3

Practical Steps for Compliance

In practice, companies need to accomplish three major sets of steps in order to ensure compliance with EU data protection laws: (1) the notification or registrations with the relevant data protection authorities (DPAs); (2) the development of internal documentation; and (3) ensuring the compliance of international data transfers. These steps have been handled separately in this chapter for the sake of discussion; however all three are closely (even intimately) correlated and cannot be separated from a compliance perspective—meaning that all are equally important in terms of compliance with the law. For example, you cannot confront the issue of interacting with DPAs (i.e., filing notifications) unless you have drafted and implemented internal documentation and are confident about compliance with the rules on international transfers.

I. INTERACTIONS WITH DPAS

Interactions with the relevant DPAs fall under three possible categories: (1) the obligation to register data processing activities; (2) the obligation to have the DPA perform a prior check on processing activities in certain specific circumstances; and, finally, (3) dealing with the DPA's general abilities to investigate, ask follow-up questions, request information, and generally act as a supervisory body.

A. Notifications to DPAs

Article 18(1) of the Directive sets out the obligation to register data processing with the relevant DPA:

> Member States shall provide that the controller or his representative, if any, must notify the supervisory authority referred to in Article 28 before carrying out any wholly or partly automatic processing operation or set of such operations intended to serve a single purpose or several related purposes.[1]

Notification to the relevant DPA is "designed to ensure disclosure of the purposes and main features of any processing operation for the purpose of verification that the

---

1. Directive 95/46/EC of the European Parliament and of the Council of 24 Oct. 1995 on the protection of individuals with regard to the processing of personal data and on the free movement of such data [hereinafter Directive], 1995 O.J. (L 281) 31 (Nov. 23, 1995), art. 18(1), at 43–44.

operation is in accordance with the national measure taken under . . . [the] Directive."[2] Generally, entities acting as data controllers are required to notify the processing of personal data to the relevant DPA for inclusion on a public register maintained by it, subject to a number of exemptions. As mentioned, controllers are legal entities that collect data from their employees and others and specify in what manner and for what purpose such data will be processed or used. Thus, companies will need to assess which entities collect data about their employees, customers, and others; who holds the data; and which entities should file a notification to the relevant DPA.

In a small number of countries, for example in Finland and Ireland, data processors are also subject to notification obligations.

1. Timing of Notifications—Prior to Processing

Controllers subject to the relevant DPA's national law must register their processing activities prior to carrying them out. In reality, as many companies are catching up with their basic notification requirements, this is a bit of a gray area—with companies pretending they are complying and DPAs turning a blind eye to the fact that many companies are notifying practices or data files that have been in place for years. Typically, this is not an issue for low-impact processing (e.g., basic human resources data); however, when files pertain to more sensitive issues (e.g., whistle-blowing hotlines, criminal background information, etc.), more care should be taken when notifying and it may be worthwhile to consult a local lawyer to verify the possible risks. It is also worth considering, when playing catch up whether processing should be suspended until the notification procedure has been finalized with the DPA.

2. Exemptions from Notification

Exemptions from notification are provided "where processing is unlikely adversely to affect the rights and freedoms of data subjects."[3] Most Member States have simplified notification procedures or exempted certain categories of data processing from the notification requirement. These exemptions depend on the country and factual circumstances (e.g., types of data processed and the purposes for processing). Most countries permit exemptions for data processing in the context of basic human resources processing (e.g., payroll and administration of basic benefits) and business contact information. Additionally, a few exclude data processing for accounting purposes (e.g., customer invoicing and billing practices). However, it is good to keep in mind that these exemptions vary in scope based on the relevant country and are not interpreted uniformly. Finally, there are exemptions for when entities have appointed

---

2. *Id.*, recital 48, at 36.
3. *Id.*, recital 49, at 36. Art. 18(2) specifies that "Member States may provide for the simplification of or exemption from notification only in the following cases and under the following conditions: where, for categories of processing operations which are unlikely, taking account of the data to be processed, to affect adversely the rights and freedoms of data subjects, they specify the purposes of the processing, the data or categories of data undergoing processing, the category or categories of data subject, the recipients or categories of recipient to whom the data are to be disclosed and the length of time the data are to be stored." *Id.* at 44.

a data protection officer (DPO) or representative and for when the processing has as its sole purpose "the keeping of a register which according to laws or regulations is intended to provide information to the public and which is open to consultations either by the public in general or by any person demonstrating a legitimate interest."[4] This exemption is further explained in Chapter 3 Section I.C.

PRACTICAL TIPS

If you would like to find out whether certain types of data processing would be exempt verify local law. It is also possible to call the local DPA and verify how the exemptions are interpreted this in practice. When contacting DPAs, it is best to do so in a personal capacity and not on behalf of an organization, as this could attract unwanted attention to the company's data processing practices. Typically, DPAs are quite willing to answer basic questions on the law and local procedures. If there are language barriers, rely on your local entity or contact persons (e.g., external counsel) to communicate in an informal way with the DPA.

A table containing a list of websites with links to national registry and notification information is contained in this book's appendix A.

3. Notification Procedure

Article 19 of the Directive specifies the minimum information that must be included in DPA notifications:

1. Member States shall specify the information to be given in the notification. It shall include at least:
   (a) the name and address of the controller and of its representative, if any;
   (b) the purpose or purposes of the processing;
   (c) a description of the category or categories of data subject and of the data or categories of data relating to them;
   (d) the recipients or categories of recipient to whom the data might be disclosed;
   (e) proposed transfers of data to third countries;
   (f) a general description allowing a preliminary assessment to be made of the appropriateness of the measures taken pursuant to Article 17 [of the Directive] to ensure security of processing.[5]

The procedures for notification of processing activities to the DPAs vary widely by country and at the moment there is no harmonized notification procedure in the European Union. In addition to the required information specified in the Directive,

---

4.   *Id.* art. 18(3), at 44. There is also an exemption from notification when processing sensitive data for legitimate activities. Although, again, national requirements on this approach vary. *Id.* art. 18(4), at 44.
5.   *Id.* art. 19(1), at 44.

notifications also typically require information on (1) how and when notice is provided to data subjects; (2) the contact person or address where individuals may exercise their rights of access, rectification, and deletion; and (3) confirmation that third-party service providers are bound by contract (or other legally binding means) and (4) that information security and confidentiality requirements are observed.

The DPAs may check the notification forms and assess any risks to individuals' data protection rights. In practice, this may be accomplished by looking at the documentation and information included in the form. However, it is also possible that DPAs may request clarification or further information following notification. Therefore, it is important to provide sufficiently detailed and accurate information to the relevant DPA during the notification procedures. This is a balancing exercise; trying to achieve factually accurate descriptions of processing activities while providing just the right amount of detail (without triggering unwanted attention of the DPAs).

4. Maintenance of Notifications

The relevant DPAs must be informed of any changes to notifications.[6] Typically, controllers have a certain period of time in which to update notifications. Some countries, for example, Ireland and the United Kingdom, require that notifications be renewed on an annual basis.

When organizations undergo mergers or acquisitions, notifications may also need to be updated. First and foremost, to reflect the proper controller following the transaction, but also to reflect the details of the notification if the processing activities have changed. This can include information on data categories, external processors and destination countries for the purposes of international data transfers. Not surprisingly, approaches of DPAs differ when it comes to such transactions. Some allow for notification regardless of the nature of the transaction; others depend on the nature of the transaction.[7]

PRACTICAL TIPS

How Do You File Notifications?

Typically, countries allow for notifications to be submitted online or through the mail as well as via fax or by using electronic signatures. If sending the notification through the mail, it is a good idea to send it as a registered letter, to maintain evidence that the notification was received. The notification forms are generally available on the DPA websites; however, only a few DPAs have translations available in English. Also keep in mind that the supporting documentation may have to be translated into the local language. The notifying entity will have to arrange for a duly authorized

---

6. *Id*. art. 19(2), at 44.
7. For example, if an acquired entity is dissolved some DPAs do not permit the transfer of the notification to the newly formed entity or acquiring company, even if the processing activities remain identical to those in the notification.

representative to sign the notifications. Finally, it is very important to keep copies of the notifications or other documents (e.g., cover letters) submitted to the DPAs. This will ensure that if there are questions about your compliance status in the future, this documentation is readily available. Often companies to do not properly store or file this information (or make it available or easy to find later), which adds to the cost of compliance and a leads to repetitive work.

How Many Notifications Must You Submit?

Some DPAs require notifications based on the "filing system" or the number of software applications (e.g., databases and information systems) in use. Therefore, if you have two human resources databases—for example, one for payroll and another for the administration of compensation and benefits—these would need to be submitted separately. The majority of countries require notifications based on the *purpose* or *objective* of processing. Therefore, this could be as broad as employment purposes or be further segmented into human resources administration and recruitment. How this separation is made in practice can also deviate: some DPAs although requiring notifications per purpose, can require separate filings based on the scope of data categories involved. For example, if a company has a customer relationship management system with names, addresses and job titles for marketing purposes, but also uses these data categories plus additional ones (tax information, order history) for management and tracking of orders, this system can require two notifications. This is because although there is a general purpose of the system—customer relationship management—the notifications require further specification on such purposes.

B.   Prior Checks—Authorization by DPAs

When processing is likely to pose risks to individuals' rights and freedoms, DPAs or the DPO in cooperation with the DPA should have the authority to check the processing prior to its commencement.[8]

Article 20 of the Directive provides in relevant part:

1. Member States shall determine the processing operations likely to present specific risks to the rights and freedoms of data subjects and shall check that these processing operations are examined prior to the start thereof.
2. Such prior checks shall be carried out by the supervisory authority following receipt of a notification from the controller or by the data protection official, who, in cases of doubt, must consult the supervisory authority.[9]

---

8.   *Id*. art. 20, at 44; *see generally id*. recitals 53 and 54, at 36.
9.   *Id*. art. 20(1) and (2), at 44.

The prior checking can be effectuated through declaration in a notification or, in some Member States, applied for through a separate procedure. Following this "check," the DPA may issue an opinion or authorization about the processing. These prior checks tend to be standard for the processing of sensitive data and in cases of certain international transfers (e.g., in a handful of countries when relying on the Commission-approved model clause contracts and in most countries when relying on distinct data transfer agreements (non–Commission-approved contracts)).

C. DPOs

Similar to the exemptions from notification, some Member States provide exemptions from notification or simplified notification procedures when a DPO has been appointed. The Directive provides that Member States may choose to exempt companies from notification if they have appointed a DPO. DPOs are to ensure compliance with applicable data protection laws in an independent manner and retain a register of the processing operations of the company.[10] The register is analogous to the notifications of processing operations that would typically be provided to and kept on file with the DPA. Therefore, DPOs must take care of the internal notifications for processing. Not all Member States have chosen to implement this exemption, but several important jurisdictions (e.g., Germany, the Netherlands, Poland and Sweden) do provide for it. The idea is that notification can be exempted or simplified where appointed people "ensure that the processing carried out is not likely adversely to affect the rights and freedoms of data subjects."[11] Practical guidance on the appointment of DPOs and their responsibilities is issued by various DPAs.

1. Timing of Your Interactions with the DPAs and Risks Associated with Notifications

Notifications are meant to ensure transparency with both the general public (including your employees and customers) and the supervising DPAs. This exercise must be balanced against a company's internal compliance in the field of data protection. In some countries, notification could trigger closer scrutiny by the DPA involving DPAs asking questions about your data protection and privacy compliance program. This will not be the case in every country, but it is important to understand where there may be additional security protocols (e.g., Poland[12] and Hungary[13]) and to ensure that your internal documentation is in order prior to notifying with the DPAs.

---

10. *Id*. art. 18(2) subparagraphs 2–4, at 44.
11. *Id*. recital 49, at 36.
12. Polish Act of 29 August 1997 on the Protection of Personal Data, as amended, at Articles 36 and 39a.
13. Hungarian Act CXII of 2011 on the Right of Informational Self-Determination and on Freedom of Information, generally § 7(1)–(4) and § 7(5) and (6) specifically. Additionally, internal data protection officers are tasked with documenting the security measures; *see* § 24(2).

Applicable Law under the General Data Protection Regulation (GDPR)

In a welcome change, the GDPR eliminates the requirement for controllers to notify processing to the DPAs. However, this requirement is replaced with a much broader obligation on the part of both controllers and processors to maintain documents on their processing activities.

Notifications/Registrations

Replacement of the notification requirement with a requirement to keep documentation is significant because every company involved in processing (both controllers *and* processors) will have a duty to keep documents about "all processing operations under its responsibility."[14]

Art. 28(2) of the GDPR builds on the information required for notifications (Article 19 of the Directive) and requires that the mandatory documentation must at least include the following information about the processing:

(a) the name and **contact details** of the controller, **or any joint controller or processor,** and of **the** representative, if any;

(b) the **name and contact details of the data protection officer, if any;**

(c) **the** purposes of the processing, **including the legitimate interests pursued by the controller where the processing is based on point (f) of Article 6(1);**

(d) a description of categories of data subjects and of the categories of **personal** data relating to them;

(e) the recipients or categories of recipients **of the personal data, including the controllers** to whom **personal** data **are** disclosed **for the legitimate interest pursued by them;**

(f) **where applicable, transfers of data to a third country or an international organisation, including the identification of that third country or international organisation and, in case of transfers referred to in point (h) of Article 44(1), the documentation of appropriate safeguards;**

(g) a general **indication of the time limits for erasure of the different categories of data;**

(h) the description **of the mechanisms referred** to in Article **22(3).**

This documentation must be available to the supervisory authority upon request.[15] An exemption to the requirement exists for companies that have a "natural person processing

---

14. Proposal for Regulation of the European Parliament and of the Council on the Protection of Individuals with regard to the Processing of Personal Data and on the Free Movement of such Data (General Data Protection Regulation) COM (2012) 11 final (Jan. 25, 2012) [hereinafter GDPR], art. 28(1), at 58.
15. *Id.* art. 28(3), at 59.

personal data without a commercial interest" or for "an enterprise or organization employ-ing fewer than 250 persons that is processing personal data only as an activity ancillary to its main activities."[16]

As with most provisions, the Commission is empowered to create standard forms for the required documentation.[17]

Prior Authorization

Again building on concepts from the Directive, the GDPR takes the prior checking requirement from Article 20 and includes a requirement for both authorization and con-sultation with the supervisory authority

> [W]here a controller or processor adopts contractual clauses as provided for in point (d) of Article 42(2) or does not provide for the appropriate safeguards in a legally binding instrument as referred to in Article 42(5) for the transfer of personal data to a third country or an international organisation.[18]

Additionally, prior consultation with the supervisory authority is required when a DPA "indicates that processing operations are by virtue of their nature, their scope or their pur-poses, likely to present a high degree of specific risks"[19] or when the supervisory authority has published a list of processing operations which are to be consulted first.[20]

DPOs

The role of DPOs is significantly expanded under the GDPR, as proposed by the Com-mission. Companies with more than 250 people or whose "core activities . . . consist of processing operations which, by virtue of their nature, their scope and/or their purposes, require regular and systematic monitoring of data subjects."[21] When a DPO is required due to size of the labor force, a group of companies may appoint a single DPO. Other companies may appoint a DPO if they choose, but it is not required.

The requirement to designate a DPO also exists pursuant to Article 35, and his or her name and contact details must be provided to the supervisory authority.[22] Articles 36 and 37 further elaborate on the DPO's role and relevant tasks and responsibilities.

Powers of the DPAs

The roles of the DPAs are strengthened and expanded in the GDPR. Additionally, in order to create the so-called one-stop-shop mechanism, the GDPR includes a procedure

---

16.   *Id.* art. 28(4), at 59.
17.   *Id.* art. 28(6), at 59.
18.   *Id.* art. 34(1), at 63.
19.   *Id.* art. 34(2)(a), at 64.
20.   *Id.* art. 34(2)(b), art. 34(4) and 34(5), at 64.
21.   *Id.* art. 35(1)(b) and (c), at 65. All public authorities or bodies are also required to appoint a DPO (*Id.* art. 35(1)(a), at 65).
22.   *Id.* art. 35(9), at 65.

whereby a lead DPA can act as the single regulator vis-à-vis companies subject to EU data protection law. Article 51(2) specifically provides:

> Where the processing of personal data takes place in the context of the activities of an establishment of a controller or a processor in the Union, and the controller or processor is established in more than one Member State, the supervisory authority of the main establishment of the controller or processor shall be competent for the supervision of the processing activities of the controller or the processor in all Member States, without prejudice to the provisions of Chapter VII of this [GDPR].

Here, the relevant lead DPA will be determined based on "the main establishment" of the relevant company.

DPA duties, as well as a specific list of "powers" are laid out in Articles 52 and 53, with a specific aim of increasing the enforcement capabilities of the DPAs. Generally, DPAs are empowered to:

- notify a party in breach of data protection obligations and order remedies;
- issue orders to comply with requests by individual data subjects to exercise their individual rights;
- order information on processing;
- ensure compliance with prior authorizations or consultations;
- issue warnings and order the correction, deletion, or destruction of personal data illegally processed;
- impose a temporary or definitive ban on processing;
- suspend international data flows;
- issue opinions on any issue related to the protection of personal data; and
- inform governments and authorities on issues of data protection.

DPAs are also empowered with certain access rights in order to investigate personal data systems and premises as well as equipment where processing occurs.[23]

Two major additions to the GDPR are the cooperation and consistency mechanisms. Cooperation duties included in Articles 55 and 56 relate to how DPAs interact with one another and are required to comply with requests of other DPAs (including joint operations). The consistency mechanism is included in Articles 57 through 63 and lays out a complex procedure to ensure uniform application of data protection when multiple DPAs are involved. As currently drafted, the GDPR contemplates a European Data Protection Board, which will act as the unifying body ensuring consistency in application of the GDPR throughout the European Union. The GDPR also contemplates situations whereby Member States' DPAs differ on issues and may take urgent—unilateral—temporary decisions. These provisions are also tempered with the powers of the Commission to take certain implementing measures.

---

23. *Id.* art. 53(2), at 79.

II. INTERNAL DOCUMENTS

A.   Notice Requirement (Information to Individuals)

The Directive calls for certain types of information to be given to data subjects to ensure transparency about the processing of their personal data. This "information requirement" exists regardless of whether personal data has been obtained directly from the individuals or not.

When data are collected directly from individuals (data subjects), the Directive requires that the following information be provided to them, unless they have already obtained it:

> (a) the identity of the controller and of his representative, if any;
> (b) the purposes of the processing for which the data are intended;
> (c) any further information such as
>> — the recipients or categories of recipients of the data,
>> — whether replies to the questions are obligatory or voluntary, as well as the possible consequences of failure to reply,
>> — the existence of the right of access to and the right to rectify the data concerning him in so far as such further information is necessary, having regard to the specific circumstances in which the data are collected, to guarantee fair processing in respect of the data subject.[24]

If personal data about the individual has been obtained from a third party and not from the data subject himself or herself, then, in addition the data categories should be provided to the data subject as well.[25] In the case that data have not been obtained directly from the data subject, information as to "whether replies to the questions are obligatory or voluntary, as well as the possible consequences of failure to reply"[26] has been omitted from the list of information to be provided to the data subject, as his or her data have already been collected. The further information to be provided in this case would specifically include "the categories of data concerned," however, and the necessity for further information disclosures to the data subject would be assessed in connection with the "specific circumstances in which the data are *processed*"[27] instead of those relating to their collection.

There is a narrow exception when the processing is "for statistical purposes" or for "historical or scientific research," and when the provision of the information is impossible or involves "disproportionate effort" or "if recording or disclosure

---

24. Directive, art. 10, at 41.
25. *Id.* art. 11(1)(c), at 42.
26. *Id.* art. 10(c), at 41.
27. *Id.* art. 11(1)(c), at 42 (emphasis added). *Compare with id.* art. 10, at 47.

is expressly laid down by law," in which cases Member States are to provide safe-guards.[28] Although it is important to note that the exceptions are extremely rare in practice (i.e., companies cannot claim disproportionate effort, merely because they do not want to provide the notice).

1. Timing

In terms of timing, if data are collected from data subjects directly, the required information should be provided upon collection of data. In the event that personal data are obtained from a third party, then the required information should be provided at the "time of undertaking the recording of personal data or if a disclosure to a third party is envisaged, no later than the time when the data are first disclosed."[29] Controllers should consider the means through which they interact with data subjects and assess the appropriate time and venue through which to provide the notice.

2. Means of Providing Notice

Information may be provided by various means and depending on the circumstances (types of data subjects, how the controller interacts with the individual). For example, it may be included in General Terms of Use or General Sale Conditions. Often companies include notices in a privacy policy or in documents addressed to new employees (human resources privacy policy, statements in work rules, etc.). When collecting data from customers or consumers, information may be presented at the bottom or back of paper or electronic forms used to collect data, or on the area of a website where it is collected.

B. Notices, Privacy Policies

Companies have corporate privacy policies that affect relationships with their employees, customers, consumers and vendors. These may take many forms and may encompass policies on the use of the Internet, websites, and other work tools (company telephones, computers, tablets).

In addition to laying out the basic approach to certain mediums, these policies may have an effect on whether or not an employee is considered to have "a reasonable expectation of privacy." One author suggests that, in the context of Internet use, "[i]f employees know the rules (and especially if they have the use of alternative means of communication for personal matters, such as an office telephone), then it would seem quite arguable that an employer should be able to displace any reasonable expectation of privacy."[30] This might not always be possible in sensitive situations in which employee privacy should be ensured, for example, in the more extreme case of giving

---

28. *Id*. art. 11(2), at 42.
29. *Id*. art. 11(1), at 41.
30. *See* Graham Smith, Internet Law and Regulation 437 (4th ed. 2007).

warnings of CCTV monitoring in bathrooms,[31] which monitoring should be pro-
scribed. A privacy policy provided to employees upon commencement of employment (in the so-called on-boarding process) is one way to provide them with required
information, and transparency should be the guiding principle here. For more details
on the different practical methods of providing notice to candidates, employees, suppliers, vendors, customers, and consumers, see Section II.D.

1. Websites

Privacy policies are one way used by websites in order to provide the information
required by the Directive and mentioned in Section II.A. Website privacy policies are
pervasive throughout the United States and companies typically associate "privacy
policy" with statements posted on the corporate website describing how "personally
identifiable information" is collected and handled via the website. This U.S. practice
has its roots in the California Online Privacy Protection Act of 2003 and is somewhat different than the Directive's notice requirement. However, in the past few years
website privacy policies are an important means of communicating with external—
especially undefined or yet to be defined—data subjects (e.g., potential customers or
job applicants). Although there is no single prescribed form for a privacy policy, the
information requirements of the Directive provide some guidance as to content. For
Safe Harbor companies, this is also a mechanism for reflecting how they follow the
Safe Harbor Principles.

In connection with search engines, the Working Party in its WP 148 discussed the
importance of being able to find a privacy policy through, for example, "links to their
privacy policy both from their home page and the pages generated in a search process
and information about cookies."[32] Privacy policies must be easily accessible to users
before making a search and the Working Party "recommends that the full privacy
policy be as complete and detailed as possible, mentioning the fundamental principles
included in data protection legislation."[33] These specifically include rights of access or
deletion of data subjects referred to in Articles 12, 13, and 14 of the Directive.[34] It can
be safely said that these sorts of elements would be helpful for the privacy policies of
other types of websites as well.

In 2012 Google changed its worldwide privacy policy, and an investigation by the
Working Party, led by the French data protection authority (the CNIL), ensued. The
following lessons for other companies' privacy policies may be drawn from the input
of the Working Party and the CNIL in the Google matter.

---

31. *Id.*
32. Working Party, *Opinion 1/2008 on Data Protection Issues Related to Search Engines* (WP 148) (Apr. 4,
2008), at 22, http://ec.europa.eu/justice/policies/privacy/docs/wpdocs/2008/wp148_en.pdf.
33. *Id.*
34. *Id.* at 23.

Concrete Applications: The Google Privacy Policy Case

In March 2012, Google consolidated all of its separate privacy policies for specific services and·products, such as Google search, YouTube, Google+, etc., into one general privacy policy. The DPAs from the European Union initiated an investigation led by the CNIL to look into the change and ensure that it was in compliance with data protection laws. From the Working Party's letter of October 16, 2012, to Larry Page of Google, it is clear that a privacy policy should reflect a company's commitment to "key data protection principles of purpose limitation, data quality, data minimization, proportionality and right to object." The Working Party found that the privacy policy did not reflect this commitment and that there was insufficient information on the purposes and categories of data to adequately inform the users how the data is collected.

Further, the Working Party found that Google's combination of data across services did not properly limit to the "scope of the collection and the potential uses of the personal data"[35]–leaving open the door for broader, combined data processing activities which would not be in line with the purpose limitation principle. Sufficient information on the purposes of data collection and the kinds of data being processed must be provided, and privacy notices should not be "too complex, law-oriented or excessively long."[36] The Working Party requires "from all large and global companies that they detail and differentiate their processing operations."[37] Also, it may be helpful to provide information as to retention periods for data collected.

The Working Party detailed recommendations for Google in its letter and in an appendix, suggesting an "architecture of layered privacy notices" in order to take into account product-specific information; the concept being that a privacy policy should be tailored to the product or service in question, and not to a range of different products and services with different impacts on the user's privacy.[38] Finally, Google was encouraged "to engage with data protection authorities when developing services with significant implications for privacy."[39]

Although the above facts come from a specific case, they give insight into the concerns of the Working Party and Member State DPAs in connection with privacy policies and processing activities that have a significant privacy impact.

---

35. Letter dated Oct. 16, 2012, from Working Party to Mr. Larry Page of Google (WP 29 Google Letter), at 1, http://ec.europa.eu/justice/data-protection/article-29/documentation/other-document/files/2012/20121016_letter_to_google_en.pdf.

36. *Id.* at 2.

37. *Id.* at 1–2.

38. *Id.* at 2. Appendix: Google Privacy Policy: Main Findings and Recommendations, http://ec.europa.eu/justice/data-protection/article-29/documentation/other-document/files/2012/20121016_google_privacy_policy_recommendations_cnil_en.pdf.

39. *Id.* at 3. For a discussion of eventual action taken by the CNIL and other European DPAs with respect to Google's privacy policy, *see* W. Gregory Voss, *European Union Data Privacy Law Developments*, 70 Bus. Law. 253 (2014). In addition, on January 30, 2015, the UK ICO announced that Google had signed an undertaking to modify its privacy policy to improve the information Google provides to consumers about the purposes and means of its personal data collection. Press Release, UK ICO, *Google to Change Privacy Policy after ICO Investigation* (Jan. 30, 2015), *available at* https://ico.org.uk/about-the-ico/news-and-events/news-and-blogs/2015/01/google-to-change-privacy-policy-after-ico-investigation/. The text of the undertaking is available at https://ico.org.uk/media/action-weve-taken/undertakings/1043170/google-inc-privacy-policy-undertaking.pdf.

C. Consent

Obtaining consent of an individual appears at first blush to be a relatively straightforward exercise. However, in the European Union, unlike the U.S. the topic of consent and the means through which organizations secure it is highly contested and very much debated.[40] The definition itself can be found in Article 2(h) of the Directive:

> '[T]he data subject's consent' shall mean any freely given specific and informed indication of his wishes by which the data subject signifies his agreement to personal data relating to him being processed.

Consent is also referenced in Articles 7, 8 and 26 of the Directive and appears in the e-Privacy Directive in relation to the placement of cookies.

1. Informed Consent

The concept of information and notice is tied to that of informed consent. WP 187 highlights that transparency is "an essential consideration in ensuring that consent is valid" and that "[t]o be valid, consent must be informed," implying that "all the necessary information must be given at the moment the consent is requested."[41]

2. "Unambiguous" Consent

Consent should be "unambiguous," based on statements or actions meant to signify agreement. It is "any . . . indication of the [data subject's] wishes . . . signif[ying] his agreement."[42] No form is prescribed for consent but it should be "freely given"[43] and "specific,"[44] and "data controllers should create and retain evidence showing that the consent was indeed given, that is, the consent should be verifiable."[45] This underscores the importance of record keeping.

Further information about consent is provided in Chapter 2 Section IV.

3. Cookies

In addition, if cookies are used by a website in order to collect data, then the e-Privacy Directive requires in most cases that the user must give his or her consent to the use of the cookie, after "having been provided with clear and comprehensive information . . . about

---

40. *See generally* Working Party, *Opinion 15/2011 on the Definition of Consent* (WP 187) (July 13, 2011), http://ec.europa.eu/justice/data-protection/article-29/documentation/opinion-recommendation/files/2011/wp187_en.pdf; *Opinion 04/2012 on Cookie Consent Exemption* (WP 194) (June 7, 2012), http://ec.europa.eu/justice/data-protection/article-29/documentation/opinion-recommendation/files/2012/wp194_en.pdf; and *Working Document 02/2013 Providing Guidance on Obtaining Consent for Cookies* (WP 208) (Oct. 2, 2013), http://ec.europa.eu/justice/data-protection/article-29/documentation/opinion-recommendation/files/2013/wp208_en.pdf.

41. WP 187, at 9.

42. *Id.* at 11.

43. *Id.* at 12–13.

44. *Id.* at 17–18.

45. *Id.* at 21.

the purposes of the processing."[46] Thus, data subjects on whose computers cookies are to be used must also be generally informed in advance about the use and purpose of cookies and provide consent, and increasingly this is done through a window that pops up on websites on the user's first connection and offers the user the choice to consent or not, consistent with the Working Party view that "in order to comply with the legislation, the relevant information notice must be provided directly to the users in a clear and understandable form before the processing takes place. It is not enough for information to be 'available' somewhere in the website that the user visits."[47] Cookie consent as well as (opt-in) consent for marketing is discussed in detail in Chapter 6.

D. Notices

PRACTICAL TIPS

Notices are subject to additional country-specific requirements. In most countries within the European Union, you need to inform data subjects that data will be transferred or disclosed, specify the jurisdictions to which personal data may be exported (in addition to informing the data subjects about the existence of transfers and possible recipients or categories of recipients), and reveal whether sensitive data will be processed. Other jurisdictions may require more detailed information, such as the contact details of the DPA. It is advisable to check notices against the background of the local national law requirements to ensure that they reflect the local requirements. It is possible to work with a general notice template that can be tailored at a regional, national, or even global level—despite national variations, however this tends to be a balancing of the specific national requirements and the desire to streamline the notice. Most importantly, notices should also be aligned with the processes or procedures of a company and accurately reflect how the data is treated. To allow notices to have a more strategic approach, it is vital that organizations consider how

---

46. Directive 2002/58/EC of the European Parliament and of the Council of 12 July 2002, concerning the processing of personal data and the protection of privacy in the electronic communications sector (Directive on privacy and electronic communications), 2002 O.J. (L 201) 37, (July 31, 2002) [hereinafter e-Privacy Directive], art. 5(3), at 44, as amended by Directive 2009/136/EC of the European Parliament and of the Council of 25 November 2009 amending Directive 2002/22/EC on universal service and users' rights relating to electronic communications networks and services, Directive 2002/58/EC concerning the processing of personal data and the protection of privacy in the electronic communications sector and Regulation (EC) No. 2006/2004 on cooperation between national authorities responsible for the enforcement of consumer protection laws, 2009 O.J. (L 337) 11, art. 2(5), at 30. Exceptions are made for cookies for the "sole purpose of carrying out the transmission of a communication over an electronic communications network" or those "as strictly necessary in order for the provider of an information society service explicitly requested by the subscriber or user to provide the service." For a discussion of these exceptions, see WP 194; see also W. Gregory Voss & Katherine Woodcock, et al., *Privacy, E-Commerce, and Data Security*, 47 ABA Section of International Law, Year in Review, at 102 (2013).

47. Working Party, *Opinion 16/2011 on EASA/IAB Best Practice Recommendation on Online Behavioural Advertising* (WP 188) (Dec. 8, 2011), at 4, http://ec.europa.eu/justice/data-protection/article-29/documentation/opinion-recommendation/files/2011/wp188_en.pdf.

their processing is structure today as well as how they would like to process personal data in the future. Otherwise, notices and other related policies may become quickly outdated and inaccurate.

For centralized companies, where policies or procedures are dictated from a single parent entity, it may be advisable to work with a global or regional privacy policy aimed at the group of data subjects (e.g., an employee privacy policy or a customer privacy policy). On the other hand, if a company operates in more decentralized manner, such as regionally (e.g., on a European basis, or in Europe, the Middle East, or Africa (EMEA)), or by country, notices may be more specified for the countries covered. It is also important to note that whether the notice takes the form of a notice, policy, (standard operating) procedure, or the like is often a question of semantics and depends the nature of the target audience and the message. Most companies choose to have separate notices for employees about how they treat their personal data and similarly choose to have separate notices for customers, suppliers, vendors, and so on. It is also possible to have internal policies on how individuals within the company who have access to (process) personal data are to treat the information. This could be a separate procedure or policy that is not drafted for wider audiences but operates as more of an internal guideline. Again, this often depends on how the company is structured and how it currently treats similar activities (e.g., information security, ethics, and behavior).

---

1. Translations

Notices also need to be supplied to individuals in a language that they can understand. This practical point is often overlooked until the last moment of implementation or rollout of a company-wide notice. It is important to remember and budget specifically for the translation into the local national language. Most notices will have to come from the employing entity (as it generally acts as the controller with respect to its employees), but notices can be drafted to come from a company group, with a specific reference to the employing entity. If working with global or regional notices, also keep in mind that the final drafts will need to be communicated to the relevant EU entities and implemented locally under local employment provisions.

For coordination purposes, each entity should have a designated contact person to handle notices and related privacy issues (e.g., an HR professional, marketing/sales team, IT manager, etc.). Having a privacy manager or steward, DPO or other person tasked with assisting or participating in the privacy initiatives of the company makes compliance more efficient—especially if that person is empowered and motivated to participate!

2. Employee Representatives or Works Councils

In many European countries, activities affecting workers—including the associated notices and policies as well as treatment of employee personal data—will need to be informed, consulted, or, in some cases, agreed with the local employee representatives or works council (so-called information and consultation requirements).[48] The precise requirements vary by country and depend on the specific processing activities. For example, whether or not the processing is part of a "new technology" in the workplace or whether there are transfers out of the European Union.[49] Taking France as an example, no information personally concerning a candidate for employment[50] or an employee[51] may be collected by a system that has not been previously brought to his or her knowledge, and the works council is informed and consulted prior to any introduction of an important new technology project that would likely have consequences on employment, professional qualification, remuneration, training, or work conditions.[52]

Typically, one should check to see whether there are works councils or employee representatives in place and consult with the local HR or employment office responsible to see how to roll out the notices or other employee documents (e.g., consents) in practice. Other employment law considerations also come into play. When considering the drafting and implementation of a notice or policy that affects workers, employee relations of the company should be considered. HR or the legal department (or external employment law advisors in more tricky situations) should be included in the drafting and implementation process as early as possible to ensure efficiency and limit disruptions.

E. Privacy and Data Impact Assessments

Although not specifically provided for in the Directive, privacy and data impact assessments are not new. Rooted in ideas of technology assessments, in a 1981 resolution,

---

48. One definition of works council is "a body or committee formed by an employer among workers within his organization for the discussion of problems of industrial relations;" *see* http://www.merriam-webster.com/dictionary/works%20council (last visited on Feb. 23, 2015). Works councils exist in multiple countries in the European Union.

49. For a succinct overview of works council requirements within the European Union, *see 10 Things You Need to Know about the Interaction between Works Councils and Data Privacy*, http://www.preslmayr.at/tl_files/Publikationen/2010/10_things_you_need_to_know_about_works_councils_and_privacy_in_europe.pdf.

50. *See* CODE DU TRAVAIL [C.TRAV.] art. L. 1221-9 (Fr.), *available at* http://legifrance.gouv.fr/affichCode.do?cidTexte=LEGITEXT000006072050&dateTexte=20140602: "Aucune information concernant personnellement un candidat à un employ ne peut être collectée par un dispositif qui n'a pas été porté préalablement à sa connaissance." ["No information relating personally to a candidate for employment may be collected by a system that has not been brought to his or her knowledge beforehand."(Free translation by the authors.)]

51. *Id.* art. L. 1222-4 (Fr.): "Aucune information concernant personnellement un salarié ne peut être collectée par un dispositif qui n'a pas été porté préalablement à sa connaissance.". ["No information relating personally to an employee may be collected by a system that has not been brought to his or her knowledge beforehand." (Free translation by the authors.)]

52. *Id.* art. L. 2323-13 (Fr.): "Le comité d'entreprise est informé et consulté, préalablement à tout projet important d'introduction de nouvelles technologies, lorsque celles-ci sont susceptibles d'avoir des consequences sur l'emploi, la qualification, la remuneration, la formation ou les conditions du travail." ["The works council shall be informed and consulted prior to any major project for the introduction of new technologies, when they are likely to have consequences on employment, qualification, remuneration, training or working conditions." (Free translation by the authors.)]

the CNIL recommended risk assessments and security studies for new personal data processing.[53] Governments worldwide and, increasingly, multinational companies rely on privacy impact assessments (PIAs) to determine the relevant risk associated with certain data processing.[54] The UK Information Commissioner's Office (ICO) has issued a comprehensive code of practice (updated in February 2014) that presents a solid introduction to PIAs, in what circumstances they should be considered, and how to undertake them in practice.[55] The European Commission issued a recommendation on May 12, 2009, as reported by the Working Party, regarding radio-frequency identification (RFID) applications, whereby Member States were asked to develop a "framework for privacy and data protection impact assessments," in conjunction with industry.[56] Such PIAs by RFID operators are to involve a pre-assessment phase and a risk-assessment phase; the latter including an identification of risks to personal data and "a resolution regarding the conditions of implementation of the RFID application under review."[57] In this case, the PIA was to lead to a PIA report at least six weeks before deployment of the RFID application, involving the RFID operator developing and publishing "*a concise, accurate and easy to understand information policy for each of their applications*,"[58] in the case of this potentially harmful-to-privacy technology.

The Working Party called the PIA a "tool designed to promote 'privacy by design,' better information to individuals as well as transparency and dialogue with competent authorities."[59]

More recently, the Working Party has recommended that "[s]pecification of requirements based on a risk analysis and/or a dedicated Privacy Impact Assessment (PIA)" be included as part of "formal 'development cycles'" by which biometric systems should be designed.[60]

---

53. *Commission nationale de l'informatique et des libertés* [hereinafter CNIL] [National Commission for Data Protection Authority], Resolution No. 81-094 of 21 July 1981 on the adoption of a recommendation relative to general measures for computer system security [Délibération n° 81-094 du 21 juillet 1981 portant adoption d'une recommandation relative aux mesures générales de sécurité des systèmes informatiques] (July 21 ,1981) (Fr.), *available at* http://www.cnil.fr/documentation/deliberations/deliberation/delib/38/.
54. The history of the PIA is outlined in *A History of Privacy Impact Assessments* from Roger Clarke, available at http://www.rogerclarke.com/DV/PIAHist.html.
55. United Kingdom Information Commissioner's Office [hereinafter UK ICO], *Conducting Privacy Impact Assessments Code of Practice*, Feb. 25, 2014, http://ico.org.uk/for_organisations/data_protection /topic_guides/~/media/documents/library/data_protection/practical_application/pia-code-of-practice-final-draft.pdf.
56. Working Party, *Opinion 9/2011 on the Revised Industry Proposal for a Privacy and Data Protection Impact Assessment Framework for RFID Applications* (WP 180) (Feb. 11, 2011), at 3, http://ec.europa.eu /justice/policies/privacy/docs/wpdocs/2011/wp180_en.pdf.
57. *Id*. at 4–5.
58. *Id*. at 6.
59. *Id*. at 7.
60. Working Party, *Opinion 3/2012 on the Developments in Biometric Technologies* (WP 193) (Apr. 27, 2012), at 29, http://ec.europa.eu/justice/data-protection/article-29/documentation/opinion-recommendation /files/2012/wp193_en.pdf.

In this case, the Working Party—which highlighted the fact that a PIA should provide solutions for mitigating data protection risks, instead of just analyzing the latter—defined the following as factors to be taken into account by the PIA during the design stage:

- The nature of the collected information;
- The purpose of the collected information;
- The accuracy of the system, assuming that important decisions for an individual could be derived from a match to a biometric pattern;
- The legal basis and legal compliance, and whether consent would be required;
- The access to the device and the internal and external sharing of information within the data controller, which would imply security techniques and procedures to protect personal data from unauthorized access;
- The less privacy-invasive measures already taken, and whether there is an alternative procedure to the biometric device (such as asking for an I.D. card);
- The decisions taken regarding retention time and deletion of data. What is the relevant period of time? Are all data collected for the same period of time? Is there an automatic decision mechanism and appropriate fallback process?
- The data subjects' rights.[61]

As we shall see, PIAs are dealt with specifically in the GDPR and, going forward, should be considered whenever special categories of data processing and/or special data protection risks are involved. More information about the conduct of privacy and data protection impact assessments is available from certain Member State DPAs such as those in France[62] and the United Kingdom.[63]

Applicable Law under the GDPR

The GDPR would increase notice requirements to individual users. In terms of conditions for consent (Article 7 of the GDPR), this new article specifies that the "controller shall bear the burden of proof for the data subject." (Article 7(1)) This highlights the importance of record keeping in order to constitute proof.

In addition, if consent is handled together with other matters in the same declaration, the requirement that consent be given must be "distinguishable in appearance from that other matter." (Article 7(2))

---

61. *Id.* at 29–30.
62. CNIL, *Methodology for Privacy Risk Management: How to Implement the Data Protection Act* (June 2012) (English Translation), http://www.cnil.fr/fileadmin/documents/en/CNIL-ManagingPrivacyRisks-Methodology.pdf.
63. *Conducting Privacy Impact Assessments Code of Practice, supra* note 55.

The GDPR picks up the point from Working Party guidance and makes it explicit in the proposed legislation that "[c]onsent shall not provide a legal basis for the processing, where there is a significant imbalance between the position of the data subject and the controller." (Article 7(4)) This would be the case, for example, when the controller is the data subject's employer.

A new requirement of transparent information and communication is added by Article 11 of the GDPR, as set out below:

1. The controller shall have transparent and easily accessible policies with regard to the processing of personal data and for the exercise of data subjects' rights.
2. The controller shall provide any information and any communication relating to the processing of personal data to the data subject in an intelligible form, using clear and plain language, adapted to the data subject, in particular for any information addressed specifically to a child.

Articles 10 and 11 of the Directive would be replaced by Article 14 of the proposed GDPR, which sets out the more extensive information to be given to the data subject. The first three paragraphs of Article 14 provide:

1. Where personal data relating to a data subject are collected, the controller shall provide the data subject with at least the following information:
   (a) the identity and the contact details of the controller and, if any, of the controller's representative and of the data protection officer;
   (b) the purposes of the processing for which the personal data are intended, including the contract terms and general conditions where the processing is based on point (b) of Article 6(1) and the legitimate interests pursued by the controller where the processing is based on point (f) of Article 6(1);
   (c) the period for which the personal data will be stored;
   (d) the existence of the right to request from the controller access to and rectification or erasure of the personal data concerning the data subject or to object to the processing of such personal data;
   (e) the right to lodge a complaint to the supervisory authority and the contact details of the supervisory authority;
   (f) the recipients or categories of the personal data;
   (g) where applicable, that the controller intends to transfer to a third country or international organization and on the level of protection afforded by that third country or international organization by reference to the adequacy decision by the Commission;
   (h) any further information necessary to guarantee fair processing in respect of the data subject, having regard to the specific circumstances in which the personal data have been collected.
2. Where the personal data are collected from the data subject, the controller shall inform the data subject, in addition to the information referred to in paragraph 1, whether the provision of personal data is obligatory or voluntary, as well as the possible consequences of failure to provide such data.

3. Where the personal data are not collected from the data subject, the controller shall inform the data subject, in addition to the information referred to in paragraph 1, from which source the personal data originate.

Although exceptions to these information requirements have been provided for (Article 14(4) and (5)), on the whole the GDPR places greater information requirements on controllers than the Directive does, both qualitatively and quantitatively, and so notices and privacy policies would need to be adjusted accordingly.

In addition, controllers, processors, and any controller's representatives, unless they are individuals without a commercial interest or firms of fewer than 250 employees for which the processing is an ancillary activity, will have requirements to maintain documentation concerning processing operations under Article 28 of the proposed GDPR. This will include, in addition to what might be expected from the new information requirements just discussed, an indication of time limits for erasure of data. (Article 28(2)(g))

The GDPR also adds a requirement of notification of a personal data breach to the supervisory authority (Article 31) and, significantly for this section, communication to the data subject when a personal data breach is "likely to adversely affect the protection of the personal data or privacy of the data subject" (Article 32(1)), describing the nature of the breach and certain other information such as recommendations for mitigating the potential adverse effects of the breach (Article 32(2)), unless the controller demonstrates to the supervisory authority's satisfaction that the data has been rendered unintelligible to any unauthorized person through technological protection measures (Article 32(3)).

Finally, under the GDPR when processing operations "present specific risks to the rights and freedoms of data subjects" (an illustrative list of certain such cases including those involving information on sex life, health, race, ethnic origin, video surveillance, etc., is provided in Article 33(2)), a data protection impact assessment shall be carried out by the controller or the processor acting on the former's behalf. (Article 33(1))

III. INTERNATIONAL DATA TRANSFERS

In the European Union, specific rules apply to cross-border transfers of personal data. To ensure the "functioning of an internal market," in the European Union, personal data can flow freely within its borders—subject to compliance with the remaining rules of the Directive.[64] Any transfer of personal data outside of the European Union to a country that is not deemed by the Commission to have an adequate level of protection is—in principle—prohibited. When a country is not deemed to provide adequate protection, a controller can take specific—contractual—safeguards to ensure protection and permit the "safe" transfer of personal data.[65] If a country does not benefit from an adequacy determination and the controller has not undertaken one of the specific safeguards, it may be possible to rely on one of the derogations

---

64. Directive, recital 3, at 31.
65. Directive, art. 26(2), at 46.

provided in Article 26(1) of the Directive. Each of these bases for transfer outside the European Union are presented next.

A.   Adequacy Determination

Under the Directive, the emphasis of the restriction on cross-border transfers is not on non–European Economic Area (EEA) countries and territories (each a Third Country) generally, as the importance of data transfers for trade and business is acknowledged.[66] Instead, transfer restrictions hinge on the *adequacy* of the Third Country's data protection laws to ensure that the EU personal data is properly ("adequately") protected under national law. Article 25 provides

> [t]he transfer to a third country of personal data which are undergoing processing or are intended for processing after transfer may take place only if, without prejudice to compliance with the national provisions adopted pursuant to the other provisions of this Directive, the third country in question ensures an adequate level of protection.[67]

Therefore, when transferring personal data out of the European Union and EEA, companies need to assess whether the destination country (or country of the "data importer") provides adequate protection for personal data from the EU perspective. In practice, few countries qualify for an adequacy determination. Many that do meet the specified requirements are countries that have implemented laws similar to or modeled on the Directive.[68] The Working Party laid out its general approach on

---

66.   *See* Directive, recital 56, at 36-37: "Whereas cross-border flows of personal data are necessary to the expansion of international trade; whereas the protection of individuals guaranteed in the Community by this Directive does not stand in the way of transfers of personal data to third countries which ensure an adequate level of protection; whereas the adequacy of the level of protection afforded by a third country must be assessed in the light of all the circumstances surrounding the transfer operation or set of transfer operations."

67.   Directive, art. 25(1), at 45.

68.   These include Argentina (*see* Commission Decision on the Adequate Protection of Personal Data in Argentina, 2003 O.J. (L 168) 19 (June 30, 2003)) and Israel (see Commission Decision 2011/61/EU of Jan. 31, 2011. on the Adequate Protection of Personal Data by the State of Israel with Regard to Automated Processing of Personal Data, 2011 O.J. (L 27) 39 (Feb. 1, 2011) restricted to automated processing); however, note the exemption of New Zealand (Commission Decision on the Adequate Protection of Personal Data by New Zealand, 2012 O.J. (L 28) 12 (Dec. 19, 2012)). Although in principle, this should not be the case: "[a] positive finding should not in principle be limited to countries having horizontal data protection laws, but should also cover specific sectors within countries where data protection is adequate, even though in other sectors the same country's protection may be less than adequate." Working Party, *Working Document on Transfers of Personal Data to Third Countries: Applying Articles 25 and 26 of the EU Data Protection Directive* (WP 12) (July 24, 1998), at 27, http://ec.europa.eu/justice/policies/privacy/docs /wpdocs/1998/wp12_en.pdf. This seems to indicate that an adequacy determination can be made for specific sectors. Although adequacy decisions have been made with respect to the transfer of passenger name record data, other sector-specific approvals have been rare. One example would be the adequacy determination for Canada, which originally was contemplated for bodies governed by the Personal Information Protection and Electronic Documents Act (PIPEDA).

adequacy early on in its Working Document on Transfer of Personal Data to Third Countries.[69]

1. Factors for a Determination of Adequacy

When assessing adequacy, the Directive stipulates that the level of protection should

> [b]e assessed in the light of all the circumstances surrounding a data transfer operation or set of data transfer operations; particular consideration shall be given to the nature of the data, the purpose and duration of the proposed processing operation or operations, the country of origin and country of final destination, the rules of law, both general and sectoral, in force in the third country in question and the professional rules and security measures which are complied with in that country.[70]

When assessing adequacy of protection of individuals' personal data, the content of the country's rules and the means or system of protection should be considered. In terms of content, adequate rules would include the six basic privacy principles (covered in Chapter 1 Section III.) and possibly the additional principles that may be necessary or relevant (e.g., protection for sensitive data, direct marketing provisions, and provisions on automated decision making), and the Commission will look to the national legal standards on personal data and whether the principles are present in the relevant domestic law. For procedural or enforcement mechanisms, the Working Party accepts that not all legal regimes expressly include data protection rules in the law nor do all have a system of externally verifying compliance with the rules such as through a supervisory authority. Therefore, when judging the adequacy of a procedural enforcement means, it is important to identify three underlying objectives: whether it (1) provides a good level of compliance, (2) supports and assists data subjects in exercising their individual rights, and (3) affords appropriate redress to damaged or injured parties (via a system of independent arbitration or adjudication).[71]

When assessing adequacy, a Third Country can ensure an adequate level of protection for personal data either through application of (1) its domestic law, or (2) international undertakings it has entered into.[72] Flowing from the latter criteria, an important factor that is taken into account is whether the relevant country has ratified Convention 108.[73] Most transfers to signatory countries will likely be considered if they are transfers to a country with an adequate level of protection, provided that the

---

69. See WP 12, *supra* note 65. This document also introduces and contemplates contractual solutions (such as binding corporate rules, Model Contracts, and other ad hoc contracts) and industry codes of conduct, in addition to outlining the basic exceptions from the prohibition on transfers to Third Countries.

70. Directive, art. 25(2), at 45–46.

71. WP 12, *supra* note 65, at 5–7.

72. Directive, art. 25(6), at 46.

73. WP 12, *supra* note 65, at 8 and 9. For a discussion of Convention 108, *see* Section I(A)(2).

importing country (1) "also has appropriate mechanisms to ensure compliance, help individuals and provide redress," and (2) is the final destination country (and not used as conduit for subsequent onward transfers).[74] The Commission also specifies the exceptional circumstances in which data flows may be suspended, for example, in case of nonenforcement by the relevant authorities.

2. Procedure for Determining Adequacy

The Commission is empowered to make the adequacy determination with respect to a Third Country.[75] The Commission makes such determination following a Working Party opinion on the country's protection of personal data. In its opinion, the Working Party conducts an analysis, taking into account the factors laid out in Chapter 3 Section III.A.1 and Section III.C.1.a.[76] Once the opinion is issued, the Commission considers the opinion and, absent objections from the EU Member States, the adequacy decision is automatically adopted. If there are objections, then the decision requires a full debate and vote. Once the decision is issued, personal data may be transferred from the European Union without additional guarantees. This determination does not affect the other conditions or restrictions of the applicable provisions from the Directive (under national law).

3. Countries Benefiting from Adequacy Determinations

Currently, adequacy determinations have been made for Andorra, Argentina, Australia (for passenger name record, "PNR"), Canada, Faeroe Islands, Guernsey, Isle of Man, Israel, Jersey, Switzerland, and the United States for companies self-certifying compliance with the Department of Commerce's Safe Harbor Privacy Principles (conditions described later) and also with respect to passenger name record (PNR) data provided to the Bureau of Customers and Border Protection.[77]

It is important to keep in mind that adequacy decisions do not necessarily provide blanket permission to transfer data to a Third Country. In certain cases, a decision permits the transfer of personal data only for limited scope (such as limited types of personal data, only automated processing, only to controllers regulated by a certain regime, etc.).

---

74. *Id.* at 9.
75. Directive, art. 25(6), at 46.
76. *See generally* WP 12, *supra* note 65, at 26–27, on the Working Party's role in the issuing of the adequacy decision.
77. The full list of the so-called white-listed countries can be found at http://ec.europa.eu/justice/data-protection/document/international-transfers/adequacy/index_en.htm, together with the relevant Commission Decisions. Please note that certain determinations of adequacy are made by Council Decisions. These typically relate to PNR and API data, as this data falls outside the "Community" pillar since it relates to issues of public security and criminal law. Thus, the decision on adequacy falls outside of the Directive under the exclusions in Article 3(2). *See* Joined cases C-317/04 and C-318/04, European Parliament v. Council of the European Union, *available at* http://curia.europa.eu/juris/document/document.jsf;jsessionid=9ea7d2dc30d65f7890da36d148cfb53887a862b95a69.e34KaxiLc3qMb40Rch0SaxuOb350?text=&docid=57550&pageIndex=0&doclang=en&mode=lst&dir=&occ=first&part=1&cid=101038.

- In Australia, for example, the decision relates to PNR data only.[78] The processing of PNR data is further discussed in Section III.A.5.
- In Canada, the Commission Decision relates only to data importers that are subject to the Canadian Personal Information Protection and Electronic Documents Act (PIPEDA).
- In Israel, the Commission Decision allows only personal data transfers that are automated or that, if not automated, are subject to further automated processing in Israel.[79]

Therefore, it is important to check the Commission Decision or Council Decision, as the case may be, prior to relying on the adequacy determination.

4. Safe Harbor Framework (Transfers to the United States)

On July 26, 2000, the Commission adopted a decision[80] recognizing the Safe Harbor Privacy Principles and the frequently asked questions (FAQs) for the U.S. Department of Commerce (DOC). This decision allows an adequacy determination for transfers of personal data to companies who have voluntarily signed up for the principles. The rules are binding for those who self-certify under Safe Harbor by way of United States Federal Trade Commission (FTC) enforcement pursuant to Section 5 of the Federal Trade Commission Act.[81] However as the FTC's competence is limited, so is the scope of entities that the framework covers—financial institutions and non-profits are excluded. Companies must publish a privacy policy that adheres to the Safe Harbor principles and must comply with such principles as well. Additionally, any relevant company must self-certify to the DOC that it is compliant and must resubmit this self-certification annually.

a. Recent Developments Concerning Safe Harbor

For many years, the European Union and certain DPAs were calling for changes to Safe Harbor, as it was felt that many companies merely signed up without properly following the principles or used the framework as a conduit for granting worldwide access to the European Union via the United States. Following the disclosures by

---

78. Council Decision 2008/651/CFSP/JHA of June 30, 2008, on the Signing, on behalf of the European Union, of an Agreement between the European Union and Australia on the Processing and Transfer of European Union-sourced Passenger Name Record (PNR) Data by Air Carriers to the Australian Customs Service, 2008 O.J. (L 213) 47 (EU) (Aug. 8, 2008).

79. Commission Decision 2011/61/EU of Jan. 31, 2011, on the Adequate Protection of Personal Data by the State of Israel with Regard to Automated Processing of Personal Data, 2011 O.J. (L 27) 39 (Feb. 1, 2011).

80. Commission Decision 520/2000/EC of July 26, 2000, Pursuant to Directive 95/46/EC of the European Parliament and of the Council on the Adequacy of the Protection Provided by the Safe Harbour Privacy Principles and Related Frequently Asked Questions Issued by the US Department of Commerce, 2000 O.J. (L 215) 7 (Aug. 25, 2000), http://eur-lex.europa.eu/LexUriServ/LexUriServ.do?uri=OJ:L:2000:215:0007:0047:EN:PDF.

81. 15 U.S.C. § 45. This Act prohibits "unfair or deceptive acts or practices in or affecting commerce." If a company does not comply with its public privacy policy or statements in its self-regulatory code/rules regarding how it collects or handles personal data, the FTC can challenge this misrepresentation as a deceptive act or practice. *See* GeoCities, Docket No C-3849 (Final Order Feb. 12, 1999), *available at* http://www.ftc.gov/sites/default/files/documents/cases/1999/02/9823015.do_.htm.

Edward Snowden on U.S. intelligence data collection programs, including the disclosure that many large companies that are Safe Harbor-certified are handing over data to such programs, the Commission set up a committee to look into Safe Harbor. On November 27, 2013, the Commission issued several documents with the aim of "restoring trust" in the flow of data from the European Union to the United States.[82] Although these documents do not bring an end to the EU-U.S. Safe Harbor program, they do highlight the extreme pressure that the Safe Harbor adequacy mechanism has been under following the Snowden disclosures.

The outcome of these documents has been a call from the Commission for action in six areas:[83]

1. Quickly adopt the EU data protection reform (GDPR);
2. Strengthen Safe Harbor (the Commission proposed 13 recommendations, including the adoption of Convention 108 by the United States[84]);
3. Strengthen safeguards for transfers of personal data in police and judicial cooperation;
4. Use the Mutual Legal Assistance and other sectoral agreements to obtain data about EU citizens (i.e., rather than via forced disclosures by U.S.-based companies having signed on to Safe Harbor, such as Facebook, Google, etc.);
5. Address EU concerns in the context of U.S. reform for privacy (meaning that the United States should also be concerned with the protections of EU citizens in addition to U.S. ones); and
6. Promote privacy internationally.

The Commission also emphasizes that standards of data protection will not be part of the Transatlantic Trade and Investment Partnership (TTIP) Agreement that the United States and the European Union have been negotiating. On October 6, 2015, the ECJ invalidated the Safe Harbor;[85] in doing so, it emphasized that DPAs can investigate and suspend transfers under the Safe Harbor Framework, which powers were denied them under the current Safe Harbor Framework.[86] EU Justice Com-

---

82. This group of documents is comprised of a strategy paper in the form of a Communication on transatlantic data flows, an analysis of the functioning of Safe Harbor from the EU perspective, and a report from the EU-U.S. working group. *See* Eur. Comm'n, *Communication from the Commission to the European Parliament and the Council on the Functioning of the Safe Harbour from the Perspective of EU Citizens and Companies Established in the EU*, COM (2013) 847, Nov. 27, 2013.

83. Press Release, Eur. Comm'n, *European Commission Calls on the U.S. to Restore Trust in the EU-U.S. Data Flows*, Nov. 27, 2013, IP/13/1166, *available at* http://europa.eu/rapid/press-release_IP-13-1166_en.htm.

84. There is increasing pressure for the United States and other countries to adopt Convention 108 as the global standard for data protection. On the Privacy Coalition's campaign to the U.S. government to support the ratification of the Convention, *see Privacy Campaign—Real Problems Real Solutions Jan. 28, 2009* (Jan. 23, 2009), *available at* http://privacycoalition.org/2009/01/privacy_campaign_real_problems.php.

85. Case C-362/14, Maximillian Schrems v. Data Protection Commissioner, http://eur-lex.europa.eu /legal-content/EN/TXT/HTML/?uri=CELEX:62014CJ0362&qid=1444143069383&from=EN.

86. *Id.*, paras. 99-102.

missioner Vera Jourová reportedly already expressed willingness to work with the U.S. Department of Commerce "to complete a revamped data agreement" to replace the current Safe Harbor Framework.[87] DPAs can investigate and suspend transfers under the Safe Harbor Framework. Furthermore, he stated that since the framework does not provide sufficient guarantees of protection, that the EC should suspend their decision.

5. PNR Data

Following the September 11, 2001, terrorist attacks in the United States, air travel and related security drastically changed. One measure that was particularly important was the ability of air carriers to transfer the personal details of passengers from arriving flights. This would allow governments to clear lists of arriving passengers for the purposes of combating terrorism and for air carriers to ensure that passengers were permitted on flights.[88] PNR contains records of each passenger's travel requirements contained in air carriers' reservation systems, including information necessary for reservations processing and control by the airlines.[89]

The United States, Canada, and Australia have all concluded agreements with the European Union for the transfer of EU passenger data in this context. These adequacy decisions have been taken via Council Decision.

As mentioned, the adequacy ruling for PNR allows for free flow of PNR data transferred from the European Union by air carriers to the relevant national customs service, subject to the conditions specified in the Council Decision, and the PNR agreement. However, this does not permit personal data, from the European Union to flow freely to Australia generally or Canada or the U.S.—outside of PIPEDA or the Safe Harbor Framework, respectively.

In practice, PNR decisions have a limited effect and do not affect most private companies other than air carriers, for example.

B.   Other Safeguards

Although an importing country may not be deemed to have an adequate level of protection for personal data, particular measures can be taken to make up for this lack of protection when sending personal data to an importing country. The Directive contemplates that transfers can be permitted when certain specific safeguards—in the form of contractual protections—are taken by the controller. These contractual safeguards are deemed appropriate and may take the form of (1) a data transfer agreement based on the Commission-approved standard contractual clauses or model contracts (Model

---

87.   See Mark Scott, *In Europe-U.S. Clash on Privacy, a Longstanding Schism*, N.Y. Times (Oct. 7, 2015), http://nyti.ms/1Q93iJM.
88.   Working Party, *Opinion 4/2003 on the Level of Protection ensured in the US for the Transfer of Passengers' Data* (WP 78) (June 13, 2003), at 6, http://ec.europa.eu/justice/policies/privacy/docs/wpdocs/2003/wp78_en.pdf.
89.   The precise data categories are specified in the agreements concluded between the European Union and Canada, the United States, and Australia. Currently, there is a proposed draft PNR Directive pending (COM (2011) 32 Final), http://ec.europa.eu/home-affairs/news/intro/docs/com_2011_32_en.pdf.

Contract), (2) binding corporate rules (BCRs), (3) industry codes of conduct, or (4) another contractual form (so-called ad hoc data transfer agreements). In exceptional situations, transfers may be allowed based on an exception to the prohibition of data transfer to non-EEA member states that do not ensure an adequate level of protection.

1. Model Contracts

The Commission is empowered to develop standard contractual clauses that provide for sufficient safeguards.[90] The Commission has issued four decisions resulting in three different versions of the Model Contracts for two types of transfers: one Model Contract for controller-to-processor transfers (C-to-P Model Contract) and two versions for controller-to-controller transfers (C-to-C Model Contract). There is a Working Document on ad hoc contractual clauses between processors, but it is still being reviewed and is not final as of the time of publishing.[91] The two versions of the C-to-C Model Contract are made up of an older version and a newer version. The newer contract includes optional business clauses (such as liability provisions), as well as provisions that were developed to make the contract friendlier to businesses.

a. Contractual Provisions

When relying on Model Contracts, the contractual provisions in the approved contracts provide the "adequate safeguards" for the controller(s) for transfers outside of the EEA. Similar to the process of an adequacy finding, the contract includes the "essential elements of protection which are missing in any given particular situation."[92] Therefore the Model Contract includes the substantive data protection rules (the privacy principles in Chapter 1 Section III) set out in an exhaustive and definite manner to permit the data importer to apply the principles in practice, combined with specific criteria to make these rules effective. The latter criteria are the three enforcement objectives mentioned earlier in Section III.A.1:

(1) to provide a good level of compliance,
(2) to support and assist data subjects in exercising their individual rights, and
(3) to afford appropriate redress to damaged or injured parties.[93]

When drafting the approved Model Contracts, the Commission has taken these factors into account and included them in the three contracts.

---

90. Directive, art. 26(2), at 46.
91. Working Party, *Working Document on 01/2012 on Draft Ad Hoc Contractual Clauses "EU Data Processor to Non-EU Sub-Processor"* (WP 214) (Mar. 21, 2014), http://ec.europa.eu/justice/data-protection /article-29/documentation/opinion-recommendation/files/2014/wp214_en.pdf.
92. WP 12, *supra* note 61, at 16.
93. *Id.* at 17–18. *See generally id.*, at 15–23.

b. Practical Considerations of Model Contract Use

Many companies choose to rely on Model Contracts and both the Commission and the Working Party promote the reliance on these particular contractual solutions.[94] Contractual bases for transfers are preferred over the derogations in Article 26(1) because the latter do not continue to cover and protect data after the transfer from the European Union; thus the contracts are deemed to be more protective of personal data.[95] In practice, the Model Contracts provide a high level of legal certainty for data controllers, as they have been drafted and approved on the EU-level and are uniformly accepted in the Member States. On the other hand, some jurisdictions require that transfers based on the Model Contracts are subject to prior authorization or a license or permit. This is the case in Spain and Austria, for example. These requirements add another level of administrative complexity and cost associated with Model Contract use. Furthermore, the provisions are very comprehensive and companies need to ensure not only that they are executing the Model Contracts but that they can comply with the provisions in practice.

Which contract is used (C-to-C or C-to-P) will depend on the respective roles of the parties involved in the transfer: specifically, whether the data importer is acting as a controller or a processor. The actual language of the contracts themselves generally is not altered or drastically altered, but the consent of the Annexes (for the C-to-C) and the Appendices (for the C-to-P) are to be filled in by the parties to specify the circumstances of the transfers. Specifically, this indicates the data categories as well as purposes for processing (more in the C-to-C context) or specific processing actions (for C-to-P transfers). Additional country requirements for the content of the attachments may be mandated, for example, in case of certain country-specific security measures or for ensuring that the Member State's national law requirements are met (e.g., this is the case in Germany for transfers to processors). See Section IV for more information on data security provisions under national law and the requirement of certain contractual provisions between controllers and processors.

2. BCRs

BCRs are internal data protection and privacy rules set out by multinational companies to facilitate transfers of personal data. They were originally developed for instances of transfers of EU personal data from the controller to other entities within the group for either processing or to another controller.[96] As of January 2013, BCRs have been

---

94. Working Party, *Opinion 05/2012 on the Cloud Computing* (WP 196) (July 1, 2012) [hereinafter WP 196], http://ec.europa.eu/justice/data-protection/article-29/documentation/opinion-recommendation/files/2012/wp196_en.pdf.

95. Commission Staff Working Document on the Implementation of the Commission Decisions on Standard Contractual Clauses for the Transfer of Personal Data to Third Countries (2001/497/EC and 2002/16/EC) SEC (2006) 95, at 2, ec.europa.eu/justice/policies/privacy/docs/modelcontracts/sec_2006_95_en.pdf.

96. Working Party, *Working Document: Transfers of Personal Data to Third Countries: Applying Article 26(2) of the EU Data Protection Directive to Binding Corporate Rules for International Data Transfers* (WP 74) (June 3, 2003), http://ec.europa.eu/justice/policies/privacy/docs/wpdocs/2003/wp74_en.pdf.

expanded to also include situations when companies act as a "processor"— i.e., when processing data on behalf of customers, such as in outsourcing scenarios.[97] BCRs are a set of rules that delineate the internal procedures for handling the processing of personal data. The substantive provisions of BCRs and the focus of the DPAs in the approval process originate from the Working Party's recommendations for contractual protections laid out in WP 12 and fully articulated in WP 74. Initially, BCRs were reserved for companies with access to lots of resources, and the approval process was very lengthy. The first BCR was undertaken by General Electric and approved in December 2005.[98] Since, BCRs have become increasingly relied upon by global companies as a mechanism for global data transfers. This marked increase is spurred on by the pressure on Safe Harbor as well as by the increasing use of decentralized and dynamic processing scenarios multinationals put in place (e.g., internal outsourcing of services and processing).

BCRs are comprised of rules—similar to a code of conduct—outlining how the company group will process personal data, including specific provisions on international data transfers. The rules are a self-certifying compliance mechanism, offering companies a certain degree of freedom in this arena. Companies can also choose the scope of coverage for such internal procedures, including which subsidiaries or affiliates are covered and what types of personal data will be included within the rules. As an example, a U.S. multinational could get BCRs to cover transfers of personal data from customers from the E.U. to its Asian affiliates, leaving the transfers to the U.S. to be covered by Safe Harbor certification or a Model Contract. BCRs are recognized by most EU and EFTA countries. Many participate in a fast track (cooperation) procedure for BCR approval.[99] Countries that do not participate in this procedure require that companies file the BCRs directly with their respective DPAs for separate review and approval.[100] In the cooperation procedure Companies must identify a lead DPA, which be the primary regulator for the approval process and facilitate the review and approval together with two other co-reviewing countries. The draft BCR and submission documents must include certain pre-defined aspects, including privacy principles, tools to show that the BCR will be effective internally and how the company will bind its entities to ensure that the BCR will be internally binding. The Working Party has issued a wide range of documents on BCRs, including checklists, suggested content and structure, and the standard application form.[101]

---

97.   *See* Working Party, *Working Document 02/2012 Setting up a Table with the Elements and Principles to be Found in Processor Binding Corporate Rules* (WP 195) (June 6, 2012), http://ec.europa.eu/justice/data-protection/article-29/documentation/opinion-recommendation/files/2012/wp195_en.pdf.

98.   *See Compliance and Privacy, GE Gains First Binding Corporate Rules UK Approval*, available at http://complianceandprivacy.com/News-GE-BCR-1.asp.

99.   Working Party, *Working Document Setting Forth a Co-Operation Procedure for Issuing Common Opinions on Adequate Safeguards Resulting From "Binding Corporate Rules"* (WP 107) (April 14, 2005), http://ec.europa.eu/justice/policies/privacy/docs/wpdocs/2005/wp107_en.pdf.

100.   As of the date of publishing these are Croatia, Hungary, Denmark, Finland, Lithuania, Poland, Portugal, Romania, Sweden & Switzerland.

101.   An overview of the Working Party documentation on BCRs is available at http://ec.europa.eu/justice/data-protection/document/international-transfers/binding-corporate-rules/tools/index_en.htm.

Although the approval procedure was historically lengthy and very costly, the introduction of the fast track procedure in 2005 has permitted increasing numbers of companies to efficiently roll out BCRs. Moreover, BCR transfers are no longer restricted to only data coming from the European Union; the Asia-Pacific Economic Cooperation (APEC) has also rolled out a similar framework to ensure data transfers, but this has yet to pick up the same amount of interest and participation.[102] The Working Party and APEC are working toward ensuring a basic level of understanding between these two systems. In the coming years, it is likely that increasing numbers of companies will turn to these self-regulating solutions to streamline compliance initiatives.[103]

3. Industry Codes of Conduct

Industry codes of conduct are contemplated in Article 27(3) of the Directive:

> 2. Member States shall make provision for trade associations and other bodies representing other categories of controllers which have drawn up draft national codes or which have the intention of amending or extending existing national codes to be able to submit them to the opinion of the national authority.

The Working Party drafted a procedure for developing these codes, which will apply throughout defined industry groups or associations (so-called community), that is active or established in a "significant number of Member States."[104] The procedure for approval is fairly straightforward; however, as of the date of publishing, only one industry group, Federation of European Direct and Interactive Marketing, has successfully had its code approved.[105] First, the relevant industry association or "community" should submit the draft code for consideration to the Working Party. The code

---

102. See generally, http://www.cbprs.org/. For more information on the background and development of the CBPRs *see* the APEC Cross-border Privacy Enforcement Arrangement, *available at* http://www.apec.org/Groups/Committee-on-Trade-and-Investment/Electronic-Commerce-Steering-Group/Cross-border-Privacy-Enforcement-Arrangement.aspx.

103. Markus Heyder, *The APEC Cross Border Privacy Rules—Now That We've Built It, Will They Come?* (Sep. 4, 2014), *available at* https://privacyassociation.org/news/a/the-apec-cross-border-privacy-rules-now-that-weve-built-it-will-they-come/. APEC and the EU are also working towards leveraging such mechanisms on a broader scale - *see* Working Party, *Letter to Ms. Chatelois, Chair of APEC Data Privacy Subgroup*, (May 29, 2015), http://ec.europa.eu/justice/data-protection/article-29/documentation/other-document/files/2015/20150529__letter_of_the_art_29_wp_on_the_joint_work_on_bcr_and_cbpr_.pdf and *Opinion 02/2014 on a Referential for Requirements for Binding Corporate Rules submitted to national Data Protection Authorities in the EU and Cross Border Privacy Rules submitted to APEC CBPR Accountability Agents (WP 212)* (Feb. 27, 2014), http://ec.europa.eu/justice/data-protection/article-29/documentation/opinion-recommendation/files/2014/wp212_en.pdf.

104. Working Party, *Future Work on Codes of Conduct: Working Document on the Procedure for the Consideration by the Working Party of Community Codes of Conduct (WP 13)* (Sept. 10, 1998), http://ec.europa.eu/justice/policies/privacy/docs/wpdocs/1998/wp13_en.pdf.

105. Working Party, *Opinion 4/2010 on the European Code of Conduct of FEDMA for the Use of Personal Data in Direct Marketing (WP 174)* (July 13, 2010), http://ec.europa.eu/justice/data-protection/article-29/documentation/opinion-recommendation/files/2010/wp174_en.pdf. *See also* the earlier negative opinion from the Working Party, *Opinion 3/2003 on the European Code of Conduct of FEDMA for the Use of Personal Data in Direct Marketing (WP 77)* (Jun. 13, 2003), http://ec.europa.eu/justice/policies/privacy/docs/wpdocs/2003/wp77_en.pdf.

should be prepared "preferably in consultation with the data subjects concerned or their representatives."[106] Then, after proper submittal to the Working Party, the draft code will be circulated to all the members of the Working Party for consultation and consideration. The Working Party will then issue an opinion on whether it meets the legal requirements or, if not, why it falls short. The Commission "may [then] ensure appropriate publicity for the codes which have been approved by the Working Party."

4. Ad Hoc Data Transfer Agreements

Article 26(2) provides that although a country may not provide adequate protection, EU Member States

> may authorize a transfer or a set of transfers of personal data to a third country which does not ensure an adequate level of protection within the meaning of Article 25 (2), where the controller adduces adequate safeguards with respect to the protection of the privacy and fundamental rights and freedoms of individuals and as regards the exercise of the corresponding rights; such safeguards may in particular result from appropriate contractual clauses.[107]

Thus, Member States may decide when to permit transfers in light of the provisions of Article 25(2). Additionally, these ad hoc contracts are subject to the prior authorization and prior consultation of the relevant DPAs. In practice, companies that are actively involved in processor-to-processor transfers rely on such contracts, as do members of U.S. financial services and nonprofits (i.e., companies or entities that are not subject to FTC jurisdiction and cannot leverage Safe Harbor for transfers). In an interesting development, Microsoft had its service agreement for its MS 365 (a cloud-based service) formally approved by the Article 29 Working Party in 2014.[108] Following this approval, the Working Party has set up a cooperation procedure through which other organizations can have their ad hoc contractual clauses reviewed and vetted as being compliant with the Model Contracts.[109]

C.   Article 26(1) Exemptions

Derogations from Article 25's principle of Third Country adequacy to permit cross-border data transfers are contained in Article 26(1). We will first look at the

---

106.   *Id.* at 2.
107.   Directive, art. 26(2), at 46.
108.   Working Party, *Letter to Mr. Nadella on the Microsoft Service Agreement*, (September 22, 2014). *See also Privacy authorities across Europe approve Microsoft's cloud commitments* (April 10, 2014) *at* http://blogs.microsoft.com/blog/2014/04/10/privacy-authorities-across-europe-approve-microsofts-cloud-commitments/.
109.   Working Party, *Working Document Setting Forth a Co-Operation Procedure for Issuing Common Opinions on "Contractual clauses" Considered as compliant with the EC Model Clauses*, WP 226, Nov. 24, 2014, http://ec.europa.eu/justice/data-protection/article-29/documentation/opinion-recommendation/files/2014/wp226_en.pdf.

interpretation of the relevant general exemptions, followed by the specific exemptions for permitting transfers.

1. Interpretation of the Article 26(1) Exemptions

Due to deviations and nonuniform application of the Article 26 exemptions, in 2005 the Working Party issued a working document on the interpretation of these exemptions (WP 114).[110] The deviation among Member States' interpretations was noted in the EC Study on Implementation.[111] The working document seeks to create an even interpretation of the exemptions with a view to inhibiting forum shopping within the European Union to avoid more rigorous application of the article in some Member States because of the nonuniform application of the rules. Prior to this, some controllers relied on the Article 26(1) exemptions as a first preference, before relying on the other bases for transfer. Logically, this would seem appropriate when looking at the articles sequentially. However, when issuing its guidance, the Working Party stated that the exemptions should be strictly interpreted in order to protect the general rule and, by extension, an individual's fundamental rights.[112]

The Additional Protocol of Convention 108, briefly discussed in Chapter 1 Section I.B., provides that parties to the Convention may dispense with the requirement of adequacy to transfer data, but "[t]he relevant domestic provisions must nevertheless respect the principle inherent in European law that clauses making exceptions are interpreted restrictively so that the exception does not become the rule."[113]

This narrow interpretation of exceptions from the general rules is also present in the case law of the European Court of Human Rights—interpreting fundamental rights in a wide manner so as to limit the scope of derogations in accordance with the effet utile principle.[114] On the EU level, this rule involves a method borrowed from international judges whereby when two interpretations of a legal instrument are possible, the judge must choose that which gives effect to the instrument (or has an effet utile), rather than that which deprives it of effect, even rejecting

---

110. Working Party, *Working Document on a Common Interpretation of Article 26(1) of Directive 95/46/EC of 24 Oct. 1995* (WP 114) (Nov. 25, 2005) [hereinafter WP 114], http://ec.europa.eu/justice/policies/privacy/docs/wpdocs/2005/wp114_en.pdf.

111. *See generally* Douwe Korff, *EC Study on Implementation of Data Processing Directive* (Sept. 2002), *available at* http://194.242.234.211/documents/10160/10704/Stato+di+attuazione+della+Direttiva+95-46-CE (referenced on http://www.garanteprivacy.it website).

112. WP 114, *supra* note 98, at 7.

113. *Id.* (citation omitted). For the source of the extract itself, *see* Additional Protocol to Convention 108 regarding Supervisory Authorities and Transborder Data Flows, art. 2(2)(a) (ETS No. 181) (Nov. 8, 2001), *available at* http://conventions.coe.int/Treaty/EN/Treaties/Html/181.htm.

114. *Id.; see also* Airey v. Ireland, ser. A, no. 32, para. 26, at 11–13, Application no. 6289/73 (Oct. 9, 1979), *available at* http://hudoc.echr.coe.int/sites/fra/pages/search.aspx?i=001-57420. In this case involving, inter alia, rights to legal aid and representation, the Court stated that "the Convention must be interpreted in the light of present-day conditions [citation omitted] and it is designed to safeguard the individual in a real and practical way as regards those areas with which it deals [citation omitted]," para. 26, at 11. For a discussion of interpretation in connection with the European Court of Human Rights and a UK statute, *see* Carmen Draghici, *The Human Rights Act in the Shadow of the European Convention: Are Copyist's Errors Allowed?*, Eur. Hum. Rts. L. Rev. 2014, 2, 154–69.

interpretations that limit or weaken such effect.[115] This power of interpretation flows from the Treaty on European Union article on the European courts, where it is provided that:

> [the ECJ] shall ensure that in the interpretation and application of the Treaties the law is observed.
>
> Member States shall provide remedies sufficient to ensure effective legal protection in the fields covered by Union law.[116]

In the context of EU legislation meant to protect individuals' fundamental rights— in this case, the Directive—it is clear that a judge would choose to limit exceptions that would weaken individual rights.

The Working Party notes that when relying on the Article 26(1) exemptions, the other provisions of the Directive still need to be respected, explaining that, "regardless of the provisions relied upon for the purpose of data transfer to a third country, other relevant provisions of the Directive need to be respected."[117] WP 114 cites situations in which sensitive data is transferred and explains that controllers will still need to comply with the provisions of Article 8 on sensitive data processing. In practice, this means that to transfer this data, controllers will still need to rely on a "legal basis" for the transfer under Article 8 (as transferring is a form of processing). Thus, even if one has a basis for the transfer under the provisions of Article 26(1), one of the bases under the provisions of Article 8 is required to permit the transfer (such as consent, processing permitted for complying with employment obligations, etc.).[118] For more on the legal basis for processing sensitive data, see Chapter 4 Section III.

The Working Party also mentions that in the case of transfers, the principles of fair and lawful processing as well as of compatible use continue to apply. Thus, the controller may need to provide notice or inform the individual about the transfer even

---

115. *See* Isabelle Pingel, sous la direction de, *De Rome à Lisbonne: Commentaire Article par Article des Traités UE et CE* (Dalloz, Paris, 2d ed., 2010), 1437 (Fr.). In a case involving discrepancies between two language versions of the ECHR, the European Court of Human Rights said that:

> Thus confronted with two versions of a treaty which are equally authentic but not exactly the same, the Court must, following established international law precedents, interpret them in a way that will reconcile them as far as possible. Given that it is a law-making treaty, it is also necessary to seek the interpretation that is most appropriate in order to realise the aim and achieve the object of the treaty, not that which would restrict to the greatest possible degree the obligations undertaken by the Parties.

Wemhoff v. Germany, Application no. 2122/64 (June 27, 1968), para. 8, at 19, *available at* http://hudoc .echr.coe.int/sites/fra/pages/search.aspx?i=001-57595.

116. *See* Consolidated Version of the Treaty on European Union, art. 19, Oct. 26, 2012, 2012 (C 326) 13, 27, *available at* http://eur-lex.europa.eu/legal-content/EN/TXT/PDF/?uri=CELEX:12012M/TXT&from=EN.

117. WP 114, *supra* note 98, at 8.

118. *Id.*

if not required explicitly under the notice requirements or the provisions on transfers. This could be the case for sensitive data or when an individual "might consider as sensitive data about him/herself in a given situation (e.g., financial data, data enabling an adverse decisions being taken against [him/her]."[119] Therefore it is important to look at the overall processing and related risks in light of fairness and what information had previously been provided to the individual about the processing. The Working Party notes that under Article 14(a) the individual may have a reason to object to a specific transfer of his or her personal data under certain circumstances.[120] See Chapter 1 Section III.C on individual rights on objecting to processing.

WP 114 makes it clear that controllers should rely on transfer mechanisms that ensure fundamental rights and safeguards continue to apply to the EU personal data when transferred to nonadequate jurisdictions. The Working Party highlights that when "significant transfers" are to take place to a country that is not deemed to provide an adequate level of protection, controllers should look to the adequate safeguard mechanisms (Model Contracts and BCRs). The Working Party elaborates that significant transfers are ones that "might be qualified as repeated, mass or structural" and should as such be effectuated within the legal framework of the safeguard mechanisms. Nevertheless it does note that "there will be cases where mass or repeated transfers can legitimately be carried out on the basis of Article 26(1), when recourse to such a legal framework is impossible in practice."[121] An example would be international transfers of money, which take place daily and en masse. One tends to also come across such transfers in the HR context, when candidates are supplying personal data to be considered for a job or in the recruitment context. Another factor is that of the relevant risks to data subjects under the circumstances—thus, the controller will need to assess whether the transfers are structural as well as the related risks to individuals under the circumstances prior to turning to the Article 26(1) exemptions. Again, reliance on the exemptions should never lead to a situation in which the data subject's fundamental rights would be compromised.[122]

2. Best Practice

WP 114 sets out a best-practice approach to transfers as follows:

- First, look to whether the importation or destination country ensures an adequate level of protection and "satisfy [one]self that the exported data will be safeguarded in that country."[123] As noted earlier, adequacy determinations include the U.S. Safe Harbor framework.

---

119. *Id.*
120. *Id.*
121. *Id.* at 9.
122. *Id.*
123. *Id.*

- If adequacy in terms of the jurisdiction is "not adequate in light of all the circumstances surrounding a data transfer" then the controller will need to look to the adequate safeguards, such as Model Contracts or BCRs.
- Only when these adequate safeguards are "truly not practical and/or feasible" can the controller then turn to the exemptions in Article 26(1).[124]

3. Consent

Article 26(1)(a) allows transfers to nonadequate jurisdictions to be made with the data subject's unambiguous consent. Here, consent must be "a freely given, specific and informed indication of the data subject's wishes" and received prior to the transfer.[125] Implied consent or the ability to opt out of a transfer is not considered valid for the purposes of this exemption. Therefore, specific consent to the specific transfer must actually be acquired in advance for the related transfer to be made.[126]

WP 114 calls attention to the overlap with Article 13 of the e-Privacy Directive and their previous advice on consent for direct marketing communications (for a discussion of the e-Privacy Directive and electronic direct marketing, see Chapter 6 Section I.). For the purposes of prior consent, its guidance together with that in WP 187 on consent are helpful in the online context. Boxes should not be already checked off for acceptance, as the checking off by the data subject would be the positive act. Furthermore, consent for the purposes of transfers within the employment context is not the preferred basis and should be consulted as a last resort. This is due primarily to the views of the Working Party and many other DPAs that consent is not deemed to be freely given in the employment context due to the subordinate role of the employee to the employer. Furthermore, consent's basis is also unreliable as data subjects must always be able to revoke their consent; hence, controllers could be in situations in which some data subjects have consented but they may at any time revoke this consent and eliminate the current basis. The Working Party noted that "[r]elying on consent may therefore prove to be . . . simple at first glance but in reality complex and cumbersome."[127]

Consent is also covered in Chapter 2 Section IV, Chapter 3 Section II. C., and Chapter 4 Section I.B. (in the latter case, in the employment context).

4. Necessary for the Performance of a Contract

The derogation in Article 26(1)(b) permits transfers when "necessary for the performance of a contract between the data subject and the controller or the implementation of pre-contractual measures taken in response to the data subject's request."[128] This derogation as well as the following ones, through Article 26(1)(e), are limited by the

---

124. *Id.*
125. *Id.* at 10.
126. *Id.*
127. *Id.* at 11.
128. Directive, art. 26(1)(b) at 46.

"necessity" of their circumstances.[129] Here, this necessity test calls for "a close and substantial connection between the data subject and the purposes of the contract":[130] Only if the data transfer is actually *necessary* for the performance of the contract or for precontractual actions taken at the request of the data subject can it take place under Article 26(1)(b).

The Working Party considers the consolidation or centralization of subsidiary employee data by multinational groups for payroll or human resource purposes "excessive since it is highly questionable" that the transfers are necessary for the performance of the employment contract between the employee and his or her employer (controller). It notes that "there is no direct and objective link" between the performance of the contract and the data transfer.[131] Moreover, WP 114 outlines that additional information or data that is not necessary for the purposes of transfers or the contract performance will never qualify under the "necessity" derogations and another basis to ensure adequacy should be found.[132]

5. Necessary for Contracts

Article 26(1)(c) allows transfers when "necessary for the conclusion or performance of a contract concluded in the interest of the data subject between the controller and a third party."[133] Similarly to the Article 26(1)(b) derogation, there is the requirement that transfers must be necessary for the conclusion or performance of a contract in the interest of the data subject. Again, there must be "a close and substantial connection between" the purposes of the contract and the data subject's interest. The Working Party considers again the outsourcing of payroll services to Third Country service providers. Here, some controllers have argued that these transfers are necessary for the performance of services as agreed in the service agreement with the payroll providers. And, furthermore, the transfers are in the data subject's interest as the service relates to the payment of employee salaries. The Working Party, however, does not consider the link between the employee's interest and the contract purposes "close and substantial." Hence, the derogation does not apply in these circumstances.

On the other hand, the Working Party considers a situation in which stock option plans are outsourced to third-party financial service providers. The Working Party does not definitively accept the application of this derogation in such

---

129. WP 114, *supra* note 98, at 12.

130. *Id.* at 13.

131. *Id.* at 13. WP 114 also mentions its PNR Opinion where it also denied the applicability of the Article 26(1)(b) derogation "to transfers of data of air passengers to the U.S. authorities, due to the scope of data transferred, certain of which cannot be deemed 'necessary' for the performance of the transport contract." *Id. See generally* Working Party, *Opinion on Transmission of Passenger Manifest Information and Other Data from Airlines to the United States* (WP 66) (Oct. 24, 2002), http://ec.europa.eu/justice/policies/privacy/docs/wpdocs/2002/wp66_en.pdf.

132. *Id.*

133. Directive, art. 26(1)(c), at 46.

situations, expressing "its reservations about the validity of this interpretation." However, it shifts the burden of overcoming these reservations to the controller; whereby the latter must satisfy a national DPA that the data transferred is necessary for the performance of the stock option service agreement. Here, the Working Party leaves this scenario open ended but makes it clear that a controller could—in theory—be able to convince a national DPA of the necessity under the circumstances.[134]

6. Public Interest Grounds and Legal Claims

Article 26(1)(d) provides for transfers when "necessary or legally required on important public interest grounds, or for the establishment, exercise or defence of legal claims."[135] The application of this basis for derogation from the requirement of an adequacy finding was considered in the Working Party's Opinion on PNR data transfers of airline passengers to the U.S. authorities. There, the Working Party found that the exception did not apply, as "the necessity of the transfer had not been established . . . and it did not appear acceptable for a unilateral decision by a third country" to specify its own public interest grounds for the basis of bulk transfers of EU personal data.[136] Any valid public interest grounds for this derogation must be found in EU law or in a Member State's national law applicable to the controller. WP 114 points out that Recital 58 of the Directive contemplates international data exchanges for tax, social security, and customs purposes. However, it notes that the public interest derogation can be relied upon only "if the transfer is of interest to the [EU] authorities [themselves]."[137]

The "establishment, safeguarding or defence of legal claims" is similarly subject to strict interpretation under the necessity test. WP 114 is abstruse on the exact circumstances in which this exception might apply, finding that it "appears to allow" a non-European parent company to transfer data relating to an employee posted to an EU subsidiary in the context of litigation, if necessary for the parent company's legal defense.[138] The Working Party does clearly state that the derogation cannot be relied upon for a transfer of all employee files to the parent in view "of the possibility that such legal proceedings might be brought one day." One thing is clear: the applicable rules on criminal and civil proceedings stemming from international treaties must be complied with when transferring under this exemption, specifically the Hague Conventions of 18 March 1970 on the Taking of Evidence Abroad in Civil or Commercial Matters and of 25 October 1980 on International Access to Justice.[139]

---

134. WP 114, *supra* note 98, at 14.
135. Directive, art. 26(1)(d), at 46.
136. WP 114, *supra* note 98, at 14–15.
137. *Id.* at 15.
138. *Id.*
139. *Id.*

7. Data Subject's Vital Interest

Article 26(1)(e) permits transfers when necessary for the protection of the data subject's vital interests.[140] This derogation applies in cases of medical emergencies when the data is directly necessary for medical treatment. An example the Working Party gives is when a data subject would be unconscious and "need urgent medical care, and only his usual doctor, established in an EU country, is able to supply these data." Again, the transfer must be necessary for the data subject's vital interest. For health data, this means that "it must be necessary for an essential diagnosis"—transfers for general medical research are outside of this scope and would need to be based on the requirements under Article 26(2).[141]

8. Public Register

Finally, Article 26(1)(f) permits transfers when "made from a register which according to laws or regulations is intended to provide information to the public and which is open to consultation either by the public in general or by any person who can demonstrate legitimate interest, to the extent that the conditions laid down in law for consultation are fulfilled in the particular case."[142] This derogation is an outlier, as it does not turn on necessity. It provides an exemption for transfers from public registers that can be "freely consulted" or "can be consulted by anyone in the country or by any person with a legitimate interest in doing so." Hence, this derogation "logically" provides for a basis to transfer personal data in the public register to people established in Third Countries. However, the transfer is conditioned, as it "should not involve the entirety of the data or entire categories of the data contained in the register."[143] This limitation is rooted in the purpose limitation principle; if the register's content were fully emptied, there is an inherent risk that the Third Country entity could use the data for purposes other than the one for which the register was established. Here, when relying on this derogation, entities from Third Countries will need to reference the national law of the Member State setting up the register to ensure that the derogation applies: "[i]n particular, these laws and regulations will define the concepts of 'intended to provide information to the public' and 'legitimate interest' on which the derogation may be used."[144] In practice, Third Country entities must be able to demonstrate their transfer purposes in a particular Member State national law setting up the public resister.

---

140. Directive, art. 26(1)(e), at 46.
141. WP 114, *supra* note 98, at 16. The Hague Conventions are *available at* http://www.hcch.net /index_en.php?act=conventions.text&cid=82 and http://www.hcch.net/index_en.php?act=conventions .text&cid=91, respectively.
142. Directive, art. 26(1)(f), at 46.
143. Directive, recital 58, at 37.
144. WP 114, *supra* note 98, at 16.

Applicable Law under the GDPR

A general principle of international transfers is included in Article 40 of the GDPR. In comparison to the Directive, it approaches the principle of international transfers in a more holistic manner, providing that any transfer—whether currently subject to processing or "intended for processing after transfer to a third country" will be "subject to the other provisions of this Regulation."[143] It also broadens the scope to include instances of onward transfers from Third Countries, ensuring these transfers are still subject to the provisions of the GDPR and that EU data protection law continues to apply to this personal data. The GDPR clearly states that compliance with the conditions on international transfers extends to *both* controllers and processors: "the conditions laid down in this Chapter are complied with by the *controller and processor*, including for onward transfers of personal data from the third country or an international organisation to another third country or to another international organization."[144]

Transfers based on a decision of adequacy of protection in the destination country are permitted under Article 41 of the GDPR. These transfers are not subject to the requirement of "any further authorization."[145] Criteria to be used by the Commission to assess and determine adequacy are also provided in such article. Three elements for the Commission to take into account are:

(1) the rule of law and relevant legislation in the Third Country,
(2) the "existence and effective functioning" of the local DPA or equivalent regulator, and
(3) the Third Country's "international commitments."

An implementing act by the Commission will specify the "geographical and sectoral application" of an adequacy decision.[146]

Interestingly, the GDPR also provides for the Commission to be granted the power to add a country or territory or processing sector within a Third Country or an international organization to a blacklist, published in the *Official Journal of the European Union* pursuant to Article 41(7),[147] of those that do not ensure adequate protection of personal data, specifically when the relevant laws do not "guarantee effective and enforceable rights including effective administrative and judicial redress for data subjects."[148] Transfers to these blacklisted countries, sectors, and territories are specifically prohibited under the GDPR.[149]

The GDPR includes a grandfathering clause, as current Commission decisions on adequacy granted under the Directive will remain in force unless and until amended, replaced, or repealed.[150]

---

145. GDPR, art. 40, at 69.
146. *Id.* (emphasis added).
147. GDPR, art. 41(1), at 69. *See also* Ch. 2 III.E, "Applicable Law under the GDPR" text box.
148. GDPR, art. 41(4), at 70.
149. GDPR, art. 41(7), at 70.
150. GDPR, art. 41(5), at 70.
151. GDPR, art. 41(6), at 70.
152. GDPR, art. 41(8), at 70.

The GDPR also shifts the order of the applicable transfer exceptions and ranks them in a more logical order than the Directive. The appropriate safeguards (including binding corporate rules) are laid out first in Articles 42 and 43, followed by the exceptional derogations from the general prohibition on transfers to nonadequate jurisdictions in Article 44.

BCRs, Model Contracts, and So On

Transfers are permitted when "the controller or processor has adduced appropriate safeguards with respect to the protection of personal data in a legally binding instrument."[151] The GDPR emphasizes both the standards of the safeguards that must be taken—and that are deemed appropriate—as well as the means by which the safeguards are provided—that is, in a contract or similar legally binding document. These safeguards are specified "in particular" to be contained in BCRs, Model Contracts adopted by the Commission,[152] or DPAs,[153] or "contractual clauses" as authorized by the DPAs.[154] The latter category continues to be subject to prior authorization. It is not clear whether this list of safeguards is to be construed as limited to these possibilities or if this is without limitation to the list.

The provisions in the GDPR on BCRs spell out that they will be approved in accordance with the new consistency mechanism. Furthermore, the requirements for what needs to be specifically present in the BCRs are outlined in Article 43(2) in subparagraphs (a) through (k). All prior authorization requirements are also removed from transfers based on BCRs and the Model Contracts, in addition to adequacy situations mentioned in Article 41.

New "Article 26" Derogations: Article 44 of the GDPR

The derogations from the general rule on transfers pursuant to adequacy are laid out in Article 44. Its provisions clearly state that when there is no adequacy or appropriate safeguards "a transfer or a set of transfers . . . may take place only on the condition that" one of the derogations is applicable.[155] This clearly establishes—somewhat in contravention to WP 114—that structural transfers may be based on the derogations and that transfers do not need to be one-time or ad hoc transfers. However, in addition to the current derogations provided in Article 26 of the Directive, the GDPR builds out a "legitimate interest" basis, which is limited in its applicability.[156] This is when the transfer is necessary for the purposes of the legitimate interests pursued by the controller or processor, which cannot be qualified as frequent or massive, and when the controller or processor has assessed the circumstances and adduced safeguards to protect the data.[157] When transferred on this basis, special consideration should be given to the type of data, purpose and duration of processing, and "the situation in the country of origin, third country"

---

153. GDPR, art. 42(1), at 70.
154. GDPR, art. 42(2)(b), at 70.
155. GDPR, art. 42(2)(c), at 71.
156. GDPR, art. 42(2)(d), at 71.
157. GDPR, art. 44(1), at 73.
158. GDPR, art. 44(1)(h), at 73.
159. *Id.*

and the destination country and any other appropriate safeguards.[158] Controllers and processors must also document the assessment of these points pursuant to the newly implemented requirement to maintain documentation,[159] and they should inform the DPA of the transfer.[160]

Codes of Conduct and Privacy Seals

The GDPR includes the articles on codes of conduct and introduces the possibility of establishing certification mechanisms and privacy seals or marks in Articles 38 and 39. As these provisions are not included in Chapter V on international transfers (which includes Articles 40 through 45), it is unclear to which extent codes of conduct and certifications mechanisms would be permitted as a sole basis for adequacy. For codes of conduct, this could be done on the basis of a Commission determination of adequacy of a specific sector. However, there is no explicit inclusion of codes of conduct in Article 41, which merely speaks about "processing sectors within that third country"—perhaps signaling that adequacy determinations would need to be approved by the Commission on a country-by-country basis even for the same sectors. Furthermore, there is no mention of privacy certification mechanisms or privacy seals in Chapter V. This leaves the future of alternative mechanisms or bases for transfer rather unclear.

IV. USE OF PROCESSORS (INDEPENDENT CONTRACTORS AND VENDORS)

Almost all controllers engage processors to process personal data. This occurs whenever external parties, such as external vendors, independent contractors, or any other third parties access personal data or process it on behalf of the controller. Thus, the relationship of the processor to the controller is typically one of a subcontractor.[163] As we have seen, the controller remains responsible for compliance with data protection law, whereas the processor is acting on the controller's behalf and under its instructions. Therefore, he Directive calls for specific provisions on the protection of confidentiality and security of processing to be concluded "in writing or in another equivalent form" between the controller and the processor. Despite the rather limited required provisions, the requirements are often included in a separate contract or a separate annex or addendum to a service agreement, often called a data processing agreement or Article 17 contract.

---

160.   GDPR, art. 44(3), at 74.
161.   GDPR, art. 28, at 58–59.
162.   GDPR, art. 44(6), at 74.
163.   In fact, the French version of the Directive uses the French term for "subcontractor" (*sous-traitant*) in place of the term "processor." *See, e.g.,* Directive, art. 17(2), at 43.

A. Processor Obligations

Generally speaking, the Directive places the bulk of compliance obligations and liability on the controller. When selecting a processor, controllers must ensure that they select a processor that is capable of respecting data protection obligations and has the necessary technical skills and organizational procedures for such compliance. Aside from the bulk of obligations and ultimate responsibility lying with the controller, the Directive recognizes two areas in which processors have certain obligations: (1) data security and (2) confidentiality of processing.

1. Data Security

The Directive provides that the obligations regarding the security of the processing shall also apply to the processor. Importantly, these data security obligations shall be defined by the law of the Member State in which the processor is established,[164] although the Directive sets out the general framework for them.

Data security requirements under the Directive are contained in Article 17, which provides in paragraph (1) that the controller must

[i]mplement appropriate technical and organizational measures to protect personal data against accidental or unlawful destruction or accidental loss, alteration, unauthorized disclosure or access, in particular where the processing involves the transmission of data over a network, and against all other unlawful forms of processing.

Having regard to the state of the art and the cost of their implementation, such measures shall ensure a level of security appropriate to the risks represented by the processing and the nature of the data to be protected.[165]

When working through a processor, the processor is also subject to the above requirements, which should be covered in the contract[166] (the data processing agreement). The controller must ensure that the processor it chooses provides "sufficient guarantees in respect of the technical security measures and organizational measures governing the processing."[167] Again, these guarantees are acquired in the data processing agreement. Thus, in the event of processing by a data processor, security requirements would apply to the controller, but the processor would also be subject to a set of security requirements with respect to its processing, as well as security and organizational measures. In such context, the burden of ensuring that the processor complies with legal requirements is placed on the controller. This burden on the controller demonstrates the

---

164. Directive, art.17(3), at 43.
165. Directive, art. 17(1), at 43.
166. Directive, art.17(3), at 43.
167. Directive, art. 17(2), at 43.

importance of the use of data processing agreements, in order to provide a contractual basis for enforcement of compliance throughout the chain of processing.

2. Confidentiality

The "confidentiality of processing" article of the Directive provides that "[a]ny person acting under the authority of the controller or of the processor, including the processor himself, who has access to personal data must not process them except on instructions from the controller, unless he is required to do so by law."[168] Processors should respect the confidentiality of the personal data and, as a practical matter, allow only authorized persons access to them. Furthermore, confidentiality requirements should be included in the data processing agreement between the controller and the processor. The French data protection authority (the CNIL) has provided a model of one such clause (obviously referring to French law), which follows:

Data-processing media and documents provided by the X Corporation to the Y Corporation remain the property of the X Corporation.

Data contained in these media and documents is strictly covered by **professional secrecy** (Article 226-13 of the Penal Code); the same applies to all the data that Y comes across of [sic] during the execution of the present contract.

In accordance with Article 34 of the French Data Processing Act modified, Y is committed to taking all the necessary precautions in order to preserve the security of information and in particular to prevent that they become garbled, damaged or communicated to unauthorized persons.

Therefore, Y commits to respecting the following obligations and making them respected by its personnel:

- not making any copy of the documents and data processing media which are entrusted to it, except for those necessary for the execution of the service envisaged in the contract, prior agreement from the record owner is necessary;
- not using the documents and processed information for purposes other than those specified in the present contract;
- not revealing these documents or information to other persons, whether they are private or public, physical or moral persons;
- taking the necessary measures in order to avoid any devious or fraudulent use of computer files during the execution of the contract;
- taking all security measures, in particular material ones, in order to ensure the preservation and integrity of the documents and information processed throughout the whole duration of the present contract;

---

168.   Directive, art.16, at 43.

- and at the end of the contract, to carry out the destruction of all the manual or computerized files which store the information that was entered.

For this reason, Y will not be able to subcontract the execution of the services to another Corporation, nor carry out a contract transfer of market in the absence of X prior agreement.

X reserves the right to perform any verification which it deems to be useful to observe the respect by Y of the above mentioned commitments.

In the event of non-observance of the above mentioned provisions, the responsibility for the holder can also be committed on the basis of provision of Articles 226-5 and 226-17 of the new Penal Code.

X will be in a position to pronounce the immediate cancellation of the contract, without damages to the benefit of the holder, in the event of breach of professional secrecy or of non-observance of the above mentioned provisions.[169]

B.   Contract between the Controller and the Processor

As previously noted, the Directive calls for a contract or a "legally binding act binding the processor to the controller," and Member State national law security requirements applicable to the processor should specifically be set out in writing. The act (or contract) referred to previously should provide in particular the following, according to the Directive:

- That the processor shall act only on the controller's instructions, and
- That the obligations regarding the security of the processing (both under the Directive and those that are defined by the *law of the Member State in which the processor is established*) shall also apply to the processor.[170] Please note that these obligations are in addition to, and do not substitute for, the controller's obligations, which continue to apply.

In order to ensure processor compliance with the above-mentioned obligations, the contract should allow for the controller to be able to audit the processor's security and confidentiality arrangements regularly, including access to premises and records, and it should settle issues such as who is to bear the costs of such audits and when they may be carried out (e.g., whether or not only during normal business hours, or with or without prior written notice). Nonetheless, the controller may contract out to the processor certain data protection compliance tasks, such as responding to requests for the exercise of data subject rights (for example, access to their data), on the

---

169.   CNIL, "Factsheet n° 12: Subcontracting" in *Guide: Security of Personal Data, 2010 edition* (2010), http://www.cnil.fr/fileadmin/documents/en/Guide_Security_of_Personal_Data-2010.pdf.
170.   Directive, art. 17 (3), at 43.

instructions of the controller. This could be provided for by the data processing contract (for routine requests). In addition, a division of responsibilities for liability for noncompliance with security and confidentiality requirements should be contained in the contract. A processor's noncompliance with such obligation should also trigger a default under the data processing agreement, allowing the controller to seek remedies (such as injunctions, damages, etc.) and potentially terminate the contract. As a practical matter, in addition to capability to meet security and organizational requirements, processor ability to honor indemnity commitments or to provide remedies in case of default should also be assessed by the controller when choosing a processor.

The UK data protection agency (UK ICO) has highlighted that a processor may be served with a law enforcement agency warrant to hand over personal data and in such an event would take on data controller responsibilities, including potentially being subject to enforcement action, for example, "if it disclosed excessive personal data in response to the warrant." Also, if the processor acts exceed the instructions coming from the controller, for example, by using the personal data for its own purposes, then it could also be considered a controller for such unauthorized use, and the contract should provide for such breach to become a default under the contract, allowing the controller to seek remedies.[171]

An important practical point is that both the security and confidentiality requirements apply to all relationships with processors, regardless of whether cross-border transfers are involved. If a processor is located in a non-EEA country that does not benefit from an adequacy determination,[172] for example, the controller must conclude the standard contractual clauses under Commission Decision 2010/87/EU[173] in order to be able to export personal data to such non-EEA country. This Controller-to-Processor Model Contract includes the requirements arising from Articles 16 and 17. Therefore, when faced with using a non–EU-based processing, executing this Model Contract provides both a basis for transfer as well as including the relevant provisions typically included in a data processing agreement. Although the processor has obligations under subparagraph (i), the Working Party highlights the fact that a controller is the party mainly responsible for data protection compliance, through the example of a small controller faced with a large processor seeking to impose his own contractual terms: "the imbalance in the contractual power of a small data controller with respect to big service providers should not be considered as a justification for the controller to accept clauses

171. *See, generally* UK ICO, *Data Controllers and Data Processors : What the Difference Is and What the Governance Implications Are* (June 5, 2014) 16–20, http://ico.org.uk/for_organisations/guidance_index/~/media/documents/library/Data_Protection/Detailed_specialist_guides/data-controllers-and-data-processors-dp-guidance.pdf.

172. *See* Chapter 3 Section III.1 for a discussion of the adequacy determination.

173. Commission Decision of Feb. 5, 2010, on Standard Contractual Clauses for the Transfer of Personal Data to Processors Established in Third Countries under Directive 95/46/EC of the European Parliament and of the Council, 2010 O.J. (L 39) 5 (Feb. 12, 2010), http://eur-lex.europa.eu/LexUriServ/LexUriServ.do?uri=OJ:L:2010:039:0005:0018:EN:PDF.

and terms of contracts which are not in compliance with data protection laws."[174] Thus, controllers faced with this situation should look for another processor willing to contract on terms compliant with the Directive terms and Member State laws.

When companies process information on behalf of other entities in the same corporate group, the same security and confidentiality requirements also apply. Therefore companies that use "shared service centers" or perform functions on behalf of other entities, for example, will need to execute data processing agreements for intercompany processing.

If further subcontracting is allowed by the controller, this should specifically be dealt with in the contract. More generally, clear instructions should be given by the controller to the processor with respect to the processing. Such instructions on the processing operations are generally included in an annex or the appendix of the C-to-P Model Contract.

The use of cloud-computing processors involves specific risks related to the need for information and control insofar as further subcontracting and cross-border transfers are concerned. As a result, the WP has highlighted that "emphasis must be placed on the features of the applicable contracts—these must include a set of standardised data protection safeguards" (including those regarding technical and operational measures and cross-border data flows), "as well as on additional mechanisms that can prove suitable for facilitating due diligence and accountability (such as independent third-party audits and certifications of a provider's services)."[175]

Let us now take a look at a few examples of relevant Member State and EEA laws (and practice) regarding controller-processor security requirements and data processing agreements.

1. France

Similarly to the Directive, France's data protection act provides that the "processor shall offer adequate guarantees to ensure the implementation of the security . . . measures mentioned in Article 34 [measures applicable to the controller]. This requirement shall not exempt the data controller from his obligation to supervise the observance of such measures."[176] Such act continues to provide that the data processing agreement "shall specify the obligations incumbent upon the processor as regards the protection of the security and confidentiality of the data and provide that the processor may act only upon the instruction of the data controller."[177]

---

174. Working Party, *Opinion 1/2010 on the Concepts of "Controller" and "Processor"* at 26 (WP 169) (Feb. 16, 2010), http://ec.europa.eu/justice/policies/privacy/docs/wpdocs/2010/wp169_en.pdf.

175. WP 196, *supra* note 89, at 8.

176. Loi Informatique et Libertés Act n° 78-17 of Jan. 6, 1978 on Information Technology, Data Files and Civil Liberties [English translation], art. 35, at 27, http://www.cnil.fr/fileadmin/documents/en/Act78-17VA.pdf.

177. *Id.*

The French data protection authority—the CNIL—has provided guidance on security guarantees applicable to subcontractors processing data, specifying that provisions such as security audits, installation visits, and the like should be made to ensure that the processor's security guarantees are "effective." Encryption technology (including data links) may be appropriate in this context. Network protection, logs, and audits for traceability and management of security clearances may be appropriate.[178] The CNIL has also underscored that the controller should have "full control" over the security of personal data for which they have responsibility, and that such control "implies knowledge of the physical location of the databases and assurance that any data transfer will be done in such a way as to guarantee their confidentiality."[179] This would be particularly relevant in the context of cloud computing and could call for contract clauses whereby the processor represents and warrants the location of the data, and undertakes not to transfer the data to any other location without the prior written consent of the controller.

One French author sets out an example clause (in French) for security obligations in the data processing agreement (which mirror in many respects the CNIL's confidentiality clause set out in Section IV.A.2), including inter alia the following elements:

- The security of data must be safeguarded, including the prevention of access by any party not previously authorized by the controller.
- Processing is limited to that which is authorized by the controller and following its instructions, and only in connection with the relevant data processing agreement.
- Subcontracting is prohibited unless prior authorization is given by the controller.
- Confidentiality requirements apply, including in connection with maintenance.
- All necessary security measures are required in order to protect the storage and integrity of the data.
- Measures must be taken to prevent fraudulent or other unintended use of the data.
- The data must be destroyed at the end of the agreement.

In addition, an obligation to cooperate with the controller and a right of inspection by the controller or by someone appointed by it (who is not a direct competitor of the processor) are provided.[180]

2. Norway

The Norwegian data protection authority has also published contract clauses in the form of a draft agreement between the controller and processor. This

---

178. *See* CNIL, "Factsheet n° 12," *supra* note 157.
179. CNIL, *Workers Being Globalised in Spite of Themselves!*, *available at* http://www.cnil.fr/english /topics/human-resources/workers-being-globalised-in-spite-of-themselves/.
180. ALAIN BENSOUSSAN, INFORMATIQUE ET LIBERTÉS 207–208 (Editions Francis Lefebvre, 2008).

agreement specifies that the "processor is obliged to give the controller access to his written technical and organizational security measures and to provide assistance" so that the controller may comply with the provisions of the Norwegian Personal Data Act of April 14, 2000, No. 31 and Personal Data Regulations of December 15, 2000, No. 1265. Prior agreement, in the form of an amendment to the data processing agreement, would be required to allow the processor to resort to subcontracting. The processor would be required to make documentation available to the controller regarding its fulfillment of security measure requirements; the controller would have access rights to the personal data being processed by the processor on its behalf; and the processor is required to report "all discrepancies." Regular security audits are provided for, as agreed upon by the controller and processor. Finally, upon termination, the processor "is obliged to return all personal data received on behalf of the controller" and covered by the agreement, and provisions for deletion and destruction of such data may be provided.[181]

3. Spain

The Spanish Royal Decree 1720/2007 sets out the Regulation (Spanish Regulation) implementing the Spanish data protection law (LOPD).[182] Article 82 of the Spanish Regulation provides for the drawing up of a "security document" between the controller and the processor.[183] Article 88 of the Spanish Regulation sets out the minimum requirements for such security document:

> Article 88. The Security Document.
>
> ...
>
> 3. The document shall contain, at least, the following aspects:
>   (a) Scope of application of the document with detailed specifications of the protected resources;
>   (b) Measures, regulations, protocols for action, rules and standards aimed at guaranteeing the level of security required herein;

---

181. Datatilsynet, *Draft Agreement—Data Processor Agreement Pursuant to the Personal Data Act*, *available at* http://www.datatilsynet.no/English/Publications/Data-processor-agreements/.

182. Real Decreto 1720/2007, de 21 de diciembre, por el que se aprueba el Reglamento de desarrollo de la Ley Orgánica 15/1999, de 13 de diciembre, de protección de datos de carácter personal [Royal Decree 1720/2007, of Dec. 21, 2007, which Approves the Regulation Implementing Organic Law 15/1999, of Dec. 13, 1999, on the Protection of Personal Data], BOE núm. 17 (Jan. 19, 2008), http://www.agpd.es /portalwebAGPD/canaldocumentacion/legislacion/estatal/common/pdfs/2014/Real_ Decreto_1720-2007_de_21_de_diciembre_por_el_que_se_aprueba_Reglamento_de_desarrollo_Ley_ Organica_15-1999_Consolidado.pdf. An English translation is http://www.agpd.es/portalwebAGPD /english_resources/regulations/common/pdfs/reglamentolopd_en.pdf, and we will refer to the text of the English translation of the Regulation.

183. *Id.*, art. 82, at 55 [English translation].

(c) Tasks and obligations of the staff in relation to the processing of personal data included in the filing system;

(d) Structure of the filing systems with personal data and description of the information systems that process them;

(e) Procedure of notification, management and response to incidents;

(f) The procedures for making backup copies and recovery of the data in the automated filing system or processing;

(g) The measures that shall necessarily be adopted for the transport of the supports or documents, as well as for their destruction, or if appropriate, their re-use.[184]

Other information may be required,[185] and the full text of the Spanish Regulation should be consulted and legal advice should be obtained prior to drafting a security document.

4. United Kingdom

The UK Data Protection Act 1998 sets out security requirements in its Seventh Principle of data protection. These requirements are of a general nature, strictly similar to those of the Directive: the contract must be in writing between the controller and processor; the processor is to act only on instructions of the controller; the processor must provide sufficient guarantees in terms of technical and organizational security measures regarding the processing; and the contract shall require "the data processor to comply with obligations equivalent to those imposed on a data controller by the seventh principle."[186]

The UK ICO has provided guidance for SMEs in regard to the security measures applicable in case of outsourcing. In deciding which measures are appropriate, "you need to take into account the sort of personal data you are dealing with, the harm that might result from its misuse, the technology that is available to protect the data and the cost of ensuring appropriate security for the data."[187] Provisions for reporting and inspection should also be implemented.[188] The UK ICO highlights that the use of model contract terms (such as those described earlier) "will satisfy the requirement (in the Seventh principle) for a written security contract and will fall within an exception to restriction on international data transfer set out in the Eighth Principle" and for

---

184. *Id.* art. 88(3), at 56–57 [English translation].

185. For additional information (in Spanish), *see* Agencia Española de Protección de Datos, Guía de Seguridad de Datos [Data Security Guide] (2010), at 58, http://www.agpd.es/portalwebAGPD/canaldocumentacion/publicaciones/common/Guias/GUIA_SEGURIDAD_2010.pdf.

186. Data Protection Act 1998 (c. 29) Sch. 1, Pt. II, para. 9–12, at 76, http://www.legislation.gov.uk/ukpga/1998/29/data.pdf.

187. UK ICO, *Outsourcing: A Guide for Small and Medium-Sized Businesses* (Feb. 28, 2012), at 3, https://ico.org.uk/media/for-organisations/documents/1585/outsourcing_guide_for_smes.pdf.

188. *Id.* at 3–4.

those reasons "model contract clauses are often used in international outsourcing arrangements."[189]

A couple of additional points highlighted by the UK ICO are worthy of note. In practice, it recommends that "the contract with your processor is enforceable in the UK (and if your processor is located in another jurisdiction, the jurisdiction of the processor)," and that you require the processor to report security breaches and other problems, and have procedures in place to deal with these appropriately.[190]

Obviously, these are just a few of the EU/EEA jurisdictions whose laws and regulations should be consulted as relevant. Nonetheless, many of the points highlighted by the different jurisdictions cited should give a good idea of what the data processing agreement (or security document) should contain.

For more information on cloud computing generally (including cloud-computing agreements), see Chapter 7 Section III.

Applicable Law under the GDPR

The proposed GDPR adds significantly to the list of obligations of the processor, and these must be reflected in controller-processor contracts, as well as provided for in the GDPR. In addition, new obligations placed on the controller should be reflected in contracts, insofar as processor cooperation is required. Examples of this include requirements of new data subject rights—the right to be forgotten and to erasure,[189] right to data portability,[190] and data protection by design and by default.[191]

The provisions regarding what should be contained in the controller-processor contract have been expanded beyond the twofold list of the Directive, discussed earlier. The relevant provision of the GDPR follows:

Article 26
Processor
... 2. The carrying out of processing by a processor shall be governed by a contract or other legal act binding the processor to the controller and stipulating in particular that the processor shall:
(a) act only on instructions from the controller, **in particular, where the transfer of the personal data used is prohibited**;
(b) **employ only staff who have committed themselves to confidentiality or are under a statutory obligation of confidentiality**;
(c) take all require measures pursuant to Article 30 [Security of processing];
(d) **enlist another processor only with the prior permission of the controller**;

---

189. *Id.* at 4–5.
190. *Id.* at 8.
191. GDPR, art. 17, at 51–53.
192. GDPR, art.18, at 53.
193. GDPR, art. 23, at 56.

(e) **insofar as this is possible given the nature of the processing, create in agreement with the controller of the necessary technical and organizational requirements for the fulfillment of the controller's obligations to respond to requests for exercising the data subject's rights laid down in Chapter III** [Rights of the Data Subject]**;**

(f) **assist the controller in ensuring compliance with the obligations pursuant to Articles 30 to 34** [respectively, Security of processing; Notification of a personal data breach to the supervisory authority; Communication of a personal data breach to the data subject; Data protection impact assessment; and Prior authorization and prior consultation]**;**

(g) **hand over all results to the controller after the end of the processing and not process the personal data otherwise;**

(h) **make available to the controller and the supervisory authority all information necessary to control compliance with the obligations laid down in this Article.**

3. The controller and the processor shall document in writing the controller's instructions and the processor's obligations referred to in paragraph 2.[192]

Article 26(2) (a) and (c) essentially are similar to the existing twofold Directive requirements, although (a) adds a reference to cross-border data transfers and (c) is merely a cross-reference to the security requirements, which have been moved to a different article and detailed in a general manner, as the GDPR would replace the various laws of the Member States in this regard. Article 26 (f) sets out cooperation provisions in areas where the processor and/or the controller will have new obligations, such as in the case of the new data breach notification requirements. Otherwise, certain new contractual requirements are similar to those discussed by the Working Party in connection with cloud-computing contracts.[193]

---

194. GDPR, art. 26 (2)–(3), at 57–58.
195. *See* WP 196, *supra* note 89.

4

Human Resources

The processing of employees' personal data by employers is extensive, as are the privacy concerns it raises. Whenever acting as an employer and processing personal data of employees (for example, in a personnel file, when granting benefits and options, for payroll purposes, etc.), organizations—specifically the employing entity—will act as the controller. Therefore, processing within the human resource (HR) context is generally the most widespread and common processing undertaken by organizations. This processing is further complicated in larger—multinational—organizations, where personal data is frequently stored, transferred, and accessed outside of the European Union. This Chapter will first deal with general provisions relating to human resources (Section I), then it will address technology and employee relationships including e-mail, video surveillance, social media, BYOD, and GPS and biometrics (Section II), and finally it will discuss the subject of sensitive data (in the EU sense of the term), including health and background check information (Section III).

I. GENERAL PROVISIONS RELATING TO HUMAN RESOURCES

Personal data processed in an employment relationship must be looked at in context. Indeed, national labor laws of the countries where employees habitually carry out their work must be investigated in addition to any analysis under the Directive. These labor laws are outside the scope of this book; however, it is important to understand at what point to turn to the relevant labor laws.[1] In addition, fundamental data protection principles (finality, transparency, legitimacy, proportionality, accuracy, and retention of the data, security, and awareness of the staff),[2] discussed in Chapter 1, Section III, apply to the processing.

---

1. The Working Party has highlighted the relationship with labor law as follows: "[D]ata protection law does not operate in isolation from labour law and practice, and labour law and practice does not operate in isolation from data protection law. This interaction is necessary and valuable and should assist the development of solutions that properly protect workers' interests." *See* Working Party, *Opinion 8/2001 on the Processing of Personal Data in the Employment Context* (WP 48) (Sept. 13, 2001), at 4 [hereinafter WP 48], http://ec.europa.eu/justice/data-protection/article-29/documentation/opinion-recommendation/files/2001/wp48_en.pdf.

2. For a discussion of these principles in an employment context, *see* WP 48, at 19–22.

A.   Records in the Employment Context

WP 48 of the Working Party sets out some examples of records in the employment context that typically contain personal data and, hence, are subject to the provisions of the Directive:[3]

- Application forms, resumes/CVs and work references
- Payroll and tax information-tax as well as social benefits information
- Sickness records
- Records on annual leave, including vacation and maternity/paternity leave, and unpaid leave/special leave records
- Annual appraisal, evaluations or assessment records
- Records relating to promotion, transfer, training
- Disciplinary records
- Records relating to accidents at work
- Information generated by computer systems (such as user names, computer or laptop terminal numbers, etc.)
- Attendance and time records
- Emergency contacts as well as beneficiaries and dependents for compensation and benefits purposes
- Reimbursement of expenses, for example travel

Other categories could include contact details or photographs for company directories and the inclusion of a responsible employee contact for a customer, client, or service ticket.

One complication arises where records are kept in manual form, as not all manual records fall under the Directive. In order for the Directive to be applicable to manual records, the records must "form part of a 'personal data filing system.'"[4] The latter is defined in the Directive as "any structured set of personal data, which are accessible according to specific criteria, whether centralized, decentralized or dispersed on a functional or geographical basis."[5] However, the Working Party comments that "[m]ost employment records are likely to fall within this definition," but in certain

---

3. *Id.* at 7.

4. *Id.* at 13. Indeed, Article 3(1) of the Directive provides that "[t]his Directive shall apply to the processing of personal data wholly or partly by automatic means, and to the processing otherwise than by automatic means of personal data which form part a filing system or are intended to form part of a filing system." Directive 95/46/EC of the European Parliament and of the Council of 24 Oct. 1995 on the protection of individuals with regard to the processing of personal data and on the free movement of such data [hereinafter Directive], 1995 O.J. (L 281) 31 (Nov. 23, 1995), art. 3(1), at 39.

5. Directive, art. 2(c), at 38. For a discussion on the different ways that Member State national laws have implemented this definition, and for the ramifications of such divergent transpositions of the Directive, *see* Douwe Korff, *Study on the Protection of the Rights and Interests of Legal Persons with regard to the Processing of Personal Data relating to such Persons*, at 19–20, Study Contract ETD/97/B-5-9500178, European Commission, Brussels, Oct. 1998, http://ec.europa.eu/justice/data-protection/document/studies/files/20000202_rights_interests_legal_en.pdf.

countries some handwritten *notes* are excluded by implementing measures, when not contained in a filing system.[6]

B. Lawfulness of the Personal Data Processing

Also interesting is the application of the criteria for lawfulness of the processing of personal data (see Chapter 2 Section IV.D) in the employment context. Lawfulness must be established under Articles 6 and 7 of the Directive. Article 8 of the Directive concerns sensitive data, which is discussed in Chapter 4 Section III. As Article 6 of the Directive refers to data quality and the collection, processing, or keeping of data, we will turn instead to Article 7.

The main legitimating criteria for personal data processing in the employment context are contained in Article 7(1) (b), (c), and (f) of the Directive. In the first such paragraph, processing is legitimate when "necessary for the performance of a contract to which the data party is subject." This is often the case in a contract of employment that requires, for example, the processing of salary and other payments. In Article 7(1)(b), processing may be lawful if "necessary for compliance with a legal obligation," such as where the employer must disclose data to the tax authorities or for social security payments. Finally, in Article 7(1)(f), processing may be legitimate where "necessary for the purposes of the legitimate interests pursued by the controller or by the third party or parties to whom the data are disclosed, except where such interests are overridden by the interests for fundamental rights and freedoms of the data subject." Here the issue is the balancing of interests of the controller with those of the data subject.

It is worth noting that there is a residual right to object to processing under Article 7(1)(f); the Working Party points out that "the worker retains the right to object to the processing on compelling legitimate grounds."[7] In practice, the exercise of this right depends on the exact circumstances of processing; it is difficult to clearly carve out the situations where it straightforwardly applies. Nevertheless, if an employee does object to processing, a distinction must be made between the personal data that the employer needs for the functioning of a proper employer-employee relationship (likely falling under Article 7(1)(b) or (c)) and the personal data processed on its legitimate interest. The employee would have to object that his or her fundamental rights would outweigh the employer's legitimate interest in a particular circumstance. If an employee objects to the processing of his or her social security or tax identification number in the personnel file, this objection would not be successful as this information is necessary for the employer to make social security or tax contributions under the law. Another example could be the objection of an employee to the processing of his or her photograph in a company directory. Here, the employee could legitimately object to this processing, as the processing is not necessary for the employment

---

6. WP 48, *supra* note 1, at 13.
7. *Id.* at 15.

relationship and the balancing of interests test would likely not be in favor of the employer's interest. (In practice, most companies request employee consent for the processing of photographs in such global directories.) It is worth noting that in the latter example, the employer would not be able to legally base the processing of photographs on the legitimate interest grounds. Therefore, the employee in this circumstance is actually objecting to illegal processing, which is a distinct objection right.

In the employment context, consent has increasingly been seen as a fallback criterion for lawfulness. As consent must be "freely given," this is difficult to prove in the work environment because of the perceived imbalance in the relationship between employer and employee and the employer's normal exercise of authority. Indeed, the Working Party is of the opinion that "where consent is required from a worker, and there is a real or potential prejudice that arises from not consenting, the consent is not valid in terms of satisfying either Article 7 or Article 8 as it is not freely given."[8] The fact that this prejudice potentially arises following a worker's refusal to give consent makes it virtually impossible for the worker to refuse to give his or her consent. The Working Party comments that "a worker must be able to withdraw consent without prejudice."[9] In practice, consent is an unreliable basis for the processing of employee personal data, as employees must be able to actually revoke such consent in practice, creating uncertainty for the employer.

C. Applicability of Data Subject Rights and Data Protection Principles in the Employment Context

Finally, it should be remembered that data protection principles and data subject rights continue to apply in the employment context. This has been underscored by the Working Party, and certain of the essential rights concerned are mentioned below.[10]

1. Notice/Privacy Policy

Employees have a right to receive confirmation that such data are being collected, the purposes for such collection, and communication of the content of such data. As highlighted in Chapter 3, Section II, it is the employer's responsibility—as a controller—to provide a notice to employees about the processing of their personal data. These notices include employee privacy policies, electronic communications policies, and so on.

2. Right of Access

Employees have the right to access their personal data under Article 12 of the Directive (see Chapter 1, Section III.2): in practice this means that employees can access their personal data processed by the employer. Employee access requests have steadily increased in the past several years, and they predominately occur in employment disputes, as employees would like to access their personnel or HR files, such as disciplinary records or evaluations. Access requests are limited in practice. For example, when

---

8. *Id.* at 23.
9. *Id.*
10. *See id.* at 3–4.

personal data of third parties—such as a manager's evaluation or a complaint from a fellow worker—are also included in the records, this information must be redacted or left out (taking into account the other individual's right to privacy). Typically, an employer would not hand over copies of records from personnel files. Depending on the applicable national law and position of the DPA, employers could instead give an overview or summary of the categories of personal data held and the related processing activities.

3. Other Individual Rights

Employees also have a right to "rectification, erasure or blocking of data the provisions of which does [sic] not comply with data protection law, in particular because of the incomplete or inaccurate nature of the data" and they can expect the employer to so notify third parties having received such data, unless such action is impossible or involves a "disproportionate effect."[11]

4. Data Quality

Data should be kept up to date (where necessary) and accurate. With the development of cloud and software as a service (SaaS) solutions, employers are increasingly able to allow employees a larger degree of control over their personal data. With the proliferation of employee electronic profiles, employers can enable employees to keep their personal data up to date.

5. Technical and Organizational Measures—Security

Employers are required to "implement appropriate technical and organizational measures at the workplace to guarantee that the personal data of . . . workers is kept secured."[12] According to the Working Party, which highlights the need to protect against unauthorized access or disclosure, security measures may include the following:

- Password/identification systems for access to computerized employment records;
- Login and tracing of access and disclosures;
- Backup copies; and
- Encryption of messages, in particular when the data is transferred outside the organization.[13]

D. International Transfers

With regard to data transfers to third countries, these should be based on adequate protection of the employees' personal data in the destination country and are subject to Articles 6 through 8 of the Directive,

> [r]ather than relying on **the derogations listed in Article 26, for example the workers' consent.** Where consent is relied on, it must be unambiguous and

---

11. *Id.* at 4.
12. *Id.* at 3.
13. *Id.* at 22.

freely given. Employers would be ill-advised to rely **solely** on consent other than in cases where, if consent is subsequently withdrawn, this will not cause problems.[14]

For a discussion of cross-border transfers of data and Article 26 derogations, see Chapter 3, Section III.

In conclusion, employee personal data is personal data, protected under the terms of the Directive, and employers must comply with data protection law in such regard. As the Working Party reminds us:

> Workers do not leave their right to privacy at the door of their workplace every morning.
> However, privacy is not an absolute right. It needs to be balanced with other legitimate interests or rights or freedoms. This also applies to the employment context.[15]

More regarding the employment context will be covered in subsequent sections.

Applicable Law under the GDPR

In its present form, Article 6(1)(b) and (c) of the GDPR maintains the bases for lawfulness currently found in Article 7(1)(b) and (c) of the Directive verbatim. With respect to paragraph (c) the GDPR specifies that the basis of the processing must be provided for in EU law (Article 6(3)(a)) or in "the law of the Member State to which the controller is subject." (Article 6(3)(b)) Furthermore, the law of the Member State must "meet an objective of public interest or must be necessary to protect the rights and freedoms of others, respect the essence of the right to the protection of personal data and be proportionate to the legitimate aim pursued."[16]

Article 7(1)(f) of the Directive would be replaced and modified in Article 6(1)(f) of the GDPR, as follows:

> (f) processing is necessary for the purposes of the legitimate interests pursued by a controller, except where such interests are overridden by the interests or fundamental rights and freedoms of the data subject which require protection of personal data, in particular where the data subject is a child. This shall not apply to processing carried out by public authorities in the performance of their tasks.[17]

---

14.   *Id.* at 4.
15.   *Id.* at 19.
16.   Proposal for Regulation of the European Parliament and of the Council on the Protection of Individuals with regard to the Processing of Personal Data and on the Free Movement of such Data (General Data Protection Regulation) COM (2012) 11 final (Jan. 25, 2012) [hereinafter GDPR], art. 6(3), at 44.
17.   GDPR, art. 6(1)(f), at 44.

These changes eliminate the basis for lawfulness built on the interests of a third party to whom the data is disclosed, provide a heightened level of protection for children (which is then further developed in Article 8 of the GDPR), and exempt public authorities carrying out their tasks from the balance-of-interest criterion.

In addition, when Article 6(1)(b) or (f) are relied upon, under Article 14(1)(b) of the GDPR, which replaces Article 10(b) of the Directive, additional information must be provided by the controller to the data subject, as follows:

> (b) the purposes of the processing for which the personal data are intended, including the contract terms and general conditions where the processing is based on point (b) of Article 6(1) and the legitimate interests pursued by the controller where the processing is based on point (f) of Article 6(1).[18]

Article 7(4) of the GDPR, setting out conditions for consent, provides as follows:

> 4. Consent shall not provide a legal basis for the processing where there is a significant imbalance between the position of the data subject and the controller.[19]

This new paragraph could be applied to prevent consent being relied upon for the lawfulness of processing in many employment relationships where the controller is the employer and the data subject is the employee. This goes in the same direction as Opinion 8/2001, discussed in this section, and even goes a bit further (or perhaps spells out the rules more clearly).

Finally, the GDPR provides the Member States with discretion to create specific rules for processing in the employment context, subject to a notification to the Commission requirement (Article 82(2)), and the Commission would be empowered to specify criteria and requirements for the safeguards of such processing under the delegated acts mechanism (Article 82(3)), in a new Article 82, the first paragraph of which is set forth here:

> 1. Within the limits of this Regulation, Member States may adopt by law specific rules regulating the processing of employees' personal data in the employment context, in particular for the purposes of the recruitment, the performance of the contract of employment, including discharge of obligations laid down by law or by collective agreements, management, planning and organization of work, health and safety at work, and for the purposes of the exercise and enjoyment, on an individual or collective basis, of rights and benefits related to employment, and for the purpose of the termination of the employment relationship.[20]

---

18.   GDPR, art. 14(1)(b), at 48.
19.   GDPR, art. 7(4), at 45.
20.   GDPR, art. 82(1), at 95.

II. TECHNOLOGY AND EMPLOYEE RELATIONSHIPS

As we have seen in Section I, the right to data protection and privacy applies both outside and inside the workplace; it must be balanced with other "legitimate interests," such as the business needs of organizations. While there is such balancing, American readers, for example, will *not* find a similar situation in the United States, where there is much less protection of privacy in the workplace than in the home, based on the notion than an employee's reasonable expectation of privacy at the workplace is much weaker than at home.[21] Data protection rules do extend to the workplace in the European Union, and worker privacy is protected as a matter of human rights, subject to such balancing.

The analysis becomes more detailed when certain forms of complicated processing are used by the employer. This section will investigate some of those other forms of processing and the data protection law relevant to them. In the process, it will explore further the relationship between employer and employee in the privacy and data protection context.

This section will first examine employee use of e-mail and the Internet and employer monitoring of such use. Next it will analyze video surveillance in the workplace, with all of the privacy risks this entails. A discussion of the use of social network services by employees (and the monitoring of such use by employers), together with the risks of such use, will follow. Then, the section will investigate bring-your-own-device (BYOD) risks and guidance, followed by a treatment of privacy and data protection issues in connection with geolocation technology and biometrics in the workplace, thereby covering a wide gamut of advanced processing of personal data in the workplace.

A. E-mail and Internet Use

Since the introduction of employee use of e-mail, employers undergo monitoring of such use to ensure that this now-established tool of communication is not being used for inappropriate purposes and, when used for other than professional reasons, does not take too much time. Employers also increasingly monitor e-mail and attachments for the protection of the security and integrity of their information systems, for spam and viruses, and for various compliance purposes. As a result the practice of monitoring and surveillance of employee electronic communications in the workplace has developed, with resulting consequences for the privacy of employees. E-mail use

---

21. For an early discussion of this, *see* Michael Higgins, *High Tech, Low Privacy*, 85 A.B.A. J. 52, 55 (May 1999). In that article, U.S. law professor Camille Hebert, author of a two-volume treatise on workplace privacy, is quoted as saying about her work, "The joke around here is, 'Why did it take you 1,700 pages to say: The employer can do it?'." *Id.*, at 54. This loss of privacy in an employment context in the digital age has been described by another U.S. law professor as follows: "The single greatest invasion of any sensible space of privacy that cyberspace has produced is the extraordinary monitoring of employees in which corporations now engage." LAWRENCE LESSIG, CODE AND OTHER LAWS OF CYBERSPACE, at 145 (1999). This section will explore how the European Union has limited this "invasion."

and monitoring sits at the intersection of two fundamental rights: the right to respect for privacy and family life (including correspondence) and the right to protection of personal data. Many national DPAs have issued guidance on the use of e-mail in the employment context and related monitoring of employees may be effectuated. In practice, it is important to verify the local rules to ensure that such practices correspond to the local provisions.

1. Working Party Guidelines for the Implementation of E-mail Monitoring

The Working Party evaluated the privacy risks of such a practice relatively early on and provided its assessment in a working document dated May 29, 2002 (WP 55).[22] It contains certain guidelines to implement monitoring measures limiting an employee's privacy justified on grounds of legitimate rights and interests such as "the employer's right to run his business efficiently . . . and . . . the right to protect himself from the liability or the harm that workers' actions may create."[23] The Working Party cites the example of an employer being the victim of a criminal offense of his or her employee as one where there are grounds for implementing monitoring. It cautions that the principle of proportionality applies to this analysis on whether measures are justified: monitoring cannot be justified merely for the *convenience* of the employer. The nature of the assessment is summarized as follows:

a. Is the monitoring activity transparent to the workers?
b. Is it necessary? Could the employer obtain the same result with traditional methods of supervision?
c. Is the proposed processing of personal data fair to the workers?
d. Is the activity proportionate to the concerns that it tries to allay?[24]

2. Transparency and Notice to Employees

Although transparency is one of the data protection principles, the others of which are discussed in Section II.A.3., it will be discussed before the others because of the particular importance accorded to it by the Working Party in the employment context.

With regard to transparency, the Working Party stresses that an employer must *inform* an employee of the presence of detection devices or equipment activated with regards to the latter's work station and of "any misuse of electronic communications detected (e-mail or Internet), unless important reasons justify the continuance of the secret surveillance, which is not normally the case."[25] Pop-up warning windows may

---

22. Working Party, *Working Document on Surveillance and Monitoring of Electronic Communications in the Workplace* (WP 55) (May 29, 2002), http://ec.europa.eu/justice/policies/privacy/docs/wpdocs/2002/wp55_en.pdf.
23. *Id.* at 4.
24. *Id.*
25. *Id.* at 4–5 (citation omitted). *See also id.* at 15.

be used for this purpose; however it is important to detail how the monitoring or surveillance takes place, its purposes, and what potential consequences the employee may face if it violates the policy.

The Working Party contemplates that employers may consider providing employees with both a professional and a private e-mail account or allowing for the use of webmail for private purposes. In this scenario, the private e-mail account or webmail would not be monitored except in "exceptional cases," but the professional e-mail could be monitored within the limits of the principles set out by the Working Party.[26] In practice, this is not the most practical solution for employers. Nevertheless, one can see that it is important to make a distinction between personal and professional use of e-mail and the Internet.

The Working Party reminds us that Articles 8 (right to respect for privacy) and 10 (right to freedom of expression) of the ECHR (the provisions of which bind all Member States of the European Union) apply in this context, and it extracts from the European Court of Human Rights case law the following principles:

a) Workers have a legitimate expectation of privacy at the workplace, which is not overridden by the fact that workers use communication devices or any other business facilities of the employer.

However the provision of proper information by the employer to the worker may reduce the workers[sic] legitimate expectation of privacy.

b) The general principle of secrecy of correspondence covers communications at the workplace. This is likely to include electronic e-mail and related files attached thereto.

c) Respect for private life also includes to a certain degree the right to establish and develop relationships with other human beings. The fact that such relationships, to a great extent, take place at the workplace puts limit to employer's legitimate need for surveillance measures.[27]

(Emphasis added.)

As we have seen, transparency means that there should be no "covert e-mail monitoring"—that is, employers should be "clear and open" about their activities, unless the relevant Member State's laws allow for this covertness in cases of necessary measures required to safeguard national security, defense, or public security; or for the prevention, investigation, detection, or prosecution of criminal offenses; or for the protection of the data subject or of the rights and freedoms of others.[28]

---

26. *Id.* at 5.
27. *Id.* at 9. For a discussion of the ECHR, *see* Chapter 1, Section I.A.
28. *Id.* at 14. These cases are taken from the Directive, art. 13, at 42.

The Working Party divides the transparency principle into two parts—an obligation to provide information to the data subject and an obligation to notify supervisory authorities before carrying out any wholly or partly automatic processing operation or set of such processing operations. In the first part, employers must provide employees with:

i. An e-mail/Internet policy describing when company communication facilities may be used for personal communications (specifying, for example, at which times and for how long they may be used).
ii. The reasons and purposes for the surveillance.
iii. The details of the surveillance measures.
iv. The details of enforcement procedures, including information about notifications of breaches of company policies and any opportunity to respond to claims.[29]

In this context, there may be employer practices or requirements to provide prior notification and/or consult with worker representatives, and employers may have to obtain their approval for implementation of such processing operations under collective agreements. Directive 2002/14/EC applies to either certain undertakings employing at least 50 employees in any one Member State or certain establishments employing at least 20 employees in any one Member State, depending on the choice made by a Member State in its implementing legislation.[30] It establishes a framework with minimum requirements for the "right to information and consultation" of employees in undertakings or establishments within the European Union,[31] covering, inter alia, "information and consultation on decisions likely to lead to substantial changes in work organisation or in contractual relations."[32]

Such changes in work organization would include surveillance of electronic communications of employees, triggering the information, and consultation requirements.[33]

In the second part, the obligation to notify the supervisory authorities before carrying out the processing means that information about the categories of data, purposes, and recipients for the processing of the data will be contained in a register accessible by employees.[34] Finally, the Working Party reminds us of an employee's right of access to personal information concerning him or her as well as the employee's right

---

29. *Id.* at 15.
30. Directive 2002/14/EC of the European Parliament and of the Council of 11 March 2002, Establishing a General Framework for Informing and Consulting Employees in the European Community—Joint Declaration of the European Parliament, the Council and the Commission on Employee Representation, 2002 O.J. (L 80) 29 (EC), art. 3(1) at 31, http://eur-lex.europa.eu/LexUriServ/LexUriServ.do?uri=OJ:L:2002:080:0029:0033:EN:PDF.
31. *Id.* art. 1(1), at 31.
32. *Id.* art. 4(2)(c), at 32.
33. WP 55, *supra* note 20, at 15.
34. *Id.* at 16.

to request rectification or erasure or blocking of data that does not comply with the Directive (e.g., where incomplete or inaccurate).[35] Paragraph 4 will explore Working Party guidance on the content of employer e-mail policies, but first the discussion of the data protection principles applied to the use of e-mail in the workplace will continue.

When drafting a notice on e-mail use in a workplace, the employees' expectation of privacy is also linked to whether private use of professional e-mail is permitted. This expands on what is noted in paragraph 2, as communications secrecy laws apply differently depending on the Member State at issue and whether private use of e-mail is permitted (this is further elaborated upon in paragraph 5). As noted, there is a general tendency to acknowledge that employees have a degree of legitimate expectations of privacy in the workplace. This is also rooted in the day-to-day realities of e-mail and other technology, such as telephone use. Employees do use company-provided technology to a certain degree for personal reasons. Furthermore, this reality is not unreasonable under the circumstances. Nevertheless, it is important to examine the purpose for monitoring together with the Member States at hand, to ensure that any notices or policies properly take into account the local laws regulating the practices.

3. Application of Data Protection Principles

These principles are taken into account by the Working Party, which bases the Working Document WP 55 on the Directive, whose data protection principles must be complied with in respect to the processing of personal data arising from e-mail monitoring. As with other relationships involving processing of personal data, employers must apply the principles from the Directive. WP 55 has laid out the basic privacy principles (see Chapter 1, Section III) of necessity, finality, transparency, legitimacy, proportionality, data quality, and security as applied to the employee monitoring context. The application of each of these principles will be discussed next.

a. Necessity

The first of the data protection principles mentioned by the Working Party is *necessity*, which imposes the requirement that the monitoring must be "absolutely necessary for a specified purpose before proceeding to engage in any such activity."[36] Where possible, an employer should implement traditional, less-intrusive methods of supervision before using such monitoring. This principle is contained throughout Articles 7 and 8 of the Directive.[37]

As an example of exceptional circumstances justifying monitoring of an employee's e-mail, the Working Party cites the case where the monitoring is necessary "to obtain confirmation or proof of certain actions on [the employee's] part," such as criminal activity, where the proof is necessary for the defense of the employer's own

---

35. *Id.* at 16.
36. *Id.* at 13.
37. Directive, arts. 7–8, at 40–41.

interests, or any activity carried out by the employer "to guarantee the security of the [information] system," such as the detection of viruses. Also, an employee's e-mail may need to be opened for purposes other than monitoring, for example, during his or her absences for vacations or for sickness.[38]

b. Finality

The second principle, *finality*, requires that data be collected for a "specified, explicit and legitimate purpose and not further processed in a way incompatible with those purposes."[39] In practice, this means that employers should pursue legitimate and pre-defined purposes when monitoring and not systematically access all communications of employees. For example, if the data processing is engaged for information system security purposes, the related data should not later be used to monitor the employee's behavior.[40] This principle is fixed in Article 6(1)(b) of the Directive.[41]

c. Transparency

The third principle, *transparency*, is discussed in paragraph 2. This principle is contained in Articles 10–12 of the Directive.[42]

d. Legitimacy

The fourth principle, *legitimacy*, refers to the requirement that there be a legitimate basis for the processing of the personal data.[43] The balancing of the legitimate interests of the employer and the fundamental rights of the employee in this context was discussed earlier in this chapter in Section I, and that concerning sensitive data will be discussed later in Section III. One example cited by the Working Party for a potential legitimate ground of the employer for processing data using monitoring is when the employer needs to protect the business from significant threats, which might involve the prevention of confidential information being disclosed to a competitor.[44] Indeed, the Working Party states that the most likely ground for the legitimacy of e-mail monitoring is found in Article 7(f) of the Directive—based on legitimate interests pursued by the controller or the third party or parties to whom the data are disclosed.[45] Nonetheless, the principle of legitimacy is embodied in the whole of Article 7 of the Directive.[46]

e. Proportionality

The fifth principle is *proportionality*. In order to comply with this principle, the monitoring must be "adequate, relevant and not excessive with regard to achieving the purpose specified," with companies fitting their policy to the type and degree

---

38. WP 55, *supra* note 22, at 13–14.
39. *Id.* at 14.
40. *Id.*
41. Directive, art. 6(1)(b), at 40.
42. Directive, arts. 10–12, at 41–42.
43. WP 55, *supra* note 22, at 16–17.
44. *Id.* at 17.
45. *Id.* at 21.
46. Directive, art. 7, at 40.

of risk they face, thereby excluding blanket monitoring of e-mails of all personnel, "other than where necessary for the purpose of ensuring the security of the system."[47] If there is a less-intrusive way to achieve the purpose, then this principle has not been respected. The Working Party suggests limiting the monitoring to traffic data on employees being monitored and time of a communication instead of content of the e-mail, if possible. It further provides that if access to content is absolutely necessary, the privacy of those outside of the company should be taken into consideration through informing them of the monitoring activities to the extent they are affected by them. This could be achieved through warning notices about the monitoring activities added to all outbound e-mails, for example. Employers could find less-intrusive ways of assessing e-mail use, rather than reviewing content, through assessing the amount of e-mail sent or received and the format of attachments. An isolated server could be used for e-mail exceeding a certain size (in terms of memory space), with a notice to the addressee that the e-mail has been redirected and may be reviewed there.[48]

This principle of proportionality (or nonexcessiveness) has its roots in Article 6(1)(c) of the Directive.[49]

f. Accuracy and Retention of Data

The sixth principle, *accuracy and retention of data*, means that data legitimately stored by the employer must be accurate, up to date, and kept for only as long as necessary (a period of no longer than three months might usually be considered justifiable). A retention period should be established by companies.[50]

The principle of accuracy may be traced back to Article 6(1)(b) of the Directive and that of limited retention of data may be traced to Article 6(1)(e).[51]

g. Security

The seventh and last of this list of principles is *security*. Employers must adopt technical and organizational measures to ensure the security of personal data held by them against outside intrusion. Antivirus protection is one example of this, and automated scanning of e-mails may be involved. System administrators and others with access to employee personal data during monitoring should be "placed under a strict duty of professional secrecy with regard to the confidential information, to which they have access."[52] Security requirements are derived from Article 17 of the Directive.[53]

---

47. WP 55, *supra* note 22, at 17.
48. WP 55, *supra* note 22, at 17–18.
49. Directive, art. 6(1)(c), at 40.
50. WP 55, *supra* note 22, at 18.
51. Directive, art. 6(1)(b) and (e), at 40.
52. WP 55, *supra* note 22, at 18–19.
53. Directive, art. 17, at 43.

In practice, employers should mitigate risks associated with the relevant monitoring practices. Such practices include certain technological measures to reduce the associated risks, such as the blocking of certain websites, reliance on purpose-specific keywords for site blocking, and e-mail searches. Here, reliance on these automated processing methods is encouraged so as to avoid identification of individuals. Most Member States' DPAs have issued guidance on how to implement the monitoring in practice.

4. Working Party Guidance on Employer E-mail Policies

The Working Party states that employers should address the following points in connection with e-mail, and that they should maintain up-to-date policies "in line with technological developments and the opinion of [their] workers":

a) Whether a worker is entitled to have an e-mail account for purely personal use, whether use of web-mail accounts is permitted at work and whether the employer recommends the use, by workers, of a private web-mail account for the purpose of using e-mail for purely personal use.

b) The arrangements in place with workers to access the contents of an e-mail, which is to say when the worker is unexpectedly absent, and the specific purposes for such access.

c) When a backup copy of messages are made, the storage period of it.

d) Information as to when e-mails are definitively deleted from the server.

e) Security issues.

f) The involvement of representative of workers in formulating the policy.[54]

5. Consideration of e-Communication Laws

In discussing law applicable to personal data processing regarding e-mail essentially derived from the Directive, it bears mentioning that e-communication laws regarding the secrecy of communications also apply to the use and monitoring of e-mail.

In this realm, the Directive is complemented and expanded by the e-Privacy Directive. Some Member States' transposition of the latter directive apply only to electronic communications service providers. This will be illustrated by three examples from relevant Member State national law.

---

54. WP 55, *supra* note 22, at 22.

a. Belgium

Belgium's Act on Electronic Communication of June 13, 2005[55] sets out provisions on the secrecy of electronic communications (including e-mail) in Article 124. Unless authorized by all persons directly or indirectly concerned, it is forbidden for one to intentionally obtain knowledge of the existence of any information transmitted by electronic communication that are not personally sent to him or her[56] or, inter alia, to store or make any use of such information.[57] Exceptions would apply to those who are an addressee of the e-mail and those who receive authorization (consent from all parties involved in the communication) or when allowed or required by law.[58] Criminal sanctions may apply if there is a violation of these provisions. In its recommendation, the Belgian DPA mentions that in the employment context, consent is unreliable as it may not be freely given. Thus, employers in Belgium must find clear legal grounds in order to access electronic communications.[59]

b. France

France's Act No. 91-646 of July 10, 1991,[60] sets out the concept of the secrecy of correspondence by electronic means. However, it is Article 226-15 of the French Criminal Code that provides sanctions in certain cases relevant to the workplace:

> Maliciously opening, destroying, delaying or diverting of correspondence sent to a third party, whether or not it arrives at its destination, or fraudulently gaining knowledge of it, is punished by one year's imprisonment and a fine of €45,000 [NB: this figure is multiplied by five—to €225,000—for legal persons (such as companies) pursuant to Article 131-38 of the French Criminal Code].

---

55. Loi relative aux communications électroniques [Act on Electronic Communications] of June 13, 2005, MONITEUR BELGE [M.B.] [Official Gazette of Belgium], ed. 2, June 20, 2005, 28070.

56. *Id.* art. 124(1), at 28103. "S'il n'y est pas autorisé par toutes les personnes directement ou indirectement concernées, nul ne peut : 1° prendre intentionnellement connaissance de l'existence d'une information de toute nature transmise par voie de communication électronique et qui ne lui est pas destinée personnellement."

57. *Id.* art. 124(4), at 28103. "4° ... stocker ou faire un usage quelconque de l'information."

58. *Id.* art. 125(1), at 28103. "§ 1er. Les dispositions de l'article 124 de la présente loi ... ne sont pas applicables: 1° lorsque la loi permet ou impose l'accomplissement des actes visés."

59. Recommandation n° 08/2012 du 2 mai 2012 d'initiative relative au contrôle de l'employeur quant à l'utilisation des outils de communication électronique sur le lieu de travail [Recommendation no. 08/2010 of May 2, 2012, on Cybersurveillance in the Workplace] COMMISSION DE LA PROTECTION DE LA VIE PRIVÉE [CPVP] [Privacy Commission], www.privacycommission.be/sites/privacycommission/files/documents/recommandation_08_2012_0.pdf. For a short discussion of this recommendation, *see* W. Gregory Voss & Katherine Woodcock, et al., *Privacy, E-Commerce and Data Security*, 47 ABA SECTION OF INTERNATIONAL LAW, YEAR IN REVIEW 99, 106–107 (2013).

60. Loin° 91-646 di 10 juillet 1991 relative au secret des correspondances émises par la voie des télécommunications, JOURNAL OFFICIEL DE LA RÉPUBLIQUE FRANÇAISE [J.O.] [OFFICIAL GAZETTE OF FRANCE], No. 162, July 13, 1991, p. 9167.

The same penalty applies to the malicious interception, diversion, use or disclosure of correspondence sent, transmitted or received by "*electronic means,*" or the setting up of a device designed to produce such interceptions.[61]

Moreover, opening an employee's e-mail has been found to be a violation of an employee's right to privacy in a case in which Nikon France fired an employee for personal use of a computer after discovering through such employee's e-mail that he was involved in a "parallel activity" on the side. In a case before the Labor Division (*Chambre sociale*) of the French Supreme Court for Judicial Matters, the court said that an employer cannot obtain knowledge of personal messages sent and received by the employee using a computer made available to him for his work, even when the employer has forbidden personal (nonprofessional) use of the computer. Thus the Labor Division disallowed a dismissal for fault based on information contained in e-mails in a "personal" folder on a computer. [62]

This result may be contrasted with the result when an employee does not indicate, through the placing of the message in a "personal" folder, or through the use of the term "private" or "personal" at the beginning of a message, the personal nature of the correspondence on an employer-supplied device, in which case the message would be presumed to be professional and not personal. In such as case the message would be available to be consulted by the employer outside the presence of the employee, and available for use as evidence, even in the event of a disciplinary proceeding. This is true for e-mails, files on a work computer, or SMS messages on a work-issued cellphone[63]. That position with respect to SMS messages was recently confirmed in a case before the Commercial Division (*Chambre commerciale, financière et économique*) of

---

61.   CODE PÉNAL [C. PÉN.] art. 226-15 and art. 131-38 (Fr.). The English text of art. 226-15 was taken from the Legifrance translation, available at http://www.legifrance.gouv.fr/Traductions/en-English/Legifrance-translations. As such translation only includes modifications up to 2005, a subsequent modification has been indicated in italics. The original French text is:

Le fait, commis de mauvaise foi, d'ouvrir, de supprimer, de retarder ou de détourner des correspondances arrivées ou non à destination et adressées à des tiers, ou d'en prendre frauduleusement connaissance, est puni d'un an d'emprisonnement et de 45 000 € d'amende.

Est puni des mêmes peines le fait, commis de mauvaise foi, d'intercepter, de détourner, d'utiliser ou de divulguer des correspondances émises, transmises ou reçues par la "voie électronique" ou de procéder à l'installation d'appareils conçus pour réaliser de telles interceptions.

62.   Cour de cassation [Cass.] [supreme court for judicial matters] soc., Oct. 2, 2001, Bull. civ. V, No. 291, p. 233 (Fr.), *available at* http://www.courdecassation.fr/jurisprudence_2/chambre_sociale_576/arret_n_1159.html. The relevant text in French is as follows:

Attendu que le salarié a droit, même au temps et au lieu de travail au respect de l'intimité de sa vie privée ; que celle-ci implique en particulier le secret des correspondances ; que l'employeur ne peut dès lors sans violationj de cette liberté fondamentale prendre connaissance des messages personnels émis par le salarié et reçus par lui grâce à un outil informatique mis à sa disposition pour son travail et ceci même au cas où l'employeur aurait interdit une utilisation non professionnelle de l'ordinateur.

63.   *See* "L'employeur peut consulter les SMS échangés via un portable professionnel" [An Employer May Consult SMS Messages Sent Using a Work Cellphone], LIAISONS SOCIALES QUOTIDIENS, No. 16780, Feb. 24, 2015, p. 1.

the French Supreme Court for Judicial Matters, involving a dispute between two brokerage firms, whereby plaintiff claimed that defendant engaged in unfair competition by soliciting and hiring away twenty of plaintiff's employees, resulting in a disruption of its activity when the employees left. In this case the SMS messages exchanged using the work cellphones of plaintiff's former employees were held to be able to be searched for legitimate reasons.[64]

c. Germany

Germany has an interesting approach, where the Telecommunication Act, 26 June 2004, as amended, lays down provisions on the secrecy of telecommunication if private use is permitted or tolerated. Section 88 of the act prohibits employers from knowingly accessing and reading electronic communication that is private (not intended for the message's reader). If personal use is allowed, exceptions exist based on the employee's sufficient consent or on the basis of a works agreement (*Betriebsvereinbarung*). If no personal use is allowed, the Act does not apply, but the practices will be subject to the Federal German Data Protection Act, 14 January 2003.

PRACTICAL TIPS

In monitoring their employees against the reasonable interest of the employee, employers should

- Ensure that the monitoring method is the least invasive means possible under the particular circumstances.
- Inform employees of the purposes for monitoring and the specific situations where monitoring will occur—include this in a clear policy available to the employees.
- Implement a proportionate monitoring process according to which the relevant e-mails of relevant employees are separated for investigation.
- Check local guidance and recommendations to ensure that monitoring is in line with local rules.
- Also verify works council requirements and other applicable employment/labor laws, such as collective labor agreements.

B. Video Surveillance

Video surveillance use has been increasing in recent years, including in the employment context. Such use involves the collection and most often the recording of personal data. As a result, video surveillance presents certain privacy concerns, and the Working Party has addressed some of these. In addition, the Working Party has sought to work toward greater harmonization in the approaches of the various Member States' laws in the area of video surveillance. The Working Party, in its WP

---

64. Cour de cassation [Cass.] [supreme court for judicial matters] com., Feb. 10, 2015, No. 13-14.779 FS-PB.

89, discusses provisions of the Directive that concern video surveillance, including the general privacy and data protection principles (see Chapter 1, Section III) and requirements for legitimacy.[65]

The Directive clearly applies to the personal data collection and processing achieved through video surveillance of individuals, other than for public or national security or defense.[66] For example, Recital 14 calls for the Directive to be applicable to processing involving "sound and image data relating to natural persons" captured and recorded.[67] As the Working Party noted, the Directive focuses on the potential for technological change in the area of video surveillance by providing that "[t]he Commission shall examine, in particular, the application of this Directive to the data processing of sound and image data relating to natural persons and shall submit any appropriate proposals which prove to be necessary, taking account of developments in information technology and in the light of the state of progress in the information society."[68]

WP 89 of the Working Party sets out various places for video surveillance systems and the various uses that may be made of them, which may be summarized by stating that video surveillance systems may be placed as follows:[69]

- Near public buildings to prevent vandalism or offenses;
- In sports arenas;
- In order to monitor traffic or transportation means in order to prevent offenses;
- Near borders or transportation means for illegal immigration monitoring and crime prevention purposes;
- Near schools to help protect minors and prevent unlawful conduct;
- In medical facilities for patient care and monitoring purposes; and
- Near shopping areas and residential areas for security and crime prevention.

Most of these examples refer to someone's workplace or public areas for security purposes. Moreover, the Working Party specifically addresses issues related to the employment context in its WP 89, referring to the general principles set out in its Working Document WP 55 (discussed earlier in Chapter 4, Section II.A),[70] and in its WP 48,[71] to the extent they are applicable to video surveillance.

---

65. Working Party, *Opinion 4/2004 on the Processing of Personal Data by Means of Video Surveillance* (WP 89) (Feb. 11, 2004) [hereinafter WP 89], at 5–7, http://ec.europa.eu/justice/policies/privacy/docs/wpdocs/2004/wp89_en.pdf.
66. Recital 16 of the Directive provides that "the processing of sound and image data, such as in cases of video surveillance, does not come within the scope of this Directive if it is carried out for the purposes of public security, defence, national security or in the course of State activities relating to the area of criminal law or of other activities which do not come within the scope of Community law." Directive, recital 16, at 32.
67. Directive, recital 14, at 32. This exclusion from the scope of the Directive also appears at Directive, art. 3(2).
68. Directive, art. 33, at 50.
69. WP 89, *supra* note 63, at 2–3.
70. WP 55, *supra* note 22.
71. WP 48, *supra* note 1.

In WP 48, the Working Party emphasizes that any monitoring of employees must be proportionate, taking into consideration the risks the employer faces and the employees' privacy and other rights. Personal data held or used must be adequate, relevant, and nonexcessive, and video surveillance must comply with the transparency requirements of Article 10 of the Directive, with employees being informed of such surveillance, its purposes, and so on.[72]

The Working Party states that "video surveillance systems aimed directly at controlling, from a remote location, quality and amount of working activities, therefore entailing the processing of personal data in this context, should not be permitted as a rule."[73] The Working Party then goes on to posit an exception to the rule when video surveillance systems are used "to meet production and/or occupational safety requirements."[74] In such cases, collective agreement rights, which often include requirements of information given to employees and prior agreement of employee representatives or trade unions as to installation arrangements, filming arrangements, and duration of surveillance, should be taken into account.[75]

Areas reserved for the private use of employees or not intended for work tasks should not be subject to surveillance. The Working Party cites the following as examples of such private areas—toilets, shower rooms, lockers, and recreation areas.[76] These areas are also places where employees—or anyone for that matter—would have a high expectation of privacy.

In addition, the finality of the collection of images should be respected. For example, "images collected exclusively to safeguard property and/or detect, prevent and control serious offences should not be used to charge an employee with minor disciplinary breaches." In cases where video surveillance images are used against employees, the latter should have access to the content of the data for their defense. Finally, information that should be provided to employees about video surveillance in the workplace should include the following:

- The identity of the controller;
- The purpose of the surveillance;
- Other information necessary "to guarantee fair processing in respect of the data subject," for example, when management would have a right to examine the data;
- The recording period; and
- When the recording would be disclosed to the law enforcement authorities.

---

72. *Id.* at 25.
73. WP 89, *supra* note 63, at 25.
74. *Id.*
75. *Id.* at 25.
76. *Id.* at 25.

This information should be clearly spelled out and the Working Party has indicated that the use of a mere symbol to provide such information about surveillance in the workplace is inadequate.[77] In public areas, such as parking lots and building entrances, signage may be sufficient; however, investigation should be made of the national laws of the relevant Member States insofar as labor law and specific video surveillance legislation may apply.

C.   Social Networking

The Directive generally applies to personal data processing by social network services (SNS),[78] in which case the SNS users are usually considered data subjects.[79] Also, an SNS user who acts for a company or association or who otherwise "uses the SNS mainly as a platform to advance commercial, political or charitable goals," does not benefit under Article 3(2) from the household activity exemption from application of the Directive to processing, and may find itself with the responsibilities of a controller for the disclosure of personal data to the SNS (another controller) and to other SNS users. As a result, data subject consent and/or legitimate grounds for processing may be required.[80]

However, the issues in the context of an employment relationship are distinct and generally involve employer monitoring of the use of SNS by employees, potential employer legal liability for such use when it infringes rights or is illegal, labor law and employment agreement provisions regarding sanctioning employees for such use, and potential risks to employers insofar as their reputation and confidential information are concerned. Some of these issues may be seen as follows.

1. Potential Employer Liability and Risks Related to Employees Using SNS

Just as employees may engage in use of e-mail contrary to law, they may also do so using SNS. Such use may involve various violations of national law, and an analysis of such legal provisions of relevant Member State laws should be conducted in order to establish the scope of the potential liability. Certain acts of an employee may result in vicarious liability of the employer, so as to support a legitimate interest of the employer in the monitoring of SNS use.

If an employee who is an SNS user limits access to his or her content on an SNS, the potential liability may disappear. Such might be the case under French law, for example, where in order for injurious words to constitute a media law violation of injurious communication (Article 23 of the Act of July 29, 1881), there must be a public (or "publicity") element for the words in question. In a recent French case, this

---

77. *Id.*
78. An SNS may be defined as "online communication platforms which enable individuals to join or create networks of like-minded users." Working Party, *Opinion 5/2009 on Online Social Networking* (WP 163) (June 12, 2009), at 4, http://ec.europa.eu/justice/policies/privacy/docs/wpdocs/2009/wp163_en.pdf. The Working Party reminds us that SNS are "information society services" under the Directive.
79. *Id.* at 5. SNS providers are considered data controllers.
80. *Id.* at 6.

public element was found not to exist because the Facebook and MSN accounts of the alleged perpetrator were accessible only to a restricted number of persons approved by her.[81] This analysis may limit available grounds for the use of SNS monitoring, and a country-by-country analysis for relevant jurisdictions should be made.

Risks involved in the use of SNS by employees include reputational ones for employers and their managers and other employees. Such use may involve defamatory or injurious communications, which, if the relevant SNS account is open to the public, may harm the reputation of the employer and its personnel. Such harm may affect the employer's ability to recruit new talent or to win new contracts or customers. In addition, SNS use may involve the disclosure of confidential corporate information that, if available to the public, and especially to competitors, may strategically harm the employer. In such a context, the preventive application of SNS use monitoring may further add legitimacy to the interests of the employer, to be balanced against the employees' fundamental rights.

2. Employer Monitoring of the Use of SNS by Employees

Generally, the points on monitoring employee e-mail (see Chapter 4, Section II.A) and video surveillance (see Chapter 4, Section II.B) apply to SNS use as well.[82] For example, an employer should evaluate whether the monitoring activity is transparent to employees. (For example, is it discussed in an employee handbook? Has the employer consulted the works councils or worker representatives about it, where appropriate? Is it the covered by an Internet policy or charter signed by the employee? Have employees been informed of the use of detection devices, of the purposes of such detection, and the use of data obtained?) The employer should also assess whether the monitoring of SNS use is necessary, fair, and proportionate. In addition, on the whole, an employer should not monitor the private SNS account of an employee except in "exceptional cases," although to a certain extent (and within certain limits), a professional SNS account established by an employer for an employee may be monitored. The personal user ID and password information for an employee's private account should not be required to be turned over to an employer. Moreover, in the employment context, grounds for processing other than consent should be privileged, because the potential prejudice to the employee who refuses to give his or her consent may have a chilling effect on such action.

The reasons for employer monitoring of the use of SNS by employees (which has to have legitimacy, such as that which may be based on the employer's legitimate interests) must be balanced against, and may be limited by, the right to respect for privacy and the right to freedom of expression of SNS users under respectively Articles 8 and

---

81. Cour de cassation [Cass.] [supreme court for judicial matters] 1e civ., Apr. 10, 2013, Bull. civ. I, No. 11-19.530 (Fr.), *available at* http://www.courdecassation.fr/jurisprudence_2/premiere_chambre_civile_568/344_10_26000.html.

82. Indeed, the discussion about the application of general data protection principles in Chapter 4 Section II.A. refers to a Working Party that covers Internet monitoring, in addition to e-mail monitoring. *See* WP 55, *supra* note 22, at 13.

10 of the ECHR (see Chapter 4, Section II.A.2). This is especially true as the various types of data with respect to an individual that are obtainable from the monitoring of the use of SNS could lead to discrimination and prejudice to fundamental rights. Examples of such data would be traffic data, location data, and data that may be used as indicia of age, sex, sexual identity, health condition, and so on, such as the recording of things on which the "Like" button is pushed or advertisements are clicked. This highlights the need for data protection principles to be respected in this context.

3. Labor Law and Employment Agreement Provisions Regarding Sanctioning Employees for SNS Use

An analysis of relevant Member State labor law, as well as any relevant employment agreement provisions, should be undertaken so as to assess the availability of sanctions for employee use (or misuse) of SNS services. Employees should be informed of the monitoring of SNS use, its purpose, the duration of the retention of data resulting from it, the extent of the monitoring, the use to be made of such data, and so on. In addition, national labor law may require certain actions to be taken before such monitoring may be used by an employer (for example, by notifying a works council or employee representatives).

D.   Bring Your Own Device

Employee use of their own devices (such as smartphones, laptops, and tablets) at the workplace, or "bring your own device" (BYOD), presents unique concerns for the employer as the latter—a controller with responsibility for compliance with data protection law—does not control such devices in the same sense as it controls the computer terminals, telephones, and other devices that it supplies the employee. As a result, operating procedures must be established in order to ensure that the employee devices are used in a manner that is not contrary to data protection and other legislation, and also in ways that do not endanger the security of company data nor risk causing the employer to incur liability (for example, for improper activities on the Internet).

The UK data protection agency, UK ICO, has provided guidance for data controllers on BYOD.[83] It highlights that **"the data controller must remain in control of the personal data for which he is responsible, regardless of the ownership of the device used to carry out the processing,"**[84] and suggests that the controller establish an Acceptable Use Policy[85] for BYOD devices, which then should be followed up with monitoring in order to ensure proper use. Security for personal data must be ensured and **"BYOD must not introduce vulnerabilities into existing secure environments."**[86] Analysis of

---

83. UK ICO, *Bring your own device (BYOD)* (Mar. 7, 2013), *available at* http://ico.org.uk/for_organisations/data_protection/topic_guides/online/~/media/documents/library/Data_Protection/Practical_application/ico_bring_your_own_device_byod_guidance.ashx.
84. *Id.* at 4.
85. *Id.* at 6.
86. *Id.*

how data is transferred between the employee's device and the employer's information system should be made, and encryption technology may be used.[87]

If Internet use is a concern (as it most certainly will be), a Wi-Fi network connection for the BYOD devices may be required and website filtering may be employed to prevent certain websites from being accessed by such devices through the employer's network.[88] But such are not the only concerns. For example, if connection between the employee's devices and the employer's network may lead to the employer processing the personal data of the employee (and others, such as family members whose data is stored on the device), the controller must "[c]onsider whether the controls [it has] in place are appropriate for any sensitive personal data being processed."[89] Furthermore, employees should receive clear information as to the purpose behind any monitoring of their BYOD use and be "satisfied that it is justified by real benefits that will be delivered,"[90] and such monitoring will generally be required to be considered "proportionate" under local Member State national labor law. In addition, the employer/controller will be responsible for ensuring that data protection principles, such as purpose limitation ("only using corporate personal data for corporate purposes,"[91] for example), are respected.

As discussed in paragraph 1(e) regarding e-mail, Member State national electronic communications law should also be consulted in connection with the use of BYOD devices.

In summary, allowing BYOD use will involve significant work upstream in the form of an audit of potential uses and risks, the establishment of a BYOD policy and BYOD procedures (including monitoring), development of other technical and organizational safeguards, and informing employees of the extent and reasons for such procedures and safeguards. Afterward, monitoring for compliance must be performed. Such planning should integrate the possibility of loss or theft of employee BYOD devices and employee use of public cloud services storage services for their BYOD devices, where data for which the employer is responsible may end up being stored.

E. Geolocation and Biometrics

Geolocation technology, including GPS, has been used by employers to track employees, and sometimes has been grounds for dismissal of employees. Biometrics may be used by employers to grant access to facilities by employees and may be used to track them as well.

---

87. *Id.* at 8.
88. *Id.* at 5.
89. *Id.* at 6.
90. *Id.* at 12.
91. *Id.*

1. Geolocation Technology

Employers who use geolocation technology to track their workers must have a legitimate ground for processing the data that results. While an employer may seek to use an employee's consent as its ground for processing, the Working Party has already shown its reserve in the employment context, based on the fact that an employee's failure to give consent might result in prejudice to such employee. Such could be the case, for example, where a prospective employee must consent in order to obtain employment. The Working Party highlights that "[t]he worker is in theory able to refuse consent, but the consequence may be the loss of a job opportunity. In such circumstances consent is not freely given and is therefore not valid."[92] It also reminds that this is area where all relevant stakeholders should be involved, and it might be appropriate to "regulate the gathering of consent statements in such circumstances" through collective bargaining agreements.[93]

In the case of geolocation technology, then, the Working Party underscores that "employers must investigate whether it is demonstrably necessary to supervise the exact locations of employees for a legitimate purpose" and then balance this against the employee's fundamental rights and freedoms. Where there is adequate justification, the employer could base the processing on the employer's legitimate interest (Directive, Article 7(f)). In any event, the "least intrusive means" should always be sought by the employer, and it should avoid "continuous monitoring" of the employee, allowing him or her to turn off the geolocation device outside of work hours. The employer should show the employee how to do so.[94]

An example of a less-intrusive means might be choosing a geolocation "system that sends an alert when an employee is crossing a pre-set virtual boundary" but is not continuously being monitored. Moreover, the Working Party points out that "[v]ehicle tracking devices are not staff tracking devices," so an employer who tracks its fleet of cars should not use such devices to track the behavior or location of employees, "for example by sending alerts in relation to speed of vehicle."[95]

It should be noted that employees' use of BYOD devices with, for example, Wi-Fi access, may also lead to the collection of geolocation data by an employer and should be included in the latter's analysis of the legitimacy of processing.

---

92. *See* WP 48, *supra* note 1.
93. Working Party, *Opinion on the Use of Location Data with a View to Providing Value-Added Services* (WP 115) (Nov. 2005), http://ec.europa.eu/justice/policies/privacy/docs/wpdocs/2005/wp115_en.pdf.
94. Working Party, *Opinion 13/2011 on Geolocation Services on Smart Mobile Devices* (WP 185) (May 16, 2011), at 14, http://ec.europa.eu/justice/data-protection/article-29/documentation/opinion-recommendation/files/2011/wp185_en.pdf.
95. *Id.*

2. Biometrics

In most cases, data from biometric technologies are personal data, and data protection principles apply to their processing.[96] Biometric information is also considered sensitive data under certain Member States' national data protection law as it is deemed as more intrusive or in a higher-risk processing category.[97]

The specific danger to privacy caused by biometrics technology has been the subject of a Working Party study.[98] Such technologies are linked to "certain characteristics of an individual," and as such pose privacy concerns.[99] In most cases, the data resulting from such technologies may be processed only if legitimate under the Directive, and a possible ground for legitimacy may be the legitimate interests of the data controller (Article 7(f) of the Directive). This might be the ground where, for example, an employer that researches dangerous viruses secures a lab through technology that grants access after scanning fingerprints and irises of employees, so that only qualified personnel may enter. In this example, the legitimate interest may significantly override the wishes of data subjects not to have their biometric data processed.[100] Note that the same cautions about the difficulty for employees to give true consent, discussed in Section I.B of this chapter, apply to biometric technologies as well, requiring controllers to seek other grounds for legitimacy of processing.

Data subjects must be informed of the collection or use of their data, they must have access to it, and it must be properly secured.[101] Special care must be taken to define and limit the purpose of the biometric data processing, respecting data protection principles.[102]

Security must be ensured for biometric data, including against data breach, using encryption technology and storage on personal devices, for example.[103]

When biometric data are no longer needed, such as when an employer has a biometric system in order to control access to a restricted area and an employee no longer needs to access that area because his or her function has changed, such employee's biometric data "must be deleted since the purpose for which they were collected no longer applies."[104]

---

96. Working Party, *Working Document on Biometrics* (WP 80) (Aug. 1, 2003), http://ec.europa.eu/justice/policies/privacy/docs/wpdocs/2003/wp80_en.pdf.

97. Section 13(5) of Slovak Act No. 122/2013 Coll. on Protection of Personal Data and on Changing and Amending of other acts, resulting from amendments and additions executed by the Act. No. 84/2014 Coll.

98. Working Party, *Opinion 3/2012 on the Developments in Biometric Technologies* (WP 193) (Apr. 27, 2012), http://ec.europa.eu/justice/data-protection/article-29/documentation/opinion-recommendation/files/2012/wp193_en.pdf.

99. *Id.* at 3.

100. *Id.* at 7 and 10–13 (on the grounds for legitimacy).

101. *Id.* at 14.

102. *Id.* at 7–10.

103. *Id.* at 30–33. For additional discussion of WP 193, *see* W. Gregory Voss, *Survey of Recent European Union Privacy Developments*, 68 Bus. Law. 205, at 209–210.

104. *Id.* at 10.

Applicable Law under the GDPR

The GDPR specifically incorporates the concept derived from Working Party opinions that "[c]onsent should not provide a valid legal ground for the processing of personal data, where there is a clear imbalance between the data subject and the controller," such as when there is a "situation of dependence," for example, "where personal data are processed by the employer of employees' personal data in the employment context."[105] In this regard, a condition for consent has been set out in Article 7(4) of the GDPR: "Consent shall not provide a legal basis for the processing, where there is a significant imbalance between the position of the data subject and the controller."[106]

With a view to uniformity, the GDPR adds a definition for "biometric data," which is defined as "any data relating to the physical, physiological or behavioural characteristics of an individual which allow their unique identification, such as facial images, or dactyloscopic data."[107] In addition, under Article 33 of the GDPR, "personal data in large scale filing systems on . . . biometric data" are considered as presenting "specific risks to the rights and freedoms of data subjects" so as to require a controller or a processor acting on the controller's behalf to carry out a data protection impact assessment with respect to such processing.[108]

III. SENSITIVE DATA

Sensitive data—or "special categories of data," as it is called in the Directive—is defined as "personal data revealing racial or ethnic origin, political opinions, religious or philosophical beliefs, trade-union membership, and the processing of data concerning health or sex life."[109] Sensitive data is treated as a separate, special category distinct from other personal data. Its processing is deemed to create greater risks and heightened consequences for individuals and their fundamental rights than the processing of other, non-"special" data. Thus, handling of sensitive data requires additional protections.[110]

The general rule is that the processing of sensitive data is prohibited and is permitted only for specific purposes and under special conditions. Criminal or judicial data and the use of national identity numbers are somewhat similarly regulated under Article 8 of the Directive. However, as we will see, their qualification and regulation under different national laws varies substantially between Member States. Other special processing situations are considered in Article 15, covering processing involving automated decision making,

---

105. GDPR, recital 34, at 22.
106. GDPR, art. 7(4), at 45.
107. GDPR, art. 4(11), at 42.
108. GDPR, art. 33(1)–(2), at 62.
109. Directive, art. 8(1), at 40.
110. Working Party, *Working Party Advice Paper on Special Categories of Data ("Sensitive Data")*, Apr. 20, 2011, at 4, http://ec.europa.eu/justice/policies/privacy/docs/wpdocs/others/2011_04_20_letter_artwp_mme_le_bail_directive_9546ec_annex1_en.pdf.

and Article 20, covering categories of data processing that presents special risks. These two latter categories are not examined here, as they are beyond the scope of this book.[111]

This section will look at the divergence in national implementation of sensitive data provisions, followed by particular consideration of certain sensitive data (health, criminal records, and national identifiers) in the employment context.

A. Divergence in National Implementation of Sensitive Data Provisions
1. Varying Categories and Treatment in Member States

The specific categories qualifying as sensitive data categories are contained in Article 8(1) of the Directive. The definition hinges on "data revealing" and "is to be understood that not only data which by its nature contains sensitive information is covered by this provision, but also data from which sensitive information with regard to an individual can be concluded."[112] Thus, sensitive data in theory casts a wide net in terms of the relevant data categories included. However, Member States' implementation of the Article 8 provisions differs substantially. Some national laws refer to data "on," "concerning," or "relating to," among others, the sensitive data categories. This difference has produced major conflicts between the national laws on what qualifies as sensitive data. This discrepancy was identified by the EC Study on Implementation, which noted:

> [t]he fact that someone regularly buys kosher or hala'l meat, or subscribes to certain magazines, or visits certain websites, may not be information 'on' or 'as to' that person's beliefs or, for example, sexual interests or 'sex life', but such a fact can be said to nevertheless '**reveal**' such sensitive information. Photographs and video-images also always 'reveal' a person's race.[113]

The Working Party in its Advice Paper on Special Categories of Data has taken the view that focusing on information from which sensitive data can be concluded is the intended approach.[114] Nevertheless, whether a photo will qualify as sensitive data or not depends on the ways and means of implementation under national law.

Some Member States have added additional categories to what is listed in Article 8(1) of the Directive, either by considering them "sensitive" or by earmarking certain categories for special handling as they are deemed to create heightened-risk processing scenarios. Such categories may include credit and financial history, social security benefits, and criminal convictions and may also be regulated in separate legislation. Genetic and

---

111. *See generally* GLOBAL EMPLOYEE PRIVACY AND DATA SECURITY LAW (Miriam H. Wugmeister & Christine Lyon, eds., 2d ed. 2011).

112. *Advice Paper on Special Categories of Data, supra* note 101, at 6.

113. Douwe Korff, *EC Study on Implementation of Data Processing Directive: Comparative Summary of National Laws*, Sept. 2002, at 84, *available at* http://194.242.234.211/documents/10160/10704/Stato+di +attuazione+della+Direttiva+95-46-CE (referenced on http://www.garanteprivacy.it); last visited on Mar. 11, 2015).

114. *Advice Paper on Special Categores of Data, supra* note 101, at 6.

biometric data is also included in some national laws, as is information on addictions.[115] Whenever such data is processed, high levels of technical and organizational protective measures should also be put in place, and special handling of this information is required.

When processing these borderline categories, which may qualify as sensitive, it is important to verify whether or not they qualify as sensitive data under applicable national law. When taking a low risk approach, it may be preferable to err on the side of caution and operate as if the information was sensitive data.

2. Preconditions for Processing

Sensitive data may be processed only as follows:

1. With the individual's "explicit consent."[116]
2. When the processing is necessary for the purposes of carrying out rights and obligations in employment law.[117]
3. Where necessary to protect the vital interests of the data subject or another individual.[118]
4. When carried out by a nonprofit body (organization) "with a political, philosophical, religious or trade-union aim."[119]
5. When the processing relates to data that are manifestly made public by the data subject or are necessary for the establishment, exercise, or defense of legal claims.[120]

The first condition, where processing is permitted based on consent, is qualified to exclude certain circumstances where sensitive data may not be processed even with consent. Specifically, Article 8(2)(a) states that consent will act as an exemption to the general prohibition "except where the laws of the Member State provide that the prohibition . . . may not be lifted by the data subject's giving his consent."[121] In practice, this basis serves to protect individuals in circumstances where consent for processing of certain sensitive data is requested but would be disproportionate, and thus illegal, under the circumstances. This, for example, could be the case if an employer

---

115.   Douwe Korff, *EC Study on Implementation of Data Processing Directive, supra* note 111, at 81. *See generally* WP 80, *supra* note 94, at 10, regarding the possible qualification of biometric data as sensitive data when revealing racial or ethnic origin, data concerning, or as an unique identifier. The Polish DPA (Generalny Inspektor Ochrony Danych Osobowych, or GIODO) has commented on court cases where employers have collected fingerprints for measuring the working time of employees. *See Czy pracodawca ma prawo za pomocą specjalnego urządzenia skanować linie papilarne pracowników w celu rejestracji godzin ich przyjścia i wyjścia z zakładu pracy?* [Does the employer have the right to use a special device to scan the fingerprints of employees to register their hours coming in and going out of the workplace?], Feb. 12, 2010. (Polish) text of opinion *available at* http://www.giodo.gov.pl/348/id_art/3358/j/pl/. The DPA took the position that the collection of fingerprints was disproportionate and consent would not be valid based on the employment relationship, and it raised the question of whether other less-intrusive means would be available.

116.   Directive, art. 8(2)(a), at 40.

117.   Directive, art. 8(2)(b), at 40.

118.   Directive, art. 8(2)(c), at 40.

119.   Directive, art. 8(2)(d), at 40–41.

120.   Directive, art. 8(2)(e), at 41.

121.   Directive, art. 8(2)(a), at 40.

requested a patient file of an employee. In Belgium, for example, sensitive data may be processed with the written consent of the data subject, save for data relating to his or her criminal background or conviction. However, when the data subject is a candidate or employee of the controller, this would obviate such consent (unless the data subject would benefit from the processing).[122]

For employers, the second basis allowing sensitive data processing when necessary to comply with employment law obligations is the most relevant. As this condition defers to labor or employment obligations of controllers, they will necessarily have to defer to their national law obligations as employers. Oftentimes, the legality of processing sensitive data turns on local business practice and questions: does the employer actually need to have the trade union membership lists, for example, for mandatory payments of union dues? If a health-care worker is on site (such as a company doctor or nurse), is he or she actually working for the controller as an employee? More likely such workers are independent contractors with a separate processing basis (and hence permitted to process the personal data on a different basis).

Sensitive data processing is also permitted where "required for the purposes of preventative medicine, medical diagnosis, the provision or care or treatment of the management of healthcare services."[123] In addition, a catchall provision says sensitive data may be processed for "substantial public interest, lay down [additional] exemptions . . . either by national law or by decision of the [DPA]."[124] In practice, this would be for fields of public health, social protections, scientific research, or government statistics. When legislating or setting out DPA guidance for this basis for processing, Member States are tasked "to provide specific and suitable safeguards" to protect data subjects' fundamental rights.[125] Member States have broadly legislated with respect to these exemptions from the prohibition on processing sensitive data. In such scenarios, national data protection laws defer to other domestic laws or rules to authorize sensitive data processing. Some Member States require that controllers request special authorization or permits for processing sensitive data in the form of a prior check or authorization.[126]

B.　Particular Consideration of Certain Sensitive Data in the Employment Context
1. Health

In contrast to the United States, there is no sector-specific regulation on the EU level regarding the processing and access of health data; these are covered by the Directive and its corresponding Member State implementing legislation instead. Health data can include information on disabilities as well as sick leave and

---

122.　*See generally* Privacy Commission (Belg.), *Protection of Personal Data in Belgium*, Apr. 23, 2012, http://www.privacycommission.be/sites/privacycommission/files/documents/protection-of-personal-data-in-belgium.pdf.

123.　Directive, art. 8(3), at 41.

124.　Directive, art. 8(4), at 41.

125.　*See* Directive, recital 34, at 34.

126.　*See* Douwe Korff, *EC Study on Implementation of Data Processing Directive, supra* note 111, at 82.

maternity/paternity periods. Within the employment context, health data may be processed based on the exemption in Article 8(2)(b): where necessary for complying with employment law provisions. Therefore, health data may generally be processed by employers on the basis of national labor or employment laws or other laws, such as social security coverage, that require the employer to collect, maintain, or track certain sensitive data. Another potential basis for the processing is the vital interests of the data subject or another person. This is relevant, for example, if there is an accident in the workplace and an employee was unable to provide consent to the disclosure of certain lifesaving information.

To provide some background, under the German Data Protection Act, health data may be processed in the exercise of pension regulations, collective agreements, and the functioning of certain benefits, such as illness and incapacity or disability at work.[127]

2. Background Checks—Criminal Data

Article 8(5) of the Directive stipulates that "data relating to offences, criminal convictions or security measures" may be processed only "under the control of official authority, or if suitable specific safeguards are provided under national law."[128] Interestingly, criminal background data is an independent provision that is not specified in the general definition of sensitive data within the meaning of Article 8(1). Therefore it is not covered under the general prohibition, as it is not consistently legislated as "sensitive data" throughout the European Union. In some countries, criminal or judicial data, including background checks, are qualified as sensitive or earmarked for special—restricted—processing. Many Western European countries operate using a system of "certificates of good conduct." The certificates are statements requested by the data subjects from the authorities. This certificate generally declares that the individual did not commit any crimes that would affect his or her character or fitness for a particular reason. These certificates are generally issued for certain specific roles or jobs (school teachers, security guards, taxi drivers, etc.). In this way, specific information on criminal history is not supplied by the authorities.[129]

In practice, this means that general background checks are not permitted, and any check of the criminal background of a job applicant or employee needs to be related

---

127. *See generally* Bundesdatenschutzgesetz [BDSG] [German Federal Data Protection Act] [trans.], Jan. 14, 2003, Federal Law Gazette I, at 66, as *amended by* art. 1 of the Act of Aug. 14, 2009, Federal Law Gazette I, at 2814, §§ 28(6) no. 3 and 28(7), http://www.gesetze-im-internet.de/englisch_bdsg /federal_data_protection_act.pdf.

128. Directive, art. 8(5), at 41.

129. In the Netherlands, an employer will not directly obtain criminal data; however, a candidate can apply for a certificate of conduct (*Verklaring Omtrent het Gedrag*) issued by the Dutch Minister of Security and Justice, which can then be provided the employer.

Such certificates may also be required for migration purposes. For a practical overview of EU countries that require such certificates, *see* Commission, *Ad-Hoc Query on a Certificate of Good Conduct when Migrants Apply for a Residence Permit*, Apr. 13, 2012, http://ec.europa.eu/dgs /home-affairs/what-we-do/networks/european_migration_network/reports/docs/ad-hoc-queries /residence/389_emn_ad-hoc_query_certificate_of_good_conduct_15march2012_wider_ dissemination_en.pdf.

to the specific position involved. In certain jurisdictions, such as Germany and the Netherlands, processing of background or criminal data requires the prior approval of the works council.

3. Social Security and National Identity Numbers

Another provision allows Member States to "determine…conditions [for processing]… national identification number" or related identifiers. Like criminal or judicial data in Article 8(5), this category is not treated explicitly as sensitive data under the Directive. As this category of data does not fit within the traditional definition of sensitive data under the Directive, it is treated differently within the national Member States. These identifiers are also used for different purposes. Some act as a social security or tax identifier, while others are used more widely as a general identifier of individuals. It is interesting to note that the Netherlands formerly used a SoFi (social security and tax identification) number, similar to a social security number in the United States. This number was phased out and replaced with a more specific unique personal identifier, known as the Citizen Service Number (*Burgerservicenummer*, or BSN number), which is more strictly regulated, to avoid the overreliance on national identity numbers.

For reference, here are a few names of national identifiers:

> Belgium—National Number
> France—INSEE code
> The Netherlands—BSN Number[130]
> Poland—Powszechny Elektroniczny System Ewidencji Ludności or PESEL
>   number
> Slovakia—Birth Number

In summary, it is important to first assess whether relevant information qualifies as sensitive or falls under a special category of personal data under national law of a Member State. Second, if it does qualify as sensitive or heightened-risk data, then you should assess what you would like to do with the information based on the relevant grounds for exemption under national laws that permit processing and transfer.

---

130. Regulated by the Wet algemene bepaling burgerservicenummer [Dutch General Law on the Citizen Service Number] [Neth.], Staatsblad van he Koninkrijk der Nederlanden [Stb.] 443 (Oct. 30, 2007)). For more information and guidance (in Dutch), *see* http://www.cbpweb.nl/Pages/med_20070719_BSN.aspx, http://www.cbpweb.nl/pages/adv_z2010-01343.aspx and http://www.cbpweb.nl/pages/adv_z2010-01343.aspx.

Applicable Law under the GDPR

Under the GDPR, the definition of sensitive data ("special categories of personal data") is consolidated and streamlined, extending to genetic data as well as to personal data concerning criminal convictions and "related security measures."[131] The legal exemptions from the prohibition to processing are also further developed to permit processing for health[132] and scientific research[133] purposes. These two exemptions are further articulated in Articles 81 and 83 of the GDPR, respectively. The exact rules relating to health and scientific research data processing have changed in recent drafts, following the amendments by the Committee on Civil Liberties, Justice and Home Affairs. However, it is clear that through the GDPR, the Commission would like to clear up some of the ambiguity surrounding the use of medical data for certain health and scientific research purposes.

There is a specific exemption for processing data on criminal convictions or related security measures when:

> [c]arried out either under the control of official authority or when the processing is necessary for compliance with a legal or regulatory obligation to which a controller is subject, or for the performance of a task carried out for important public interest reasons, and in so far as authorised by Union law or Member State law providing for adequate safeguards.

Again, such complete databases may be maintained only "under the control of official authority."[134]

The exemption for processing by associations, foundations, and nonprofit bodies "with a political, philosophical, religion or trade-union aim" is slightly adjusted to permit disclosures within the body of the organization, so that consent of the data subject is necessary only when data is disclosed "outside that body."[135]

---

131. GDPR, art. 9(1), at 45.
132. GDPR, art. 9(2)(h), at 46.
133. GDPR, art. 9(2)(i), at 46.
134. GDPR, art. 9(2)(j), at 46.
135. *Id.*, art. 9(2)(d), at 46.

5

Privacy and Company Compliance

I. WHISTLE-BLOWING HOTLINES

Following the adoption of the Sarbanes Oxley Act (SOX)[1] in 2002, U.S. companies and their global subsidiaries, affiliates, and foreign companies listed on the U.S. market were required to set up audit committees and implement procedures to report violations relating to accounting, internal accounting controls, and auditing matters.[2] This approach was enlarged by the Dodd Frank Wall Street Reform and Consumer Protection Act (Dodd Frank)[3] and by recent momentum behind corporate governance programs. Many companies set up global whistle-blowing hotlines to take reports of misconduct within their companies and to handle compliance issues and complaints.

In the European Union, these hotlines create tension for companies; on one hand, multinational groups need to comply with SOX provisions, but on the other hand, they need to ensure that personal information processed within the hotlines, as well as the reporting and investigation process is in compliance with EU data protection rules. Furthermore, there is an added complexity, as the hotlines are driven by U.S. laws and not by EU Member State national laws. Therefore, no specific legal provisions (in most EU countries) call for such hotlines. Thus, hotlines, when set up for European subsidiaries based on U.S. laws, act as an extraterritorial application of U.S. law. An example of this would be a foreign, non-U.S. company with a bond listing on the NYSE bond marketplace required to comply with SOX requirements.

A. Cultural and Employment Concerns

In Europe, hotlines are often met with confusion or suspicion. As a result of cultural differences, the essence of these hotlines is not always translated in Europe in the same way as it is perceived in the United States, which has a long history of whistle-blowing laws and relevant protections. In many countries, hotlines are viewed as creating an

---

1. Sarbanes-Oxley Act of 2002, Pub. L. No. 107-204, 116 Stat. 745, July 30, 2002, *available at* http://www.gpo.gov/fdsys/pkg/PLAW-107publ204/html/PLAW-107publ204.htm.
2. *Id.* at § 301 (4)(A)–(B), 116 Stat. 776–777, 15 U.S.C. § 78j–1 (m)(1)–(6).
3. Dodd-Frank Wall Street Reform and Consumer Protection Act, Pub. L. No. 111-203, 124 Stat. 1376, 12 U.S.C. § 5301 *et seq.*, July 21, 2010, at § 21, http://www.gpo.gov/fdsys/pkg/PLAW-111publ203/pdf/PLAW-111publ203.pdf.

atmosphere of distrust, suspicion, and denouncement, as evoked by former Working Party Chair Peter Schaar:

> I am personally keen to underline that this assessment must be read in the specific European context. It is certainly useful at this stage to recall that anonymous reporting evokes some of the darkest times of recent history on the European continent, whether during World War II or during more recent dictatorships in Southern and Eastern Europe. This historical specificity makes up for a lot of the reluctance of the EU Data Protection Authorities to allow anonymous schemes being advertised as such in companies as a normal mode of reporting concerns.[4]

In addition to data protection concerns, hotlines are also affected by employment or labor law requirements. Many countries require information or consultation with the local works councils or local employee representatives. National language is another concern that companies must keep in mind. If a company has a large number of workers, for example in an industrial context, providing hotlines only in English will not suffice to serve all workers. Most external hotline providers have broad linguistic capabilities in order to handle calls, but this affects costs. Furthermore, notices and policies on the hotlines must be provided in the local languages.

EU data protection laws are often triggered as the result of EU personal data collected in the framework of hotlines within the employment and business context. Thus, the relevant hotline is subject to the same principles discussed in Chapter 1 Section III. The French data protection authority (the CNIL) published guidelines on November 11, 2005,[5] following attempts by McDonald's and Exide Technologies to establish hotlines in France.[6] Shortly thereafter, the Working Party issued its own opinion on the treatment of hotlines on February 1, 2006.[7] This section will examine

---

4. Letter from Mr. Peter Schaar, Chair of Working Party, to Mr. Ethiopis Tafara, Director, Office of International Affairs, Securities and Exchange Commission, July 3, 2006, http://ec.europa.eu/justice/policies/privacy/docs/wpdocs/others/2006-07-03-reply_whistleblowing.pdf.

5. CNIL, *Guideline document adopted by the "Commission nationale de l'informatique et des libertés" (CNIL) on 10 November 2005 for the implementation of whistleblowing systems in compliance with the French Data Protection Act of 6 January 1978, as amended in August 2004, relating to information technology, data filing systems and liberties.* (Nov. 11, 2005), http://www.cnil.fr/fileadmin/documents/en/CNIL-recommandations-whistleblowing-VA.pdf. Please note that the CNIL has issued a standard authorization decision no. AU-004 that now permits companies to self-certify.

6. *See* CNIL, Decision No. 2005-110 McDonald's France and CNIL (May 26, 2005) (Fr.), *available at* http://www.cnil.fr/documentation/deliberations/deliberation/delib/73/ and CNIL, Decision No. 2005-111 (May 26, 2005) Compagnie européenne d'accumulateurs and CNIL (Fr.), *available at* http://www.cnil.fr/documentation/deliberations/deliberation/delib/74/.

7. Working Party, *Opinion 1/2006 on the Application of EU Data Protection Rules to Internal Whistleblowing Schemes in the Fields of Accounting, Internal Accounting Controls, Auditing Matters, Fight against Bribery, Banking and Financial Crime* (WP 117) (Feb. 1, 2006), http://ec.europa.eu/justice/policies/privacy/docs/wpdocs/2006/wp117_en.pdf.

the following: the legal basis for processing in connection with a hotline; the rules on data quality and proportionality and notice and transparency requirements; and the management of these reporting systems, touching on the transfer issues that are inherent with their use.

B. Legal Basis for Hotlines

To be lawful, a hotline must have a legitimate basis for processing under the national law of the Member State(s) in which it is implemented. Reflecting back to the discussion in Section II.D, two possible legitimate bases apply to hotlines: (1) compliance with a legal obligation, and (2) the legitimate interest of the controller (or third party to whom the data is disclosed).

Arising from the implementation of antibribery laws, reporting systems for internal controls are required within the financial sector and in certain EU countries. However, extraterritorial application of U.S. law does not qualify under this particular basis. Hotlines may be put in place due to "legally binding obligations of national law in the same fields as those covered by SOX."[8] Local provisions of law could give rise to the need for a hotline, but if a company is rolling out a compliance hotline on the basis of SOX, it cannot rely on the national provision if this is not applicable to it.

For the most part, companies rely on their legitimate interests as a basis for the implementation of a hotline. This is based on the importance of implementing good corporate governance within organizations and ensuring transparency, solid financial and accounting practices, and the company's interest in enabling employees to report certain irregularities.[9] In EU countries where no specific national law requires a hotline, it is generally acknowledged that "data controllers still hold a legitimate interest in implementing . . . [hotline] schemes" in the fields of accounting, internal controls, auditing matters, antibribery, and banking and financial crimes.[10] It is important to remember that this legal basis must be balanced against the fundamental rights of data subjects. Hotlines must ensure the protection of the individuals whose personal data is processed within the hotline, i.e., the reporting individuals and individuals reported about or implicated in a report.

C. Proportionality and Data Quality: Limiting the Scope of the Hotline

The Working Party has made several recommendations to ensure that personal data collected is proportional to the purposes pursued by the hotline. It recommends the following.

---

8. *Id.* at 8.
9. *Id.*
10. *Id.*

1. A Limit on the Number (Type) of People Who Are Able to Use the Hotline to Submit a Report

Based on the nature of the company rolling out the hotline, it should carefully consider whether it is appropriate to limit the number of people who can submit a report. Meaning, should the hotline really extend and be available to all employees, or would it be more appropriate to make it available to just those who would be likely to have information on accounting, internal controls, auditing matters, antibribery, and banking and financial crimes?[11] In some circumstances, companies have extended availability of their hotlines to even external persons like auditors, suppliers, or business contacts, who may be in a better position to report on instances of bribery or irregularities in accounting. The scope of the possible reporting individuals should be assessed based on the circumstances.

2. A Limit on the Number (Type) of People Who May Be Incriminated via the Hotline

Companies should consider whether it is appropriate under the circumstances to limit the number of people who may be incriminated. In some circumstances, it does not make sense to include all employees of the company who can be reported about through the company's hotline. For example, should the company receptionist or cleaning crew be excluded?[12] Companies will need to closely examine the type of complaints they would like to process in hotlines and balance the scope against the categories of data subjects concerned, essentially looking at whether the hotline should extend to all employees or whether it should be limited to only management, accountants, and so on. This generally depends on the type of company and business involved. Increasingly, companies have their hotlines open to everyone to allow non-employees to submit reports and to be reported on. An example would be the situation where a supplier or contractor is violating antibribery laws.

3. Preference for Identified versus Anonymous Reports and Promoting Confidentiality of a Hotline

A hot-button issue for hotlines in the European Union is the possibility of submitting reports anonymously. For the cultural reasons outlined in Mr. Schaaf's letter mentioned earlier, this is a practice that comes under additional scrutiny in the European Union. As an example, it is completely prohibited in Spain. The Working Party notes that investigations are made more difficult because there is no identified person for asking follow-up questions. Anonymity does not necessarily prevent others from identifying the whistle-blower, and it is easier to organize the protection of whistle-blowers when their identity is known. Additionally, there is a risk that the organization could develop a culture of receiving anonymous malicious reports, and the

---

11. *Id.* at 10.
12. *Id.*

"social climate within the organisation could deteriorate."[13] For these reasons, the Working Party recommends that reports be submitted on identified bases, balancing any retaliation concerns with the confidential treatment and promotion of the hotline and reports. In principle, the Working Party specifies that only identified reports should be communicated using hotlines, but it recognizes the need and reality of certain businesses in which anonymity is required. Thus, anonymous reports can take place but should be as an exception to the general rule of identification.

In practice, companies should avoid the promotion of anonymous reporting or, at least, avoid the appearance of promoting or advertising anonymous reporting. U.S. companies quite frequently advertise in codes of conduct or business policies that anonymous reporting is possible via hotlines. In Europe, this wording will need to be altered to state that a company encourages reporters to identify themselves, but if they do not feel comfortable with this, anonymity may be an option. WP 117 explains that people will be more comfortable identifying themselves when they are aware that their identity will be kept confidential. Confidentiality should be highlighted within the scheme, and reporting individuals should be made aware that their identity will not be disclosed to third parties, including the employee's line management or the incriminated person. The scheme should also make clear that the identity of reporting individuals will be need to be disclosed to the relevant people for investigation and any subsequent judicial proceedings.[14]

Anonymous reports should be treated with special caution within a hotline. For example, the first recipient of the report (not necessarily the person taking the report) should consider whether the report should be taken or admitted into the hotline and whether it is appropriate to circulate the report. Anonymous reports should be treated in a swifter manner than standard identified reports. This does not mean that the reports should not be properly investigated, but organizations should consider such reports with caution as they could be misused.[15]

4. Scope of Reporting: Proportionality and Accuracy within Hotline

As hotlines are meant to ensure a suitable level of corporate governance, the data processed should be limited to the facts directly linked to this purpose. Companies should clearly delineate the type of information and complaints that may be collected through a hotline. The Working Party has stated that companies should limit "the type of information to accounting, internal accounting controls or auditing or banking and financial crime and anti-bribery."[16] There are wider reporting possibilities under EU Member State national laws; however, this varies by country. If one wants to roll out a truly EU-wide system, the scope would necessarily need to be limited

---

13. *Id.* at 11.
14. *Id.*
15. *Id.*
16. *Id.*

to allegations around accounting, auditing, banking/financial crimes, and antibribery instances. If companies would like to benefit from instances of wider reporting possibilities, such as violations of company codes of conduct, environmental laws, sexual harassment, or workplace protection laws, they will need to check for each country to ensure the permitted breadth under national laws.

If reports or facts are collected that do not relate to the permitted scope, these should be forwarded through the proper management channels for follow-up and action.

5. Data Retention

Personal data collected and processed within the hotline should be deleted within two months from the completion of the investigation. If legal proceedings or disciplinary actions arise,[17] the personal data may be kept for longer until the conclusion of the proceedings and the statutory period for appeal. These are determined by the applicable national laws. Any unsubstantiated reports or facts should be deleted immediately.[18]

In practice, companies prefer to retain reports and results of investigations in archives as part of their records management programs. Archiving of reports and access to these reports is covered by provisions of relevant national law.

D. Transparency and Notice

Flowing from the information requirements in the Directive (Articles 10 and 11), the controller of a hotline needs to provide sufficient notice to all data subjects involved in the scheme. In practice, this means that individuals need to be notified about the existence of the hotline, its objectives, and how the hotline works, including how reports may be filed and how they are followed up and investigated. The latter point is important because the notice should outline how reports are taken, processed, investigated, and closed or passed on, as well as any relevant recipients of the personal data contained in the reports in the hotline. As in standard notices, the hotline notice should include information on rights of access, rectification, and deletion. The hotline notice should also include the fact that the whistle-blower's identity will remain confidential throughout the process and that abuse or malicious reporting can result in action against the reporter. This statement should be tempered with the fact that individuals reporting in good faith will not face sanctions.

E. Rights of Implicated Persons

All data subjects within the scope of the hotline should have their fundamental rights to protection of personal data upheld. This includes individuals who are named in any relevant report (each known as an implicated person). When companies rely on

---

17.   This may consist of legal proceedings against the incriminated person or against the whistle-blower if he or she has maliciously submitted a report. The latter proceedings arise in defamation suits.
18.   WP 117, *supra* note 7, at 12.

their legitimate interests for investigating reports as the legal basis for processing, they must balance these interests against the rights of the individuals named in the corresponding report. This means that persons named in the report should receive notification about the processing and be able to apply their individual rights vis-à-vis the personal data processed about them.

1. Notice—Communication about Implication in Report

The required notification communication should be issued in compliance with the rules of Article 11 of the Directive. Importantly, where the personal data is collected from external individuals submitting a report, they will also need to receive notice. This expands the notice requirement beyond merely employees when hotlines are open to external parties for reporting and similarly, for being reported on. Individuals who have been reported to the hotline should receive notice "as soon as practicably possible after the data concerning them are recorded."[19]

In practice, notice to an implicated person can be delayed "where there is substantial risk that such notification would be jeopardise the ability of the company to effectively investigate the allegation or gather the necessary evidence," i.e., to prevent destruction or alteration of evidence for the duration of the risk.[20]

The Working Party highlights that this exception should be applied "restrictively," but it is difficult to imagine in what scenario notifying the implicated person would not trigger the destruction or alteration of evidence of a crime—perhaps when the report includes all the necessary facts and evidence?

F. Right of Access

The hotline will have to include a specific procedure allowing implicated persons to access and correct or update their personal data in the corresponding report where outdated, inaccurate, or incomplete. The rights and freedoms of other people involved in the hotline may be restricted to ensure the confidentiality of the hotline and the whistle-blower. Again this restriction should be applied on a case-by-case basis. The implicated person should never gain access or information about the whistle-blower on the basis of his or her right of access. However, where malicious reporting has occurred, the whistle-blower's identity may be disclosed.

Other data subjects should also be granted similar rights. This would be the case, for example, when a report is filed whereby certain witnesses or bystanders are named in a certain factual situation.

G. Confidentiality and Information Security Measures

The company should "take all reasonable technical and organizational precautions to preserve the security of the data when it is gathered, circulated or conserved"[21] in the

---

19. *Id.* at 13.
20. *Id.* at 13–14.
21. *Id.*

hotline. These measures must be appropriate (proportionate) in light of the purposes of investigating the issues and must meet the information security requirements under the national laws of the relevant EU Member States. If an external service provider is running the hotline or is involved in the investigation of the reports, a data processing agreement pursuant to Article 17 of the Directive must be in place (see Chapter 3 Section IV).

Confidentiality of reporting should be guaranteed and third parties should be prevented from accessing the identity of the reporter. The hotline must include measures to guarantee that the whistle-blower's identity remains confidential and is not disclosed to the implicated person throughout the duration of the investigation, unless it is a case of a malicious report, where the implicated person would like to file a defamation or libel suit. Furthermore, national laws on corporate governance may provide for a specific measure for protecting the whistle-blower from retaliation in the form of certain discriminatory or disciplinary measures.

H. Management of Hotlines and Internal Handling

Companies should carefully consider the procedures for operating hotlines and how the hotlines and investigations will be managed. Third-party service providers may be used, as long as they commit to the Directive's Articles 17 and 16 requirements. See Chapter 3 Section IV.

Companies must have a separate, independent organization within the company for handling reports and leading investigations. The people in this department must be specially trained and dedicated, "limited in number and bound by specific confidentiality obligations."[22] The people handing these procedures should be separated from other departments—human resources, for example.

Furthermore, all information processed should be sent only to the persons within the group who need to know it, i.e., specifically responsible people, or for taking follow-up measures on the facts reported. All information should be treated confidentially and subject to security measures.

I. External Hotline Providers

Even if the hotline is outsourced, companies remain responsible for the processing of personal data within the hotline. External service hotline providers act as processors for the purposes of the application of the Directive. This means they will have to comply with specifications on processors such as acting only under the instructions of the controller and ensuring information security, confidentiality, and organizational measures for the protection of personal data. They should also apply the data retention periods as per instructions or obligations of the controller. The providers should communicate the information only to designated persons within a company. Additionally, companies should be in a position to audit or verify the processor's

---

22. *Id.* at 15.

compliance with the data processing agreement, its instructions, and compliance with data protection laws.

J. Preference for EU Treatment of Investigations

Due to the framework of hotlines, reports and personal data are often shared throughout the global company group.

> Taking the proportionality principle into account, the nature and seriousness of the alleged offence should in principle determine at what level, and thus in what country, assessment of the report should take place. As a rule, the Working Party believes that groups should deal with reports locally, i.e. in one EU country, rather than automatically share all the information with other companies in the group.[23]

WP 117 acknowledges exceptions, including broader communication of reports or facts when "communication is necessary for the investigation, depending on the nature or seriousness of the reported misconduct, or results from how the group is set up."[24] If a report incriminates another legal entity within the group or the company's local management, then data can be justified to being passed on; however, the communication should be subject to confidential and secure conditions.

K. Transfers

When an external provider is used for collection and processing of personal information within the hotline or when information is communicated to other affiliates within the company group outside of the European Union, the provisions on international transfers contained in the Directive will apply. In practice, most third-party hotline providers are Safe Harbor compliant or have facilities within the European Union to ensure that personal data is not transferred out of the European Union for the purposes of taking hotline reports.

Companies should keep these requirements in mind when drafting Model Contracts, preparing Safe Harbor certifications, or developing a BCR program. Similarly, notifications with the respective DPAs are required. Please note that many Member States have specific restrictions on the implementation of whistle-blowing hotlines (prior checking) and require additional formalities for the notification of such activities.[25]

---

23. *Id.* at 16.
24. *Id.*
25. For an in-depth look at hotlines and the EU challenges from a U.S. perspective, *see* D.C. Dowling, Jr., *Sarbanes-Oxley Whistleblower Hotlines across Europe: Directions through the Maze*, 42 Int'l Law. 1 (2008), at 12, http://eb.whitecase.com/files/News/005738d8-0cf4-424c-8b1a-419393eab02d/Presentation/NewsAttachment/54486b2d-b48b-4337-a73c-3f7554c7f92f/Alert_GlobalHR_090808_whistleblower.pdf.

National Guidance on Hotlines from DPAs

Belgium
Privacy Commission Recommendation No. 1/2006 (Nov. 29, 2006): www.privacycommission .be/sites/privacycommission/files/documents/recommandation_01_2006.pdf

France
CNIL Guideline Document for the Implementation of Whistleblowing Systems in Compliance with the French Data Protection Act of 6 January 1978, as amended in August 2004, relating to Information Technology, Data Filing Systems and Liberties (Nov. 11, 2005), http://www.cnil.fr/fileadmin/documents/en/CNIL-recommandations-whistleblowing--VA.pdf. Please note that the CNIL has issued a standard authorization decision no. AU-004 that has simplified the authorization process. http://www.cnil.fr/documentation/ deliberations/deliberation/delib/83/

Germany
Ad Hoc working group, Dusseldorfer Kreis, Whistleblowing–Hotlines: Firmeninterne Warnsysteme und Beschäftigtendatenschutz, https://www.datenschutz-hamburg.de/ uploads/media/Handreichung_Whistleblowing-Hotlines.pdf.

Ireland
Irish Data Protection Commissioner's Guidance "Whistleblower" schemes and Compliance with the U.S. Sarbanes-Oxley Act http://www.dataprotection.ie/docs /Whistleblower/303.htm

The Netherlands
Dutch DPA's Opinion (Jan. 16, 2006), http://www.cbpweb.nl/Pages/uit_z2004-1233 .aspx

Spain
Creación de sistemas de denuncias internas en las empresas (mecanismos de "whistleblowing"), http://www.agpd.es/portalwebAGPD/canaldocumentacion/informes_juridicos/ otras_cuestiones/common/pdfs/2007-0128_Creaci-oo-n-de-sistemas-de-denuncias-internas-en-las-empresas-mecanismos-de-whistleblowing.pdf.

II. AUDITS AND FOREIGN CORRUPT PRACTICES ACT (AND OTHER ANTIBRIBERY/ANTICORRUPTION LEGISLATION)

A. Background on Corruption Compliance and Data Protection

The legal environment for anticorruption and antibribery (ACB) and anti–money laundering/counterterrorist financing (AML) has been changing rapidly due to a shift in a government focus on ethics. Globally, many intergovernmental organizations and groups have come out against corruption. Adding to these efforts, governments are actively trying to stop the flow of funds by terrorist groups and laundering of funds acquired through illegal activities.[26] Companies must establish their economic and financial stability through compliance solutions. At the same time, companies must ensure legal compliance and solidify their reputation for both the public and their stakeholders. Increasingly, the AML and ACB fights are coming together in corporate compliance programs. AML and ACB are both echoed in company codes of conduct, in ethics policies, and in the form of due diligence and risk assessments carried out by companies. Corporate compliance departments must balance competing compliance obligations; the most frustrating can be the conflicts with EU data protection rules.

The tension between, on the one hand AML and ACB laws, and on the other hand, data protection laws and regulations, arises when corporations seek information and documentation for their compliance efforts and reporting obligations when an individual's personal data is involved. Even more frustrating is the lack of guidance that exists to provide companies with solutions and balance to their compliance approach. Currently, there is no clear guidance provided for these issues; however, best practices are beginning to incorporate data protection concerns. Here we will present the regulatory landscape of data protection in ACB and AML compliance efforts and provide some practical considerations for companies to take into account. We will begin with a brief general introduction to ACB and AML laws and then present the data protection issues that typically arise in connection with the application of these laws.

B. A Short Overview of ACB and AML Laws

ACB legislation has its roots in the U.S. Foreign Corrupt Practices Act[27] (FCPA) of 1970. Although the FCPA was deemed as an important piece of legislation, the United States felt that it put U.S. businesses at a disadvantage compared with foreign companies as they were no longer able to engage in the payment of foreign

---

26. These bodies include the United Nations, World Bank, International Monetary Fund, World Trade Organization, Organization of American States, Council of Europe, and the European Union. OECD Convention. United Nations Convention against Corruption, Dec. 14, 2005, *see* http://www.unodc.org/documents/treaties/UNCAC/Publications/Convention/08-50026_E.pdf; United Nations Convention against Transnational Organized Crime and the Protocols thereto, Sept. 23, 2003, https://treaties.un.org/doc/Publication/MTDSG/Volume%20II/Chapter%20XVIII/XVIII-12.en.pdf; Paul Allan Schott, Reference Guide to Anti-Money Laundering and Combating the Financing of Terrorism And Supplement on Special Recommendation IX (International Bank for Reconstruction and Development, The International Monetary Fund and the World Bank, 2d ed. 2006), http://siteresources.worldbank.org/EXTAML/Resources/396511-1146581427871/Reference_Guide_AMLCFT_2ndSupplement.pdf; Inter-American Convention against Corruption, adopted Mar. 29, 1996, *available at* http://www.oas.org/juridico/english/Treaties/b-58.html;
OECD Convention on Combating Bribery of Foreign Public Officials in International Business Transactions, Feb. 15. 1999, http://www.oecd.org/daf/anti-bribery/ConvCombatBribery_ENG.pdf; Council of Europe, Criminal Law Convention on Corruption, Jan. 27, 1999, *available at* http://conventions.coe.int/Treaty/en/Treaties/Html/173.htm.
27. 15 U.S.C.A. §§ 78dd-1 (2010).

bribes. Now, this seems strange, but in many European countries, bribes were even acknowledged as an annual expense of a company. In 1997, the OECD Convention on Combating Bribery of Foreign Public Officials in International Business Transactions[28] was signed and Western countries were now on board with a global ACB standard. Since then, there has been an ever-increasing concern for global businesses to ensure ACB compliance. The passage of the UK Anti-Bribery Act of 2010[29] evidenced this far-reaching concern. Furthermore, the Commission has published a decision establishing an anticorruption reporting mechanism for periodic assessment,[30] driven in part by the commitments established in the Stockholm Program.[31] The program outlines policy plans for justice and home affairs for EU Member States from 2010 through 2014, and it includes both ACB and AML commitments.

Similarly, following the September 11, 2001 attacks on New York's World Trade Center, AML legislation grew and was marked by a rapidly changing regulatory environment for controls on financial transactions. The intergovernmental organization, the Financial Action Task Force (on Money Laundering) (FATF),[32] has issued recommendations on AML (FATF Recommendations).[33] These are also taken into account by the EU Directive 2005/60/EC[34] which has been implemented by Member States and which is currently in the process of revision.[35] The United States

---

28. Convention on Combating Bribery of Foreign Public Officials in International Business Transactions, OECD, Dec. 17, 1997, S. TREATY DOC. No. 105-43, reprinted at 37 I.L.M. 1, 4 (1998), http://www.oecd .org/daf/anti-bribery/ConvCombatBribery_ENG.pdf.
29. Bribery Act, 2010, c. 23 (U.K.), *available at* http://www.legislation.gov.uk/ukpga/2010/23.
30. Commission Decision of June 6, 2011, Establishing an EU Anti-Corruption Reporting Mechanism for Periodic Assessment (EU Anti-Corruption Report) C(2011) 3673 final (June 6, 2011), http://ec.europa .eu/dgs/home-affairs/what-we-do/policies/pdf/com_decision_2011_3673_final_en.pdf.
31. Eur. Council, *The Stockholm Programme—An Open and Secure Europe Serving and Protecting Citizens,* 2010 O.J. (C 115) 1, 23 (May 4, 2010), *available at* http://eur-lex.europa.eu/legal-content/EN/TXT/ PDF/?uri=CELEX:52010XG0504(01)&from=EN. The European Council invites the Commission to: "develop indicators, on the basis of existing systems and common criteria, to measure efforts in the fight against corruption, in particular in the areas of the acquis (public procurement, financial control, etc) and to develop a comprehensive anti-corruption policy, in close cooperation with the Council of Europe Group of States against Corruption (GRECO). The Commission should submit a report in 2010 to the Council on the modalities for the Union to accede to GRECO."
32. *See* http://www.fatf-gafi.org/.
33. FATF, *International Standards on Combating Money Laundering and the Financing of Terrorism & Proliferation: The FATF Recommendations* (Feb. 16, 2012), http://www.fatf-gafi.org/media/fatf/documents/ recommendations/pdfs/FATF_Recommendations.pdf.
34. Directive 2005/60/EC of the European Parliament and of the Council of 26 October 2005 on the prevention of the use of the financial system for the purpose of money laundering and terrorist financing, 2005 O.J. (L 309) 15 (Nov. 25, 2005) [hereinafter AML Directive], *available at* http://eur-lex.europa.eu/ legal-content/EN/TXT/PDF/?uri=CELEX:32005L0060&from=EN.
35. *See* Commission, *Report from the Commission to the European Parliament and the Council on the application of Directive 2005/60/EC on the prevention of the use of the financial system for the purpose of money laundering and terrorist financing* COM (2012) 168 final (Apr. 11, 2012), http://ec.europa.eu/ internal_market/company/docs/financial-crime/20120411_report_en.pdf.

has the Bank Secrecy Act of 1970[36] as well as the Money Laundering Control Act of 1986.[37] Increasingly, AML compliance efforts are coming more in line with the ACB—specifically, by way of due diligence and risk assessment requirements.

C. How Personal Data Fits In

The definition of personal data is quite broad under the Directive, which casts a wide net for data protection within compliance programs. Specifically, there are two main areas where data protection risks arise: risk assessments and due diligence. Both of these compliance tools are interlinked, as risk assessments sometimes come in the form of due diligence. Additionally, both AML and ACB guidance encourage companies and governments to use these tools for compliance.

1. Risk Assessments

Risk assessments in corruption compliance involve looking into a company's business and circumstances, including geographic locations and industrial sectors of operation to assess risk for foreign bribery and money laundering. For both ACB and AML, understanding risks within business is fundamental for compliance programs. The FATF Recommendations take a risk-based approach to company compliance efforts. The recent revision of the FATF Recommendations on AML strengthened obligations for high-risk situations.[38] Thus, it is essential that companies are able to understand the degree of risks presented for AML in order to properly follow the FATF Recommendations. Countries generally use the FATF Recommendations, but these are also directed at financial institutions. The outcome of the risk assessments will determine the compliance program, including the level of customer due diligence (CDD) necessary to achieve compliance.[39]

Financial institutions must identify certain risks and criteria that permit risk assessments to take place. This entails focusing on particular customers and customer groups as well as on specific transactions. Once there is an initial assessment, this process may continue after certain activities or when a customer's full risk profile develops. Additionally, financial institutions may adjust customer profiles based on information received from authorities, and they are subject to reporting obligations in case of suspicious activity.[40] This system inherently encourages the creation of customer and group profiles and reporting, which invokes concerns similar to those that arise from hotlines.

---

36. Currency and Foreign Transactions Reporting Act of 1970, Pub. L. No. 91-508, 84 Stat. 1118 (1970) (codified at 31 U.S.C. §§ 321, 5311–5314, 5316–5322 (1988 & Supp. V 1993)).
37. Pub. L. No. 99-570, 100 Stat. 3207 (1986) (codified at 18 U.S.C. §§ 1956–57 (1988)).
38. FATF, International Standards on Combating Money Laundering and the Financing of Terrorism and Proliferation, *supra* note 32.
39. *Id.* at 15.
40. *Id.* at 19.

The Working Party has drafted several letters and issued recommended guidance on the proposed amendments to the AML/ACB overhaul.[41] In its recommendation, the Working Party encourages financial institutions to include prior assessments of privacy impact prior to implementing risk assessments and management programs. The recommendations for PIAs are directed both toward financial institutions and countries prior to implementing laws.

An analogous recommendation for the use and reliance of risk assessments is also outlined in the UK guidance on the Bribery Act. The guidance highlights commonly encountered risks in business opportunities and business partners. Business opportunity risk occurs in high-value projects, projects with multiple contractors or middlemen, or in circumstances in which projects are not undertaken at market prices or with clear and legitimate objectives.[42] Further, risks with business partners may be higher if using intermediaries when dealing with foreign officials or JV partners, as well as in relationships with politically exposed persons (PEPs) where the proposed business involves or is linked to an official.[43] Risk assessments inherently will involve procedures within due diligence, as this is the main mechanism in which companies are able to identify and mitigate the risks posed.

2. Due Diligence

Due diligence is the main mechanism that companies' compliance departments use to identify and mitigate risks within businesses. This is true for both AML and ACB, thus it affects financial institutions and companies alike that are dealing abroad. The actual form of due diligence will depend on the company or financial institution and the regulations that apply to them. For AML compliance, financial institutions use CDD, as well as know your customer (KYC) due diligence and reporting of suspicious transactions (STRs). In ACB compliance, companies use interrogative questionnaires, investigations, and general research on associated persons (partners, agents, etc.).[44] Both ACB and AML compliance involve financial profiling and possible forms of blacklisting of individuals. The FCPA includes obligations to determine whether individuals (partners, agents, representatives, etc.) are qualified persons or persons with professional ties to the government, as well as reputations with local countries, local bankers, clients, and other businesses. Other internal controls include reporting

---

41. *See, e.g.,* Working Party, *Opinion 14/2011 on Data Protection Issues Related to the Prevention of Money Laundering and Terrorist Financing,* and its Annex (WP 186) (June 13, 2011) [hereinafter collectively WP 186], http://ec.europa.eu/justice/data-protection/article-29/documentation/opinion-recommendation/files/2011/wp186_en.pdf and http://ec.europa.eu/justice/data-protection/article-29/documentation/opinion-recommendation/files/2011/wp186_en_annex.pdf.

42. *The Bribery Act 2010: Guidance about Procedures Which Relevant Commercial Organizations Can Put into Place to Prevent Persons Associated with Them from Bribing (Section 9 of the Bribery Act 2010),* Ministry of Justice (U.K.), (Feb. 11, 2012) [hereinafter UK Bribery Act Guidance], at 26, https://www.gov.uk/government/uploads/system/uploads/attachment_data/file/181762/bribery-act-2010-guidance.pdf.

43. *Id.*

44. UK Bribery Act Guidance, *supra* note 42, at 28.

mechanisms (such as hotlines, as we have seen previously) and investigations (like private background checks and verification of individuals based on publicly available information or databanks). Increasingly companies are outsourcing risk determination and due diligence onto partners and agents, requiring them to clear or attest that their local business partners, suppliers, and vendors, are not in violation of such laws. In this way, companies are able to pass on some level of risk; however, this increases the proliferation of these practices.

Within the context of both corporate mechanisms for risk assessments and due diligence, the potential for processing personal data arises. As soon this is done by an EU-based company or in the European Union by a foreign company, EU data protection rules apply. As such, companies must also ensure that their compliance efforts, either in AML or ACB or both, are done in compliance with EU data protection rules.

D. Data Protection Issues
1. Legal Basis for Processing

ACB and AML compliance processing activities (such as those outlined earlier) must rely on a legal basis for processing. Therefore, the compliance activities must be processed lawfully under a certain basis provided by law. Generally, the main bases are the consent of the data subject, i.e., the individual, where necessary for the performance of a contract, where necessary to comply with a legal obligation, or where necessary to uphold the legitimate interest of the company. Furthermore, the processing of sensitive data is generally a prohibited subject to more narrow exceptions like consent.

For most AML and ACB activities, and processing in general, it is tempting for companies to rely on the consent of the relevant individuals or on the legitimate interests of the company as a basis for the legitimacy of processing personal data. However, the Working Party has noted that within the context of AML, these bases pose serious issues. First, the legitimate interests of the company are not transparent, especially considering that many risk assessments occur intrabank. This means that the risk assessments are carried out based on a financial institution's subjectively determined need. This need is directly in conflict with the foreseeability of the law under Article 8 of the ECHR.[45] Furthermore, consent is deemed not to be freely given in most AML situations as the Working Party considers that data subjects typically do not have the power to revoke consent because there is no option to opt out of CDD. Within the context of AML litigation, the Working Party encourages the following bases for processing: legal obligations to which the controller is subject (Article 7 (c) of the Directive[46]) and the performance of a task carried out in the public interest or in

---

45. ECHR, art. 8.
46. Directive, art. 7(c), at 40.

the exercise of official authority vested in the controller or in a third party to whom the data is disclosed (Article 7(e) of the Directive[47]).[48]

Although these bases are not problematic at first blush, most AML as well as ACB regulations and conventions are open-ended with respect to the specifics of what companies need to do in practice. This leaves companies the flexibility to choose how to implement risk assessments and due diligence. Most concrete suggestions for compliance risk assessments and due diligence are provided in soft law, such as international recommendations on which the laws are based or guidance from regulators or authorities. Thus, reliance on the legal obligations may be difficult for companies in practice. Furthermore, the AML recommendation of the Working Party is in contradiction to the Working Party Opinion on Reporting Hotlines, which accepts the balance of legitimate interests of a company.[49]

2. Controller/Processor Determinations

Companies' roles in AML and ACB compliance will not always be clear. This is particularly so when companies are working with a network of affiliates and subsidiaries or when the compliance obligations are based on non-EU legislation. The FCPA is a good example of this. In some situations, groups can find that a parent company is in fact a data controller based outside of the European Union. Additionally, with the outsourcing of due diligence, companies will find themselves subject to the requirements associated with the use of processors. It is essential that companies consider the roles in which affiliates and parent companies will act with respect to their AML or ACB compliance. When external companies provide research and due diligence about partners and agents, companies should be sure to document their relationship and ensure that the research company—in its role as the processor—is aware of the data protection laws that govern the processing.

3. Notices

Companies processing personal data are required to provide information notices to the relevant data subjects whose information they are processing.[50] In the context of providing notices to customers, partners, and agents in AML and ACB compliance, the provision of notices requirement is often overlooked. Compliance with the provision of notices is not always practical for businesses. Generally the best approach is to ensure that company privacy policies include their compliance efforts and outline the methods by which personal data will be processed. Alternatively, companies may develop specific notices for compliance efforts, which can be changed accordingly with the compliance program as it develops and changes. These notices should ensure transparency by outlining internal data protection measures and how these

---

47. Directive, art. 7(e), at 40.
48. WP 186 Annex, *supra* note 41, at 8.
49. *See id.*; WP 117, *supra* note 7, at 8.
50. Directive, arts. 10–11, at 41–42.

fit in with AML/ACB compliance programs.[51] Particularly, these policies should include:

- The nature of processing operations and categories of data used;
- The purposes of processing;
- The legal basis for processing;
- The role of the controller and the processor, if relevant, in the data processing activities;
- Outlining safeguards for personal data; and
- Additional information that may be relevant under the circumstances, including when third-party disclosures will be made (to financial intelligence units, other group companies, or governmental authorities), procedures on how to exercise individual rights of access, correction and deletion, sources of data, whether responses and provision of information are required or not, data retention periods, and the effects of profiling, where relevant.[52]

The Working Party highlighted that it would be efficient to have notices and policies made public, allowing all relevant persons to have access to the procedures in place, lending to transparency.[53]

4. Proportionality and Purpose Limitation

A fundamental tension exists between AML and ACB compliance and data protection laws. Companies need sufficient and descriptive detail about individual clients, customers, business partners, agents, and so on in order to have accurate and reliable compliance documentation. At the same time, the overinclusion of personal information on individuals risks violating data protection laws. Under the data quality principles of Article 6 of the Directive, personal data must be proportionate, accurate, up to date, relevant, complete, and not excessive in relation to the purposes for which it is collected or subsequently processed.[54] When carrying out risk assessments or due diligence that include personal details on individuals, companies need to ensure proportionality; this means ensuring a balance between the rights of the individual to privacy and the protection of his or her information and the company's interest in documenting compliance with its AML or ACB commitments. Oftentimes this balance is difficult to achieve, as companies would prefer to collect more information than necessarily required for compliance. Nevertheless, by restricting the collection to only the information required, companies will be able to enjoy a certain degree of comfort with respect to privacy and AML/ACB compliance.

---

51. *See generally* WP 186 Annex, *supra* note 41, at 13–16.
52. *Id*. at 13.
53. *Id*. at 13, and 15.
54. Directive, art. 6, at 40.

5. Retention Policies

Personal data should not be kept in an identifiable format for longer than is necessary to achieve the purposes for which the data was collected or subsequently processed and it must not be processed in a way that is inconsistent with these purposes. Companies need to ensure that they keep information for only as long as necessary to fulfill their obligations. Oddly, the AML Directive includes a minimum retention period for companies to keep information on compliance with its obligations.[55] The Working Party has recommended in its Opinion 14/2011 that Member States and the European Union consider also specifying retention maximums, in order to provide guidance on retention periods. Retention periods and policies cannot specify that data can be kept forever.[56]

6. Data Transfers

As has been explored earlier, special rules apply to data transfers outside the European Economic Area (EEA) to countries that have not been officially recognized as providing an adequate level of protection equivalent to the protection level under EU law. There are concerns with the sharing of personal data collected in AML and ACB compliance. Often, companies transfer the results of risk assessments and due diligence back to U.S.- or non–EU-based parent companies. There are also concerns with intergovernmental cooperation in the field of AML and ACB compliance, as authorities are increasingly sharing information on individuals with one another in the fight against corruption. The Working Party recommends a balanced data-sharing scheme, which is to say a push regime where the information is actively provided by the EU-based authorities upon request or upon a need for the relevant information.[57]

E. Summary

Despite the fundamental tension between AML/ACB compliance obligations and data protection rules, it is possible to reconcile both within a company's compliance program. Although the legal basis for processing personal data in risk assessments and due diligence is not entirely clear in every jurisdiction, it is anticipated that data protection concerns will be included in any future AML directive that results from the current revision process for the AML Directive and in any ACB best practice guidance at the EU level. More importantly, companies should be clear about what role they play when processing personal data for compliance and should ensure that any third-party actors, i.e., processors, are also contractually bound by confidentiality and information security commitments. Furthermore, companies should work to develop privacy notices and statements regarding their AML/ACB processing to ensure transparency and comply with relevant notice requirements. Companies

---

55.   AML Directive, art. 30.
56.   WP 186 Annex, *supra* note 40, at 22–23.
57.   WP 186 Annex, *supra* note 41, at 26, 27.

should also ensure that all data collected for compliance initiatives are proportional and narrowed to the scope necessary. This also applies to the duration of data storage for compliance, as companies should not keep personal data longer than necessary. Finally, companies need to ensure that information sharing between group companies and especially with third parties and partners internationally is in compliance with EU data protection law. This means providing for transfer mechanisms and procedures for the sharing of information.

6

Customers and Marketing

I. DIRECT ELECTRONIC MARKETING AND THE E-PRIVACY DIRECTIVE

General marketing practices involving the processing of personal data of individuals are governed by the Directive and its corresponding principles. Article 14(b) of the Directive grants an individual the right

> [t]o object, on request and free of charge, to the processing of personal data relating to him which the controller anticipates being processed for the purposes of direct marketing, or to be informed before personal data are disclosed for the first time to third parties or used on their behalf for the purposes of direct marketing, and to be expressly offered the right to object free of charge to such disclosures or uses.[1]

This right permits all individuals to object to, or opt out of, processing for direct marketing purposes and the disclosure of their personal data to third parties for the same purposes. This opt-out basis, together with the core principles of the Directive should be applied to personal data in the context of marketing activities, together with any applicable national laws regulating marketing practices.[2] In practice, this means that companies must comply, inter alia, with the notice requirement and have an applicable legal basis under Article 7 for processing.[3]

However, where electronic communications are used to directly transmit advertising or marketing materials to customers and consumers, the Directive is supplemented by the e-Privacy Directive. In addition to regulating Internet Service Providers and providers of "publicly available electronic communications service," the e-Privacy Directive seeks to protect the "legitimate interests" of legal persons

---

1. Directive 95/46/EC of the European Parliament and of the Council of 24 Oct. 1995 on the protection of individuals with regard to the processing of personal data and on the free movement of such data [hereinafter Directive], 1995 O.J. (L 281) 31 (Nov. 23, 1995), art. 14(b), at 43.
2. *See* Directive, recital 71, at 38: "this Directive does not stand in the way of a Member State's regulating marketing activities aimed at consumers residing in territory in so far as such regulation does not concern the protection of individuals with regard to the processing of personal data."
3. The various legal bases for processing are discussed in Chapter 2 Section IV.

and the "fundamental rights" of natural persons.[4] Thus, the e-Privacy Directive sits at a peculiar crossroads of telecommunication regulation and privacy and data protection. Here, we will specifically look at the EU rules on direct marketing by electronic communications, including e-mail, fax, automated calling, and electronic messages, such as multimedia message service (MMS) and short message service (SMS) (e-marketing). It is important to keep in mind that in addition to compliance with the e-Privacy Directive, organizations will also have to comply with the provisions of the Directive (95/46/EC). Here, the discussion will begin with (1) an introduction to the e-Privacy Directive, followed by (2) a discussion of the e-Privacy Directive specifically applied to e-marketing issues, and it will finish with (3) an exploration of a code of conduct used in the direct marketing sector—that of the Federation of European Direct Marketing (FEDMA).

A. Privacy, e-Marketing, and the e-Privacy Directive

The e-Privacy Directive is a successor to Directive 97/66/EC that covered personal data and privacy in the telecommunications sector.[5] The e-Privacy Directive brought personal data and privacy in telecommunications into the Internet era, with its adoption in 2002.[6] Although the e-Privacy Directive contains provisions on e-marketing, it is also concerned with privacy and the protection of personal data (including location data and telecommunications traffic data) in the electronic communications sector, including mobile and fixed-line telecommunications services.

The e-Privacy Directive applies to e-marketing, dealing with a gamut of issues in this sector such as (a) an opt-in requirement to receive commercial communications and the concept of prior consent, (b) spam or "unsolicited communications" and the existing customer exception, (c) recent guidance on the existing customer exception to the general rule, and (d) notice and transparency requirements. Each will be examined in order.

1. An Opt-in Requirement to Receive Commercial Communications and the Concept of Prior Consent

The e-Privacy Directive is, accordingly, the EU legislative instrument that established the characteristic opt-in principle of EU law with respect to e-marketing. It sets out

---

4. Directive 2002/58/EC of the European Parliament and of the Council of 12 July 2002, concerning the processing of personal data and the protection of privacy in the electronic communications sector (Directive on privacy and electronic communications), 2002 O.J. (L 201) 37, (July 31, 2002) [hereinafter e-Privacy Directive], recital 12, at 38.

5. Directive 97/66/EC of the European Parliament and of the Council of 15 December 1997 Concerning the Processing of Personal Data and the Protection of Privacy in the Telecommunications Sector, 1998 O.J. (L 24) 1 (Jan. 30, 1998) [hereinafter Directive 97/66/EC].

6. *See* GRAHAM SMITH, INTERNET LAW AND REGULATION 437 (4th ed. 2007), para. 7.3.1 (§ 7-011), at 692. The 1997 Directive was seen as "out of date" almost as soon as it appeared and "it was far from clear how—if at all—it would apply to the internet and other developing technology." As an example, the e-Privacy Directive extended provisions on "unsolicited calls" to e-mail. *Compare* Directive 97/66/EC, *supra* note 5, art. 12, at 6 *with* e-Privacy Directive, *supra* note 4, art. 13, at 45.

the requirement that "prior consent" of the relevant recipients ("subscribers" or, since amendment of the e-Privacy Directive described later, "subscribers or users") must be obtained for "electronic mail for the purposes of direct marketing."[7] This opt-in requirement is aimed at prohibiting spam. "Electronic mail" is defined broadly to include "any text, voice, sound or image message sent over a public communications network which can be stored in the network or in the recipient's terminal equipment until it is collected by the recipient."[8] As such, it includes SMS messages as well.[9] The Directive 2009/136/EC[10] that amended the e-Privacy Directive makes it clear that MMS messages "and other kinds of similar applications" are covered, too.[11]

The Working Party discussed the opt-in principle in early advice, indicating that its application to e-mail is merely a continuance of an earlier policy aimed at the use of automated faxes and calls.[12] Consent to the receipt of a communication must be given *before* sending the e-marketing communication and may not be obtained through a general communication asking for consent. Again, the Working Party highlights that the request for consent must include a "legitimate, explicit and specific" purpose.

Pre-checked boxes on websites are not acceptable for indicating consent, as is the case for when consent is implied "unless opposition is made," which would be considered an "opt-out."[13] More generally, the Working Party highlights that the necessary consent to receiving e-marketing communications is "not specific to communications for direct marketing purposes" and may be obtained through many means. One practical example is the checking of a box to accept general terms and conditions when registering for a website, where consent to the sending of e-marketing is expressly sought. Again, the consent must comply with general requirements—such as it being "informed, specific and freely given."[14] Where consent is sought for giving data to third parties, this should be asked for specifically.[15] This would include situations when asking to send data to partners or affiliates, for example.

---

7. e-Privacy Directive, *supra* note 4, art. 13(1), at 45.

8. *Id.* art. 2(h), at 43.

9. *See id.* recital 40, at 41.

10. *See* Directive 2009/136/EC of the European Parliament and of the Council of 25 Nov. 2009, amending Directive 2002/22/EC on universal service and users' rights relating to electronic communications networks and services, the e-Privacy Directive, and Regulation (EC) No. 2006/2004 on cooperation between national authorities responsible for the enforcement of consumer protection laws, 2009 O.J. (L337) 11 (Dec. 18, 2009).

11. *Id.* recital 67, at 20.

12. *See* Working Party, *Opinion 5/2004 on Unsolicited Communications for Marketing Purposes under Article 13 of Directive 2002/58/EC* (WP 90) (Feb. 27, 2004), at 3–4, http://ec.europa.eu/justice/policies/privacy/docs/wpdocs/2004/wp90_en.pdf.

13. *Id.* at 5.

14. *Id.* at 4–5.

15. *Id.* at 5.

The Working Party later underscored this latter concept, reminding us that "consent based on individuals' silence" is not suitable.[16] It gives an example of an online book-seller sending an e-mail to the members of its customer loyalty program telling them that their data will be handed over to an advertising company and giving them two weeks to respond, failing which they would be considered to consent. In this case the consent would not be "valid, unambiguous consent."[17]

2. The Existing Customer Exception

Article 13 of the e-Privacy Directive on "unsolicited communication" (spam) allows for an exception to the opt-in consent requirement. This exception applies to existing customers, where either a natural or a legal person receives an e-mail address from a customer in connection with a sale of a good or service, then that e-mail address may be used by the same person for the direct marketing of "its own similar products or services" so long as the customers are "clearly and distinctly" given the opportunity to opt out, without charge, both at the time of the collection of the customer's e-mail and address and upon each communication. Therefore, when there is an existing customer relationship, an organization may send e-marketing communications to the customer when it relates to similar products or services.

The provisions of this exception have been described as "quite limited," as they would not cover, for example, the case where a company "buys in an email mailing list."[18] Only the company's existing customers are covered—those for whom it has already collected an e-mail address in connection with the sale of its own goods and services. What this covers in practice is more difficult to distinguish: does the organization need to have an established contract for the sale of goods or services in order to send such e-marketing communications? Could an organization utilize prospects or business partners that it is in close contact with? The safest case would be where the contact is an existing customer under contract. Nevertheless, for an organization's marketing department, such rigid constraints may not be practical; for example, if a prospective customer provides a business card, does that qualify as opt-in consent, or should that individual be asked to sign a consent form in addition? Furthermore, what is a similar product or service? If a consumer buys a dress through an online retailer, can that retailer now send e-marketing communications relating to its men's suit line?

As such e-marketing practices occupy a border area between regulation of marketing and advertising and the protection of an individual's personal data, much ambiguity exists. It is always good to assess local business practices and to keep in mind that circumstances differ substantially when working in the business-to-business sector versus when dealing directly with consumers. Business-to-consumer e-marketing

---

16. *See* Working Party, *Opinion 15/2011 on the Definition of Consent* (WP 187) (July 13, 2011), at 24, http://ec.europa.eu/justice/data-protection/article-29/documentation/opinion-recommendation/files/2011/wp187_en.pdf.

17. *Id.*

18. *See* GRAHAM SMITH, *supra* note 6, para. 7.3.3 (§ 7-013) at 693.

should be conducted carefully to ensure that consumer information is protected and consumer preferences are being respected. Companies need to treat such relationships with particular care and attention as brand and organizational reputation is more exposed in such circumstances.

In addition to the opt-in requirement and its relevant exemption, all e-marketing communications must include an opt-out method that is easy to use. Any refusal by the customer of use of his or her e-mail in this connection must be respected.[19] Again, as mentioned above, the provisions of the Directive with respect to the legitimate collection of personal data (and, more generally, its privacy principles) must be complied with.

3. Recent Guidance on the Existing Customer Exception

On April 2, 2013, the Working Party issued an opinion on purpose limitation (WP 203),[20] which specifically dealt with the existing customer exception in Article 13. In WP 203, the Working Party indicated that this provision (it recalls that such Article 13 does not apply to "[m]ore traditional means of direct marketing" such as postal mail, with respect to which the Directive would apply) showed how the data subject's reasonable expectations and the data collection context may have an impact on an assessment of legal grounds for compatibility of processing.[21] While further processing of the data for marketing may be lawful, it may be subject to different safeguards, taking into consideration the context and the relationship between the controllers and the data subject. One case for this may be the "sharing of information with data brokers or other third parties in order to develop more effective segmentation in direct mailings."[22] In addition, the Working Party notes that data subjects have the right to object to any processing for direct marketing under Article 14(b) of the Directive, free of charge, and that infrastructure must be set up so that this right can be effectively exercised.[23]

4. Notice/Transparency

More generally, if direct marketing via e-mail is used, the e-mail must not "disguise or conceal the identity of the sender on whose behalf the communication is made,"[24] which would violate Article 6 of the e-Commerce Directive.[25] That article provides,

---

19. Directive 2009/136/EC, *supra* note 10, art. 1(25), at 31 (containing the amended art. 13(2) of the e-Privacy Directive).

20. Working Party, *Opinion 03/2013 on Purpose Limitation* (WP 203) (Apr. 2, 2013), http://ec.europa .eu/justice/data-protection/article-29/documentation/opinion-recommendation/files/2013/wp203_en.pdf.

21. *Id.* at 34

22. *Id.* at 34–35.

23. *Id.* at 35.

24. Directive 2009/136/EC, *supra* note 10, art. 2(7), at 31 (containing the amended art. 13(4) of the e-Privacy Directive).

25. Directive 2000/31/EC of the European Parliament and of the Council of 8 June 2000 on Certain Legal Aspects of Information Society Services, in Particular Electronic Commerce, in the Internal Market (Directive on Electronic Commerce), 2000 O.J. (L 178) 1 (Jul. 17, 2000) [hereinafter e-Commerce Directive].

in relevant part, that at a minimum, "commercial communications" that are part of an "information society service"[26] should meet the following conditions:

(a) the commercial communication shall be clearly identifiable as such;

(b) the natural or legal person on whose behalf the commercial communication is made shall be clearly identifiable.[27]

Thus, a direct marketing e-mail (or SMS or MMS) must clearly indicate that it is a commercial communication and disclose the party on whose behalf it is sent.

5. Protections

Unlike the Directive, which secures the fundamental rights of natural persons, the e-Privacy Directive protects the rights of natural persons and the "legitimate interests" of legal persons as well. This section will now discuss the protection of these "legitimate interests," and then examine the possibility of opt-out registers as one specific form of protection, before turning briefly to certain exclusions.

a. Protection of the "Legitimate Interests" of Legal Persons

The e-Privacy Directive, as amended, provides that Member States shall ensure that "legitimate interests" of legal persons who are subscribers shall also be protected insofar as unsolicited communications are concerned, and that both natural and legal persons affected by an infringement of the domestic law provisions adopted under Article 13 shall have recourse to legal proceedings, in addition to any applicable administrative remedies, and it allows an "electronic communications service provider" to bring proceedings in defense of its legitimate interests as well.[28] In the latter case, Directive 2009/136/EC recognizes that such party makes substantial investments fighting spam and is "better able to detect and identify spammers."[29]

b. Opt-out Registers

Where Member States set up an "opt-out" register for unsolicited communications to a legal person (mostly business users), the provisions of Article 7 of the e-Commerce Directive apply.[30] That article provides that an allowed unsolicited commercial communication shall be clearly and unambiguously indicated as such "as soon as it is received by the recipient." In addition, "Member States shall take measures to ensure that

---

26. An "Information Society service" means "any service normally provided for remuneration, at a distance, by electronic means and at the individual request of a recipient of services." Directive 98/48/EC of the European Parliament and of the Council of 20 July 1998, 1998 O.J. (L 217) 18 (Aug. 5, 1998), amending Directive 98/34/EC of the European Parliament and of the Council of 22 June 1998, Laying Down a Procedure for the Provision of Information in the Field of Technical Standards and Regulations, 1998 O.J, (L 204) 37 (Jul. 21, 1998), art. 1(2) at 21 (amending art. 1 of Directive 98/34/EC by adding in a new para. 2).
27. *Id*. art. 6(a)–(b), at 11.
28. Directive 2009/136/EC, *supra* note 10, art. 1(25), at 31 (containing the amended arts. 13(5)–(6)).
29. *Id*. recital 68.
30. *Id*. recital 45.

services providers undertaking unsolicited commercial communications by electronic mail consult regularly and respect the opt-out registers in which natural persons not wishing to receive such commercial communications can register themselves."[31] Thus, the e-Privacy Directive recalls the obligation (contained in the e-Commerce Directive) to consult and respect the opt-out register. Many countries around the world,[32] as well as in Europe, have set up different types of opt-out registers to varying degrees of success. Some registers are for calls, SMS messages, or e-mails. Additionally, some countries require that organizations check these lists to ensure that their contact databases properly reflect individual preferences—thereby shifting the burden onto companies to keep their mailing or marketing lists up to date and correct.

c. Certain Exclusions

Finally, Directive 2009/136/EC makes it clear that the e-Privacy Directive does not apply to "closed user groups" or "corporate networks,"[33] meaning that it should not apply to intranets or to in-house chat functions, for example. However, such networks are not typically those used for unsolicited commercial communications!

B. A Sectoral Code of Conduct in the Direct Marketing Area: The FEDMA Code of Conduct and Annex

In connection with direct marketing, the FEDMA has established a European Code of Practice for the Use of Personal Data in Direct Marketing. The Working Party has opined on this code (or at least on part of it), and we will now look at this attempt at self-regulation. The Working Party opinions were rendered under the authority of the Directive's Article 27(3) dealing with Community codes of conduct. That provision provides as follows:

> Draft Community codes, and amendments or extensions to existing Community codes, may be submitted to the Working Party referred to in Article 29. This Working Party shall determine, among other things, whether the drafts submitted to it are in accordance with the national provisions adopted pursuant to this Directive. If it sees fit, the authority shall seek the views of data subjects or their representatives. The Commission may ensure appropriate publicity for the codes which have been approved by the Working Party.[34]

A FEDMA Code was submitted in 2003 and the Working Party rendered an opinion in WP 77 on it during that year. There it found that the Code was in accordance with Article 27, dealing with significant matters such as the right to object

---

31. e-Commerce Directive, *supra* note 25, art. 7, at 11.
32. *See*, *e.g.*, the Do-Not-E-Mail registry provision of the CAN-SPAM (Controlling the Assault of Non-Solicited Pornography and Marketing) Act of 2003, 15 U.S.C. § 7708.
33. Directive 2009/136/EC, *supra* note 10, recital 55, at 18.
34. Directive, art. 27(3), at 47.

to processing for direct marketing purposes and inclusion of specific provisions intended to protect children (such as when they provide data in order to participate in promotional games). In addition, a Data Protection Committee was created by FEDMA to monitor the FEDMA Code's application.[35] During the period from 2005 until 2010, FEDMA corresponded with the Working Party about an annex to the FEDMA Code that was to cover on-line marketing (Annex). Comments were made, redrafting was done by FEDMA, further meetings were held about a completely revised version of the Annex, and finally, in 2010, a new version of the Annex was submitted to the Working Party by FEDMA.[36]

In its WP 174 about the Annex,[37] the Working Party noted that the Annex closely follows the structure of the FEDMA Code that it had already approved, and that the content of the Annex improves the other document's quality and clarifies issues.[38] The Working Party concluded that it was satisfied that the Annex is in accordance with the Directive and the e-Privacy Directive. The Working Party did caution that Directive 2009/136/EC may require amendment to the Annex, especially regarding cookies and spyware.[39]

II. BEHAVIORAL MARKETING AND COOKIES

EU privacy and data protection law affects companies engaged in the online environment, whether through the use of behavioral marketing (or advertising) or, more generally, through the use of "cookies."[40]

A. Terms Used

In the e-Privacy Directive, the term "cookie" is not specifically defined. However, the e-Privacy Directive speaks about "devices" stored on "terminal equipment" of users. The UK data protection agency (UK ICO) has described a "cookie" as follows:

> [a] small file, typically of letters and numbers, downloaded on to a device when the user accesses certain websites. Cookies are then sent back to originating

---

35. Working Party, *Opinion 3/2003 on the European Code of Conduct of FEDMA for the Use of Personal Data in Direct Marketing* (WP 77) (Jun. 13, 2003), http://ec.europa.eu/justice/policies/privacy/docs/wpdocs/2003/wp77_en.pdf.

36. FEDMA, *European Code of Practice for the Use of Personal Data in Direct Marketing Electronic Communications Annex* (Jun. 2010), http://ec.europa.eu/justice/policies/privacy/docs/wpdocs/2010/wp174_annex_en.pdf.

37. Working Party, *Opinion 4/2010 on the European Code of Conduct of FEDMA for the Use of Personal Data in Direct Marketing* (WP 174) (July 13, 2010), http://ec.europa.eu/justice/data-protection/article-29/documentation/opinion-recommendation/files/2010/wp174_en.pdf.

38. *Id.* at 4.

39. *Id.* at 5–6.

40. For an understanding of cookies in the marketing context, *see, e.g.*, DAVE CHAFFEY & FIONA ELLIS-CHADWICK, DIGITAL MARKETING, STRATEGY, IMPLEMENTATION AND PRACTICE 168–70 (5th ed. 2012).

website on each subsequent visit. Cookies are useful because they allow a website to recognise a user's device.[41]

The e-Privacy Directive regulates the use of cookies, citing personal privacy concerns, as an example:[42]

[s]py ware, web bugs, hidden identifiers and other similar devices [that] can enter the user's terminal without their knowledge in order to gain access to information, to store hidden information or to trace the activities of the user and may seriously intrude upon the privacy of these users.[43]

The "terminal" referred to above is generally a computer or a mobile device, such as a tablet or a smartphone.

B. Applicable Law

As cookies are essential to behavioral marketing, we will commence our analysis with the relevant EU law applicable to cookies, but before we do, a word about applicable law. We have examined the application of the Directive generally to the processing of personal data. As we have seen, applicable law under the Directive focuses on the location of the equipment or processing within the European Union (See Chapter 2 Section I.). In the case of cookies, if a collection of personal data is made through the use of cookies by a party outside of the European Union, the Working Party has long considered that the user's computer on which the cookie is placed may be considered to be the "equipment" under Article 4(1)(c) of the Directive. Assuming that it is located on the territory of a Member State, the national law of that Member State would apply to the question of how the user's personal data may be collected using such a cookie.[44] This view has been cited more recently in WP 179,[45] which also provides an example in which a cloud service provider would be subject to EU data protection law if it uses specific equipment in the European Union—for example, if the service "installs cookies with the purpose of storing and retrieving personal data of users."[46] The cloud service provider would then have to comply with information and other requirements of the Directive.[47]

---

41. UK ICO, *Guidance on the Rules on Use of Cookies and Similar Technologies* (2012), at 2, *available at* http://ico.org.uk/for_organisations/privacy_and_electronic_communications/the_guide/cookies.
42. Directive 2009/136/EC, *supra* note 10, recital 24, at 19.
43. *Id.* recitals 24–25, at 19.
44. Working Party, *Working Document on Determining the International Application of EU Data Protection Law to Personal Data Processing on the Internet by Non-EU Based Web Sites* (WP 56) (May 30, 2003), case A, at 11, http://ec.europa.eu/justice/policies/privacy/docs/wpdocs/2002/wp56_en.pdf.
45. Working Party, *Opinion 8/2010 on Applicable Law* (WP 179) (Dec. 16, 2010), at 21, http://ec.europa .eu/justice/policies/privacy/docs/wpdocs/2010/wp179_en.pdf.
46. *Id.* ex. 8, at 22.
47. *Id.*

C. Cookies under EU Privacy and Data Protection Law

Prior to amendment of the e-Privacy Directive, the use of cookies was to be limited to cases where there was a legitimate purpose and with the user's knowledge.[48] Users were to be given clear information as to the purposes of processing using the cookie in compliance with the Directive and the opportunity to refuse, although access to certain website content could be made conditional on accepting a cookie if for a legitimate purpose.[49]

1. Changes to the Law Since Directive 2009/136/EC

Since the adoption of Directive 2009/136/EC, which amended the e-Privacy Directive, informed consent[50] in compliance with the 1995 Directive must be obtained prior to installing a cookie on a subscriber's or user's "terminal equipment."[51] One author has described this shift as one "changing the notice and consent requirements from informed opt-out to an almost (but not quite) informed opt-in," citing the amended Article 5(3) of the e-Privacy Directive.[52] This prior informed consent requirement has been implemented into Member State national law,[53] but an exception is allowed for technical cookies and cookies strictly required to provide a service explicitly requested by a subscriber or a user:

> This shall not prevent any technical storage or access for the sole purpose of carrying out the transmission of a communication over an electronic communications network, or as strictly necessary in order for the provider of an information society service explicitly requested by the subscriber or user to provide the service.[54]

As a result, certain cookies are subject to this requirement, and other technical cookies are not. The French data protection authority (CNIL) provided advice on this issue, indicating that "flash" cookies and local web storage would be subject to the requirement, and cookies used like a shopping cart on an e-commerce site, Session

---

48.   Directive 2009/136/EC, *supra* note 10, recital 24, at 19.

49.   *Id.* recital 24, at 19.

50.   "Consent" refers to that term as used in the Directive. For further information about consent, *see* Chapter 2 Section IV.A.

51.   Directive 2009/136/EC, *supra* note 10, art. 2(5), at 30 (containing the amended art. 5(3) of the e-Privacy Directive).

52.   *See* Robert Bond, *The EU E-Privacy Directive and Consent to Cookies*, 68 Bus. Law. 215 (2012).

53.   *See, e.g.,* Belgian law: *Loi relatif au statut du régulateur des secteurs des postes et des télécommunications belges* [Belgian Telecom Act] *of Jan. 17, 2003*, Moniteur Belge [M.B.] [Official Gazette of Belgium], *as amended* July 25, 2012, art. 129, [at 1 ?], *available at* http://www.ibpt.be/ShowDoc .aspx?objectID=948&lang=fr. *See also* Article 32 II of *Loi 78-17 du 6 janvier 1978 relative à l'informatique, aux fichiers et aux libertés* [Law 78-17 of Jan. 6, 1978 on Information Technology, Data Files, and Civil Liberties][the French Data Protection Act], J.O., Jan. 7, 1978, p. 227 (Fr.), http://www.cnil.fr/fileadmin/ documents/en/Act78-17VA.pdf (English translation), as implemented by *Ordonnance n° 2011-1012 du 24 août 2011 relative aux communications électroniques* [Ordinance No. 2011-1012 on Electronic Communications], Aug. 24, 2011, J.O., No. 0197, Aug. 26, 2011, 14473, art. 37 (Fr.).

54.   Directive 2009/136/EC, *supra* note 10, art. 2(5) at 30 (containing the amended art. 5(3) of the e-Privacy Directive).

ID cookies, or other cookies strictly necessary in order to provide requested services or content, for example, would not be subject to the requirement.[55] As the amended e-Privacy Directive was implemented under Member States' national law, frustratingly, there is a breadth of variance in approaches to cookies within the European Union. Many DPAs have issued their own guidance, with some taking more strict approaches and others having a more relaxed view. Interestingly, in the Netherlands, the cookie law was interpreted so strictly that the law was subsequently amended.

2. UK ICO Guidance on the Use of Cookies

Following the amendments to the e-Privacy Directive, the UK ICO issued updated guidance on the use of cookies in May 2012. There it emphasized that the amendments were prompted by the concerns about online tracking and spyware, and that the rules were meant to protect Internet users' privacy "even where the information being collected about them is not directly personally identifiable."[56] The guidance sheds light on what kinds of cookies might benefit from the "technical cookies" exemption, discussed later. Here is a summary of the table contained in the UK ICO's guidance:[57]

Exception Probably Applies	Exception Probably Does Not Apply
A shopping cart cookie	Analytical cookies counting unique visits
Certain security cookies such as those in connection with online banking services	Advertising cookies
Cookies that help navigation—such as those that help load pages quickly and effectively "by distributing the workload across numerous computers"[58]	Personalization cookies that recognize a returning user and tailor the site to them

The UK ICO discusses the "prior" informed consent requirement, when it is not possible to obtain set cookies before users have been able to understand what cookies are being used and to decide on whether or not to give their consent to the use of cookies. For example, in the cases where websites currently set cookies upon a user entering their websites, then the websites should "be able to demonstrate that they are doing as much as possible to reduce the amount of time before the user receives

55. CNIL, *Ce que le "Paquet Télécom" change pour les cookies* [*What the Telecoms Package Changes for Cookies*], Oct. 26, 2011, *available at* http://www.cnil.fr/la-cnil/actu-cnil/article/article/ce-que-le-paquet-telecom-change-pour-les-cookies/.
56. UK ICO, *Guidance on the Rules on Use of Cookies and Similar Technologies*, *supra* note 41, at 2.
57. *Id.* at 13.
58. *Id.*

information about cookies and is provided with options" and that the information will be "readily available."[59] Where persistent cookies are used, these should have their lifetime shortened or be made into session cookies, pursuant to the proportionality requirement.[60]

Furthermore, the UK ICO indicated that explicit opt-in consent is not always necessary (although it may be required for sensitive information, such as health data). Implied consent, where there is "some action taken by consenting individual from which their consent can be inferred," such as by navigating through the pages of a website or clicking on a button, so long as users have "a reasonable understanding that by doing so they are agreeing to cookies being set."[61] Nonetheless, providing this information in a lengthy or complicated notice would likely not suffice. Obtaining explicit consent provides "regulatory certainty"—that is, being sure that you comply with the law.[62] In evaluating what type of notice should be given, one should consider the intended audience of the website, the audience's expectations on how information will be received, and tailoring the language to the audience.[63]

The UK ICO gave the example of one way of indicating consent—by the user clicking through a clear notice that cookies are used (and indicating the nature of that use) before using the website.[64] The UK ICO presents the example of an employer indicating consent through the choice of browser options and providing an employee with a terminal expressly to accomplish a work task "where to effectively complete the task depends on using a cookie type device."[65] In this case, it might be reasonable to accept the employer/subscriber consent, whereas when the employee uses the computer, and acceptance of the cookie would "involve unwarranted collection of personal data of that employee," it might not.[66]

As one can see, the UK ICO has taken a more pragmatic approach—whereas other DPAs, such as the CNIL or the Working Party, may be considered to have been more rigid in their interpretations.

It should be noted that the e-Privacy Directive allows that consent may potentially be expressed through browser settings. According to Directive 2009/136/EC, "[w]here it is technically possible and effective, in accordance with the relevant provisions of [the Directive], the user's consent to processing may be expressed by using the appropriate settings of a browser or other application."[67] However, for the moment

---

59.   *Id.* at 6.
60.   "Persistent cookies" last from one browser session to another, while "session cookies" expire at the end of the browser session, and so may be considered less of a risk to privacy. *See id.* at 4–5.
61.   *Id.* at 7.
62.   *Id.*
63.   *Id.* at 8.
64.   *Id.* at 9.
65.   *Id.* at 10.
66.   *Id.*
67.   Directive 2009/136/EC, *supra* note 10, recital 66, at 20.

this approach has not been generally accepted within the European Union (see the later discussion of behavioral advertising).

3. Working Party Guidance on Consent—WP 194 and WP 208

The Working Party also provided guidance on the definition of consent, following the adoption of Directive 2009/136/EC and the confusion raised by the new obligations. In WP 194, the Working Party explained that informed consent is not required if the cookies are used "for the sole purpose of carrying out the transmission of a communication over an electronic communications network."[68] The Working Party states that "transmission of the communication must not be possible without the use of the cookie," in order for it to fall within this exemption.[69]

A first alternative criterion was established for fitting within the exemption based on this language (Criterion A). For Criterion A to be met, three factors were identified as "strictly necessary" to fit within the exemption: (1) "the ability to route the information over the network" (identifying communication endpoints); (2) "the ability to exchange data items in their intended order" (numbering packets); and (3) "the ability to detect transmission errors or data loss."[70]

The second alternative criterion for exemption (Criterion B) is based on the case where a cookie is "strictly necessary in order for the provider of an information society service explicitly requested by the subscriber or user to provide the service."[71] In order to satisfy Criterion B, two tests must be met: (1) the service must be "explicitly requested by the user," by taking positive action (and not just being passive), and the service has to have a "clearly defined perimeter"; and (2) the cookie is "strictly needed" in order to provide the service—that is, if it is disabled, "the service will not work."[72]

The Working Party distinguishes cookies by their different forms and their duration—persistent versus session cookies:

> A cookie that is exempted from consent should have a lifespan that is in direct relation to the purpose it is used for, and must be set to expire once it is not needed, taking into account the reasonable expectations of the average user or subscriber.

Usually cookies that meet Criteria A and B will expire at the end of the session, but this is not always the case. In connection with a shopping cart, an e-commerce merchant could set a cookie to expire within a couple hours or after the end of the

---

68. Working Party, *Opinion 04/2012 on Cookie Consent Exemption* (WP 194) (June 7, 2012), at 3, http://ec.europa.eu/justice/data-protection/article-29/documentation/opinion-recommendation/files/2012/wp194_en.pdf.

69. *Id.* at 3.

70. *Id.* at 3–4.

71. *Id.* at 2.

72. *Id.* at 3.

browser session in order to meet a user's expectation that he or she could later resume the transaction, if his or her browser accidentally closed, for example.[73]

Multipurpose cookies do exist (e.g., tracking and remembering user preferences); however, if one of the purposes is exempted (i.e., user preferences), user consent is still needed if the other purpose does not qualify for an exemption. A solution might be to use a separate cookie for each purpose.[74] The Working Party concludes by setting out cookies that are not exempted from consent, namely "social plug-in tracking,"[75] "third party advertising"[76] cookies, and, in general, "first party analytics"[77] cookies. The first two of these cookies are specifically identified as being used in behavioral advertising.

Slightly over a year after WP 194, and following the UK ICO advice, the Working Party published guidance on obtaining consent for cookies.[78] The Working Party reiterated consent requirements and clarified that in order for consent to be valid it must consist of specific information, be given prior to processing, be unambiguous (the data subject's active choice must leave no doubt as to his or her intention), and be freely given (the data subject must have an actual choice).[79]

For active choices, the Working Party noted that tools such as banners, splash screens, modal windows, and browser settings may be used. Insofar as browser settings are concerned, the key is that the user should be "fully informed" and have "actively configured" the browser, thus indicating active behavior.[80] Presumably this refers to "do not track" preferences (or personalized browser settings, where the general setting is to automatically reject third-party cookies); however, this has not yet been widely accepted in practice.

D. Online Behavioral Advertising

Online behavioral advertising is highly dependent on the use of information that is considered personal data in Europe. The Working Party first dealt with online behavioral advertising in its opinion WP 171, issued before the amendments of Directive 2009/136/EC.[81] This will provide us with an introduction to the subject.

1. Introduction

In WP 171, the Working Party described behavioral advertising and the legal framework surrounding it. It also detailed the obligation to obtain prior informed consent.

---

73. *Id.* at 5.
74. *Id.* at 6.
75. *Id.* at 9.
76. *Id.* at 9–10.
77. *Id.* at 10.
78. WP 208.
79. *Id.* at 3.
80. *Id.* at 4–5.
81. Working Party, *Opinion 2/2010 on Online Behavioural Advertising* (WP 171) (Jun. 22, 2010), http://ec.europa.eu/justice/policies/privacy/docs/wpdocs/2010/wp171_en.pdf.

In this opinion, the Working Party expressed its deep concern about the "privacy and data protection implications" of behavioral advertising,[82] and it highlighted the "high level of intrusiveness into people's privacy" of behavioral advertising,[83] which it defined as follows:

> *Behavioural advertising* is advertising that is based on the observation of the behaviour of individuals over time. Behavioural advertising seeks to study the characteristics of this behaviour through their actions (repeated site visits, interactions, keywords, online content production, etc.), in order to develop a specific profile and thus provide data subjects with advertisements tailored to match their inferred interests.[84]

The main actors in behavioral advertising are publishers of websites, advertisers, and advertising network providers (ad network providers) who connect these publishers with advertisers.[85] Increasingly, companies are seeking out such solutions to provide more tailored content but also to receive more detailed information on consumers and their practices and preferences. The user's behavior is tracked using "tracking cookies" placed on the user's computer by a third party other than the website publisher, so-called third party cookies. The Working Party highlights that practice, although web browsers typically make it possible to block these third-party cookies, through a practice called *respawning*. However, new enhanced tracking technologies that cannot be deleted through typical browser privacy settings have been used to "restore" cookies that been refused or deleted. These are referred to as "'Flash Cookies' (local shared objects)."[86] In its WP 171, the Working Party uses the term "cookies" to refer to "all technologies which are based on the principle of storing and accessing information on the user terminal equipment," unless otherwise specified.[87]

2. Application of the e-Privacy Directive

Article 5(3) of the amended e-Privacy Directive applies to cookies, as do Recital 66 of Directive 2009/136/EC and Recitals 24 and 25 of the e-Privacy Directive, and the provisions of the Directive apply to "matters not specifically covered by the e-Privacy Directive wherever personal data are processed."[88] The e-Privacy Directive applies whether or not the information collected is personal data, so it is independent of that concept and (as WP 171 underscores) its Recital 24 refers to the user's terminal as part of his or her "private sphere," thus invoking the protection of the ECHR.[89] Nonetheless, a cookie's

---

82. *Id.* at 21.
83. *Id.* at 4.
84. *Id.*
85. *See id.* at 5.
86. *Id.* at 6-7.
87. *Id.*
88. *Id.* at 7–8. Citation omitted.
89. *Id.* at 9.

collection of IP addresses and processing of unique identifiers often involves the processing of personal data, even when dynamic IP addresses are used, as data subjects may be "singled out" as individuals and allow their profiles to be linked to personally identifiable information, even if their names are not known.[90]

3. Responsibilities of the Various Actors in Behavioral Advertising and Guidance

The responsibilities of the actors in behavioral advertising, as distilled by the Working Party in WP 171, may be summarized as follows:[91]

a. Summary of Responsibilities of Behavioral Advertising Actors

Type of Player	Responsibilities
Ad network providers	Must obtain informed consent of data subject under the e-Privacy Directive; if personal data is collected, it will also have the responsibilities of a data *controller* under the Directive, with the bulk of compliance obligations.
Publishers	Responsibility regarding the transfer of the IP address that takes place when individuals visit the website—considered data *controllers* for these actions; however, they do not bear the bulk of the Directive compliance obligations because they do not hold personal data. Nonetheless, they may be considered *joint controllers* (and have the corresponding responsibilities—including an obligation to inform the data subject about the processing, for example, regarding the transfer of IP address for the purpose of displaying ads and further data processing carried out by the ad network provider—this is analyzed on a case-by-case basis) if they collect and transmit personal data about their visitors (name, address, age, location, etc.) to the ad network provider. In such cases, service agreements should be used to divide up the controller roles and responsibilities.
Advertisers	Capturing "targeting information" such as demographic data (e.g., "young mothers" or "extreme sports fan") and combining it with online surfing behavior of the data subject, then considered an independent data *controller* for that part of the data processing, with the corresponding responsibilities.

---

90. *Id.*
91. *See Id.* at 10–12.

b. Guidance on Consent for Ad Networks

The Working Party considers that the practice of informing data subjects about the use of cookies for behavioral advertising in ad network providers' and publishers' general terms and conditions or privacy policy does not meet the requirements of Article 5(3) of the e-Privacy Directive. The Working Party considers that the use of browser settings (as discussed in Recital 66 of Directive 2009/136/EC) will satisfy the prior informed consent requirement only in "very limited circumstances." In this context, the Working Party states that if the default browser settings allow the collection and processing of data subject information, the mere acquisition of such browser settings cannot imply consent of the data subject. The choice of the data subject to block cookies should not be bypassed, for example, through respawning using flash cookies. Finally, the Working Party considers that "[c]onsent in bulk for any future processing without knowing the circumstances surrounding the processing cannot be valid consent."[92] The Working Party thus suggests that browsers whose default settings reject third-party cookies and require affirmative action on the part of the data subject to accept the use of cookies and the continued transmission of information "may be able to deliver valid and effective consent."[93] In addition, "clear, comprehensive and fully visible information" must be provided (through the browser or together with other "information tools") in order to obtain informed consent.[94] The Working Party suggests the use of a "privacy wizard" (as a way to exercise choice) when a browser is first installed.[95]

Consent should be valid for a limited period of time (e.g., for one year) and this period should not be prolonged; additional information should be provided to the data subject; and the consent should be revocable (with clear information provided as to the means of revocation).[96] Moreover, the Working Party is of the view, inter alia, that ad network providers should not offer interest categories intended to influence children, in light of the problems associated with obtaining consent from the children's parents or legal representatives.[97]

c. Guidance on Information and Other Requirements for Ad Networks

Regarding information requirements, data subjects should be informed of the purposes of processing and the identity of the ad network provider. In addition, information should be provided regarding the recipients of the data, the fact that the cookies will allow the ad provider to collect information about visits to other websites, the ads that they have been shown, which ones have been clicked on, timing, and the existence of a right of access. Providing a minimum of such information "directly on the screen,

---

92. *Id.* at 14. (citation omitted).
93. *Id.*
94. *Id.* at 15.
95. *Id.* at 13–14. This is the case with Windows 8 OS, for example.
96. *Id.* at 16–17.
97. *Id.* at 17.

interactively, easily visible and understandable" may be the best way to comply with the principle set out in Recital 25 of the e-Privacy Directive. Ad network providers should inform data subjects periodically about the fact that monitoring is taking place, and, as we have seen, publishers may have information disclosure obligations as well.[98]

At a minimum the information that users are provided should include the following:

[w]ho (i.e. which entity) is responsible for serving the cookie and collecting the related information. In addition, they should be informed in simple ways that (a) the cookie will be used to create profiles; (b) what type of information will be collected to build such profiles; (c) the fact that the profiles will be used to deliver targeted advertising and (d) the fact that the cookie will enable the user's identification across multiple web sites.

This information could be provided through layered interactive on-screen notices.[99]

The Working Party recalls that the other principles relating to data quality (purpose limitation and retention principles) also apply to such processing. Furthermore, if an individual asks for a deletion of his or her profile or withdraws consent, the ad network provider must promptly erase or delete the data subject's information. Similarly, data subjects' individual rights also apply in this sphere and they should be informed about any tools available (such as cookie ID numbers) that may help them exercise these rights.[100] In addition, data controllers have data security obligations and must take "technical and organisational measures," and they may have to notify national DPAs of the processing if required under national law as well as comply with Articles 25 and 26 of the Directive for cross-border data transfers.[101]

d. Guidance on Sensitive Data

The Working Party highlights serious risks of infringement to personal data if special categories of data (data revealing race, ethnic origin, political opinions, religious or philosophical beliefs, and trade union membership, and data concerning health or sex life) are used in order to serve behavioral advertising, and so the Working Party discourages the offer or use of interest categories that would reveal sensitive data.[102] The Working Party cautions that under Article 8 of the Directive, which prohibits the processing of sensitive data "except in certain, specific circumstances," separate prior opt-in consent in accordance with Article 8(2)(a) may be the only possible ground to

---

98. *Id.* at 17–19.
99. *Id.* at 24.
100. *Id.* at 20–21.
101. *Id.* at 21.
102. *Id.* at 19.

legitimize data processing, and that opt-out mechanisms or the use of browser settings would not meet legal requirements.[103]

4. EASA/IAB Code—Best Practice Recommendation on Online Behavioural Advertising

On August 3, 2011, the Working Party published an open letter addressed to the Internet Advertising Bureau (IAB) Europe and the European Advertising Standards Alliance (EASA),[104] commenting on its draft self-regulatory Framework for Online Behavioral Advertising, referred to as the Best Practice Recommendation on Online Behavioural Advertising (the EASA/IAB Code).[105] On December 15, 2011, the Working Party sent an additional letter to the IAB and EASA highlighting their failure to answer the Working Party's questions contained in its prior letter.[106]

The Working Party issued its Opinion 16/2011 on the EASA/IAB Code on December 15, 2011.[107] The Working Party highlighted the fact that the online behavioral advertising industry "relies heavily on cookies and similar technologies" in order to obtain information on the user's device, as noted earlier.[108] While acknowledging that some "interesting approaches" came from the EASA/IAB Code, such as the Education principle,[109] the Working Party found that such Code's system of using an icon as an information notice, linked to an information website (www .youronlinechoices.eu), on which users could opt out by selecting company names from a list of advertising networks, was insufficient for the purposes of obtaining informed consent, and did not meet the requirement set out in the amended e-Privacy Directive. Nonetheless, the icon system could be used to complement other notices or as additional information after consent has already been provided. The Working Party also stated that the use of the word "advertising" next to the icon was not enough to inform the user of the purpose of the cookies for behavioral advertising

103. *Id.* at 20. When the Working Party speaks of separate consent, it means consent "separate from other consent obtained for processing in general."

104. Letter from the Jacob Kohnstamm, Chairman, Working Party, to the OBA Industry—IAB Europe and EASA, (Aug. 3, 2011), http://ec.europa.eu/justice/data-protection/article-29/documentation/other-document/files/2011/20110803_letter_to_oba_annexes.pdf.

105. *EASA Best Practice Recommendation on Online Behavioural Advertising, Setting Out a European Advertising Industry-Wide Self-Regulatory Standard and Compliance Mechanism for Consumer Controls in Online Behavioural Advertising* (Apr. 13, 2011), http://easa-alliance.org/binarydata.aspx?type=doc/EASA_BPR_OBA_12_APRIL_2011_CLEAN.pdf/download.

106. Letter from Jacob Kohnstamm, Chairan, WP 29, to the OBA Industry—IAB Europe and EASA, (Dec. 15, 2011), http://ec.europa.eu/justice/data-protection/article-29/documentation/other-document/files/2011/20111215_letter_oba_industry_en.pdf.

107. Working Party, *Opinion 16/2011 on EASA/IAB Best Practice Recommendation on Online Behavioural Advertising* (WP 188) (Dec. 8, 2011), http://ec.europa.eu/justice/data-protection/article-29/documentation/opinion-recommendation/files/2011/wp188_en.pdf.

108. *Id.* at 3.

109. *Id.* at 4.

(at a minimum "personalised advertising" should be referred to), and should include "correct and complete" information (for this, see the earlier discussion of WP 171).[110]

a. Use of Opt-out Cookie System and JavaScript

The Working Party found that the EASA/IAB Code, "instead of seeking users consent, claims to provide for a way of exercising 'choice'," which is effectively an opt-out measure, contrary to the requirements of Article 5(3) of the amended e-Privacy Directive. Even if the user uses the opt-out cookie system provided in this Code, there would still be an "ongoing technical exchange of information" between his or her terminal and the ad network, which is one problem, among others. The information website provided by the EASA/IAB uses JavaScript functions that allow the tracking of an individual, without notice, further highlighting this system's incompatibility with relevant law.[111]

b. Other Areas of Concern

The Working Party disagrees with the assertion on the EASA/IAB information website that the information used for providing behavioral advertising is not personal data, and it recalls that in any event "Article 5(3) of the revised e-Privacy Directive is applicable independently of whether the information stored or accessed in the user's terminal equipment consists personal data or not."[112] In its discussion, the Working Party clarifies that not all cookies would require informed consent, recalling the exempted cookies: a *"secure login session cookie,"* a *"shopping basket cookie,"* and *"[s]ecurity cookies,"* although providers of information society services would still have an obligation to inform users.[113]

c. Alternatives to Pop-up Screens for Obtaining Consent

The Working Party detailed alternatives to pop-up screens as a means to obtain consent:

- A static information banner requesting consent, with a link to a privacy statement;
- A splash screen that appears on entering a website and explains the cookies that will be placed if the user consents;
- A default setting prohibiting transfer of data to third parties and requiring a user to affirmatively take action (such as to click) to indicate consent;
- A default browser setting that would prevent collection of behavioral data ("do not collect").[114]

---

110. *Id.* at 4–5.
111. *Id.* at 6–7.
112. *Id.* at 8.
113. *Id.* at 8–9.
114. *Id.* at 9–10.

5. UK CAP Rules on Online Behavioral Advertising

Prior to this, on November 21, 2012, the UK Committee of Advertising Practice (CAP), the UK body responsible for drafting and maintaining UK advertising codes, issued new rules on online behavioral advertising contained in Appendix 3 to the CAP Code.[115] These rules require third parties (i) to give clear and comprehensive notice about the collection and use of behavior data on their website, including with respect to opting out (including via a link to a mechanism to do so) (Rule 31.1.1); (ii) to give clear and comprehensive notice that they are collecting and using web viewing behavior data for behavioral advertising purposes, in or around the relevant ad (again with a link for opting out) (Rule 31.1.2); (iii) not to create interest segments targeting children 12 or younger (Rule 31.1.3); and (iv) to obtain explicit consent before using technology to collect and use information about "all or substantially all websites that are visited by web users on a particular computer" for behavioral advertising purposes.[116]

E. Relationship with the GDPR

As the law in the area of cookies and behavioral advertising arises primarily under the e-Privacy Directive, as amended, a section on Applicable Law under the GDPR will not be provided here. Nonetheless, it should be kept in mind that provisions regarding information requirements, privacy principles, and data subject rights under the GDPR, described elsewhere in this book, will have an impact on the use of cookies and behavioral advertising. Please consult the relevant sections for further information.

---

115.   Committee of Advertising Practice, *Appendix 3 Online Behavioural Advertising, available at* http://www.cap.org.uk/Advertising-Codes/Non-broadcast-HTML/Appendix-3-Online-Behavioural-Advertising.aspx.

116.   *Id.*

7

Development of New Technologies

The Working Party has commented that "[e]ach new phase of technological development presents a challenge for the protection of personal data and the right to privacy."[1] That statement was made in 1999 and it then referred to the use of the Internet as a new phase of technological development. EU data protection law, as embodied by the Directive, is meant to be *technologically neutral* (as it will be with the proposed GDPR, if and when the GDPR is adopted). That is, its provisions apply regardless of the technology used to process personal data. This approach has the advantage of allowing for the application of current legislation to new technologies developed after the legislation's adoption. Many new technologies have developed since the Directive's adoption in 1995; however, determining how the Directive's application to those new technologies works in practice can still be a struggle. The Working Party has consistently, albeit not always clearly, issued guidance contributing to the understanding of how existing law applies to such technologies.

Both biometrics and GPS technology have been discussed previously in the employment relationship context.[2] However, we will now turn to new technologies generally and present some of the practical concerns and issues at a high level.

I. BIOMETRICS AND FACIAL RECOGNITION

The Directive does not specifically refer to biometrics. However, the French Data Protection Agency—the CNIL—has provided information on biometrics in the context of the Directive at least since 1999 and has translated into English part of its annual report for 2001 on the issue.[3] The CNIL favors the use of biometric technologies that are "not based on storing the templates in a database," such as using a microchip card that is kept by the data subject or devices such as a mobile phone or computer for which he or she has exclusive use. It also warns that a biometrics element that "leaves traces" such as DNA or fingerprints may have an incidence on liberties and privacy,

---

1. Working Party, *Working Document: Processing of Personal Data on the Internet* (WP 16) (Feb. 23, 1999), at 2, http://ec.europa.eu/justice/data-protection/article-29/documentation/opinion-recommendation/files/1999/wp16_en.pdf.
2. *See* Chapter 4 Section II.E.
3. CNIL, *22nd Annual Report for 2001, Extracts of Chapter 3 "Current Debates": A Century of Biometrics* (July 2002), http://www.cnil.fr/fileadmin/documents/en/AR-22-biometrics_VA.pdf.

but that an element "leaving no trace," such as the outline of a hand, the retina, and voice recognition technologies "should be preferred," absent a "particular imperative requirement of security."[4]

A. Working Party Guidance

Moreover, the Working Party issued a working document on biometrics as early as 2003.[5] The Working Party highlighted the "special nature" of biometric data in that it relates to "the behavioural and physiological characteristics of an individual and may allow his or her unique identification."[6] The Working Party set out the then different uses for biometrics: automated authentification/verification and identification, especially for entry control, whether the space is a physical one or a virtual one. It also enumerated some of the then current forms of biometrics—such as DNA and fingerprint testing—and warned about potential reuse of data by third parties for their own purposes if society increases the use of biometric databases for "routine applications" and about the public becoming desensitized to the data protection risks and impact on the data subject's life due to widening use of biometrics.[7] Biometric identifiers are not always used in isolation and are often combined for security purposes or may be used with other identifying methods, such as passwords, PIN codes, smart cards, and so on.

Although the Working Party considered that, in most cases "measures of biometric identification or their digital translation in a template form . . . are personal data," if they are "stored in a way that no reasonable means can be used by the controller or by any other person to identify the data subject," they should not be considered personal data.[8] The application or lack of application of the Directive appears to hinge on this analysis. However, as discussed later in the section on big data, when looking at anonymization, the Working Party generally considers biometric data to be personal data when it is possible to identify the individual to whom the data relates. It is worth noting that the household use exemption from the Directive may apply, when dealing in applications purely in domestic use by a natural person (for example, a personal smartphone or computer with a fingerprint reader).

In 2012, the Working Party provided new guidance on biometric technologies.[9] Here, it highlighted the potential dangers in processing, due to the close tie to an individual's personal physical characteristics.[10] As a result, in order for such processing

---

4. *Id.* at 12.
5. Working Party, *Working Document on Biometrics* (WP 80) (Aug. 1, 2003), http://ec.europa.eu/justice/policies/privacy/docs/wpdocs/2003/wp80_en.pdf.
6. *Id.* at 2.
7. *Id.*
8. *Id.* at 5.
9. Working Party, *Opinion 3/2012 on the Developments in Biometric Technologies* (WP 193) (Apr. 27, 2012), http://ec.europa.eu/justice/data-protection/article-29/documentation/opinion-recommendation/files/2012/wp193_en.pdf.
10. *See id.* at 3.

to occur legally, it must be legitimate under the Directive, and the proper securing of such data is necessary.[11]

B. Complying with the Directive

When dealing with biometric processing, most analyses turn on the proportionality of the collection and processing—if there is a less-intrusive way to achieve the purposes, the test fails.[12] In addition, the Working Party gives an example of inappropriate reuse of biometric data. If such data are collected for access control, they should not be further used for workplace surveillance or in order to determine the data subject's emotional state, for example. In discussing the relevant privacy principles in WP 193, the Working Party highlighted the principles of purpose limitation, proportionality, necessity, and data minimization, stating that these should be kept in mind when the purposes of an application are defined.[13]

1. Proportionality and Purpose Limitation

In analyzing the application of the principle of proportionality, one will search for (i) the necessity of the use of the biometric system in order to fill a need, and not just its convenience or cost efficiency; (ii) the likely effectiveness of the biometric system in meeting the need; (iii) whether the benefit of the use of such technology is relatively important compared to the loss of privacy; and (iv) whether there is a less "privacy intrusive" method in order to fulfill the need.[14] In the analysis, the purpose of the processing will play a major role. Thus, the use of facial recognition or DNA data may be very effective in the identification of serious crime suspects, but it may not be justified in more large-scale use (such as widespread facial recognition without the knowledge of data subjects), because of the potential negative effects on privacy.[15]

2. Legal Grounds for Processing

a. Performance of a Contract

Under the basis provided in Article 7(b), if necessity for the performance of a contract is the legal grounds, in general this will apply only when "pure biometric services" are provided (such as submitting hair samples for DNA testing), and it "cannot be used to legitimate a secondary service that consists in enrolling a person into a biometric system."[16]

b. Controller's Legitimate Interest

A data controller's legitimate interest under Article 7(f) of the Directive may be used only as the legal grounds for processing when, as may be the case with security for high-risk areas (e.g., access to a laboratory where research on dangerous viruses is

---

11.   *Id.* at 10–14.
12.   *Id.* at 6.
13.   *Id.* at 7.
14.   *Id.* at 8.
15.   *Id.* at 9.
16.   *Id.* at 12.

being conducted), the controller's interest "objectively prevails over the data subjects' right not to be enrolled in a biometric system," where no valid (less invasive) alternative is available without directly having an impact on security. For these grounds to apply to general security requirements for property or individuals, there must be the "concrete existence of a considerable risk."[17]

c. Individual's Consent

Regarding the data subject's consent pursuant to Article 7(a) of the Directive, an example is given of certain of these principles in the context of online photographs, such as in social media, photo management, or sharing applications. Photographs in these cases may not be further processed, for example, in order to extract biometric templates or enroll them into a biometric system for automatic facial recognition without a "specific legal basis" (such as consent under Article 7(a) of the Directive) for the additional purpose, and such additional processing must then be done in such a way that biometric data are deleted when no longer needed.[18] If consent is the legal grounds for processing biometric data, it must be a "freely given, specific and informed indication of the data subject's wishes," and thus it cannot be obtained through "mandatory acceptance of general terms and conditions," nor through "opt-out possibilities," and it must be revocable.[19] In addition, the Working Party considers that, in many cases, unless a "valid alternative like a password or a swipe card" is offered, consent to processing of biometric data may not be considered as freely given.[20]

3. Security Measures—Technical and Organizational Measures to Protect Personal Data

Security measures for biometric data must be "adequate and effective." The Working Party calls for "a high level of technical protection for the processing . . . using the latest technical possibilities."[21] The data processed must be accurate at enrollment and when linking the data to the data subject. (One reason given for this need for accuracy is the prevention of identity fraud.) Only required information (not all available information) should be processed, and data should not be kept beyond the time it is needed for the purposes for which it was collected or legally further processed. For example, if an employee has access to a restricted area using biometric technologies and his job responsibilities change so that he no longer needs such access, the employer should delete his corresponding biometric data.[22]

---

17. *Id.* at 13.
18. *Id.* at 7.
19. *Id.* at 10.
20. *Id.*
21. *Id.* at 28.
22. *Id.* at 9–10.

4. Privacy by Design and Privacy Impact Assessments

In addition, privacy by design principles should be implemented throughout the value chain of biometric systems, and the Working Party recommends a risk analysis and/or privacy impact assessment (PIA) as an early step:[23]

1. Specification of requirements based on a risk analysis and/or a dedicated PIA.
2. Description and justification on how the design fulfills the requirements.
3. Validation with functional and security tests.
4. Verification of compliance of the final design with the regulatory framework.

A PIA should evaluate how the main risks of biometric data—identity fraud, purpose diversion, and data breach—can be avoided or limited by the relevant biometric system.[24] Furthermore, the Working Party recommends that specific technical and organizational measures be taken.[25]

C. Facial Recognition in Online and Mobile Services

The Working Party issued an opinion in WP 192,[26] shortly after Facebook's launch of its tag suggestions for photos on the use of facial recognition in online and mobile services.[27] In that opinion, the Working Party confirmed that "[w]hen a digital image contains an individual's face which is clearly visible and allows for that individual to be identified it would be considered personal data," adding that a reference template created from such an image would also be considered personal data.[28] Thus, the provisions of the Directive apply to this specific form of biometric data.

Informed consent of the data subject is generally required prior to the processing of his or her image for facial recognition, and he or she should be informed of the use prior to uploading an image to the social network service (SNS), and the registered users of the SNS must be given an option to consent (or not) to their "reference template" (which is created from the image and used for future identification and comparison) being enrolled into the identification database.[29] In WP 192, the Working Party provides recommendations regarding lawfulness of processing, security, data

---

23. *Id.* at 28–29.
24. *Id.* at 30–31.
25. *Id.* at 30–34.
26. Working Party, *Opinion 02/2012 on Facial Recognition in Online and Mobile Services* (WP 192) (Mar. 22, 2012), http://ec.europa.eu/justice/data-protection/article-29/documentation/opinion-recommendation /files/2012/wp192_en.pdf.
27. *See* Justin Mitchell, *Making Photo Tagging Easier*, Dec. 15, 2010 (last updated on June 30, 2011), *available at* https://www.facebook.com/notes/facebook/making-photo-tagging-easier/467145887130.
28. WP 192, *supra* note 26, at 4.
29. *Id.* at 5–6.

minimization, and the exercise of the right to access, and these may be looked to for guidance by interested parties.[30]

II. GPS AND GEOLOCATION

As we have already seen, GPS and geolocation technologies have specific interest in the employment relationship. These technologies also have interest in the context of new mobile telephone technology. Often such devices incorporate either GPS or geo-locational technology using the relevant cell-phone network to follow a device's (and by extension, the device's user's) movements.

GPS and Geolocation technology is increasingly used via telephone networks (here, primarily cellular networks) for the purposes of proposing local products or services to the device's user. The "location data" produced by such technology is covered by the Directive, as complemented by the e-Privacy Directive regarding privacy in communications. We have already seen the importance of the e-Privacy Directive, as amended, regarding both direct mail and behavioral advertising and the use of cookies.[31] Specific provisions of the e-Privacy Directive also deal with location data, which is defined as "any data processed in an electronic communications network or by an electronic communications service, indicating the geographic position of the terminal equipment of a user of a publicly available electronic communications service."[32] Terminal equipment could include mobile devices such as a smartphone or a cell-network-connected tablet.

Article 9(1) of the e-Privacy Directive requires that location data other than traffic data relating to users or subscribers may be processed only when made anonymous or with the informed consent of the users or subscribers "to the extent and for the duration necessary for the provision of a value added service."[33] Informed consent requires that prior information be provided of the type of location data processed, the purposes and duration of processing, and whether the data will be transmitted to a third party for the purpose of the service. Users or subscribers must be able to withdraw such consent at any time[34] and must be able to temporarily refuse the processing for each connection to the network or each transmission of a communication, free of charge through a "simple means."[35] Such processing of location data other than traffic data is restricted to "persons acting under the authority of the provider of the public communications network or publicly available communications service or of

---

30. *Id.* at 7–9.
31. *See* Chapter 6 Sections I and II.
32. Directive 2002/58/EC of the European Parliament and of the Council of 12 July 2002, concerning the processing of personal data and the protection of privacy in the electronic communications sector (Directive on privacy and electronic communications), 2002 O.J. (L 201) 37, (July 31, 2002) [hereinafter e-Privacy Directive], art. 2(c), at 43, as amended by Directive 2009/136/EC art. 2(2) (a), at 29.
33. *Id.* art. 9(1), at 45.
34. *Id.*
35. *Id.* art. 9(2), at 45.

the third party providing the value added service, and must be restricted to what is necessary for the purposes of providing the value added service."[36]

- A "value added service" is defined as "any service which requires the processing of traffic data or location data other than traffic data beyond what is necessary for the transmission of a communication or the billing thereof."[37] For example, this could include a smartphone application using location technology.
- "Traffic data" is "any data processed for the purpose of the conveyance of a communication on an electronic communication network or for the billing thereof."[38]

A. Guidance on Geolocation Services

The Working Party has twice given guidance on geolocation services: once on the use of location data in order to provide value-added services[39] and a second time with respect to geolocation services on smart mobile devices.[40] In the first case, the Working Party distinguishes the use of GPS—"locating people at their own request," from value-added services—"on their being located (at the request of a third party)."[41] In this context it sees that

> [t]he key issue for the processing of location data has thus moved on from being a question of storage (essentially: on what conditions should location data be stored by electronic communications operators?) to being a question of use (how can we ensure that data are used for supplying value-added services in accordance with the principles applicable to the processing of personal data?).[42]

The Working Party confirms that since location data "always relate to an identified or identifiable nature person" it is personal data subject to the provisions of the Directive. It gives the logic for the specific inclusion of location data in Article 9 of the e-Privacy Directive: location data is a "particularly sensitive matter involving the key issue of the freedom to come and go anonymously," with specific rules requiring consent of, and information to, users or subscribers prior to processing of such data.[43]

---

36. *Id*. art. 9(3), at 45.
37. *Id*. art. 2(g) at 43.
38. *Id*. art. 2(b), at 43.
39. Working Party, *Opinion on the Use of Location Data with a View to Providing Value-Added Services* (WP 115) (Nov. 2005), http://ec.europa.eu/justice/policies/privacy/docs/wpdocs/2005/wp115_en.pdf.
40. Working Party, *Opinion 13/2011 on Geolocation Services on Smart Mobile Devices* (WP 185) (May 16, 2011), at 14, http://ec.europa.eu/justice/data-protection/article-29/documentation/opinion-recommendation/files/2011/wp185_en.pdf.
41. WP 115, *supra* note 39, at 3.
42. *Id.*
43. *Id.*

To comply with Article 10 of the Directive and Articles 6 and 9 of the e-Privacy Directive, either the provider of the value-added service or, if such party is not in direct contact with the data subject, the electronic communications operator should provide the data subject with specific information in a clear, complete, and comprehensive manner. This can be accomplished either through the service's general terms and conditions or directly when the service is used.[44] The following information is relevant when requesting location data:

- The controller's identity, as well as that of his or her representative, if applicable;
- Purposes of processing;
- The type of location data being processed;
- The duration of processing;
- Information about transmittal of data to a third party for provision of the service;
- The right to data access and rectification;
- The right to withdraw consent or temporarily refuse processing of such data, and applicable conditions for exercising this right; and
- The right to cancel the data.

As mentioned, prior informed consent is required for the processing of location data. The Working Party rules out acquiring consent via the acceptance of "general terms and conditions for the electronic communications service offered."[45] However, it does state that specific actions coupled with adequate advance information about the data processing provided to an individual may indicate his or her consent to being located "on an ongoing basis."[46]

The Working Party highlights that data subjects should be able to withdraw consent at any time and may temporarily refuse processing. Service providers should regularly remind them that their terminal equipment "has been, will be or can be located." In addition, once the service has been provided, the data subject's location data (unless made anonymous) should not be stored, unless necessary for billing or interconnection payment reasons. Finally, security measures ensuring confidentiality and integrity of location data must be implemented, and access of authorized persons to the data should be logged.[47]

B. Geolocation Services on Smart Mobile Devices

In WP 185, the Working Party describes new geolocation technologies and the privacy risks involved in the constant location monitoring of smart mobile devices (whether

---

44. *Id.* at 4–5.
45. *Id.* at 5.
46. *Id.* at 5–6.
47. *Id.* at 7–8.

through cellular base stations, GPS, or WiFi access points), allowing geolocation service providers to develop extensive profiles of users.[48] The Directive applies to the location data processing and the e-Privacy Directive "only applies to the processing of base station data by public electronic communication services and networks (telecom operators)."[49]

The Working Party highlights that for companies that provide location services and applications through a combination of GPS, WiFi, and cellular base station data, these services and applications are considered as "information society services" that are explicitly excluded from the e-Privacy Directive, due to their exclusion from the definition of "electronic communications services" in Article 2(c) of the revised Framework Directive—Directive 2002/21/EC. The Working Party gives the example of a user sending GPS data using the Internet. In such cases, the data is transmitted independently of the GSM cellphone network. In this case, "[t]he telecommunications service provider acts as mere conduit." Thus, "[i]t cannot gain access to GPS and/ or WiFi and/or base station data communicated to and from a smart mobile device between a user/subscriber and an information society service without very intrusive means such as *deep packet inspection*." Even though the e-Privacy Directive does not apply in such circumstances, the Directive *does* apply according to the Working Party, which refers to its analysis from WP 185 on the Concept of Personal Data.[50]

The Working Party divides up the functions in connection with "online geolocation services provided by information society services": (i) controllers of geolocation infrastructure, (ii) providers of geolocation applications and services, and (iii) developers of the operating system of a smart mobile device, although any one company may perform more than one such role.

In the first and second functions, both act as a data controller:

(i)   A service provider using mapped WiFi access points acts much like a telephone operator, processing location data from cellular base stations and processing personal data when calculating the smart device location.

(ii) The application provider in providing the application showing the location of friends or contacts, regardless of whether this information is downloaded onto a device, is also acting as a controller.

For the third function, app developers may qualify as controllers if one "interacts directly with the user and collects personal data" (for example, if it collects user

---

48.   WP 185, *supra* note 37, at 7.
49.   *Id.* at 7.
50.   *Id.* at 8–11.

registration information or when the developer processes personal data from geolocation apps, "independently from the application providers."[51]

When acting as a controller, as we know, the Directive provisions apply to such geolocation processing activities. Here, prior informed consent is the main ground to make the processing legitimate. Default operating system settings for location services should be set to "OFF" so that the user must take action in order to allow the use of location data. Again, consent should be specific, and if purposes of processing change, the controller should seek renewed specific consent. Due to risks of "secret monitoring," if a geolocation capacity on the device is switched to "ON," the device should continuously warn the user that geolocation is "ON," for example, through the use of an icon that is permanently visible. Users should be reminded periodically (at least once a year) even when they have used the service of the nature of the processing of their personal data, and they should have an easy way to opt out and to withdraw consent. Finally, the Working Party considers that the collection and processing of service set identifiers is not necessary for providing geolocation services, and so would be considered excessive based on mapping of WiFi access point locations.[52]

The Working Party highlights information requirements, and comments that information must be clear and aimed at a "broad audience," and not just the "technically skilled."[53] Data subjects have the right to access their location data collected from their smart devices in a "human readable" format, detailed in geographic locations and not just base station number, for instance. They should also have access to profiles created on the basis of their location data and they have rights to update, rectify, or erase such information. One way to handle this requirement is to provide the data subject direct online access to their information—this method of direct access by data subject is rapidly increasing and more organizations are relying on such methods to permit access as well as accuracy of the data.[54] Location data and profiles based on them must be deleted "after a justified period of time."

The Working Party also provides further technical recommendations; if "demonstrably necessary" for an operating system developer or geolocation infrastructure controller to collect anonymous location history data in order improve service, this data should be nonidentifiable (even indirectly). If a randomly attributed unique device identifier (UDID) number is used to identify a device, this should be stored only for a maximum of 24 hours for operational purposes, after which it should be further anonymized. Once a WiFi access point MAC address is "associated with a new location," the previous location should be immediately deleted.[55]

---

51. *Id.* at 12–13.
52. *Id.* at 13–17.
53. *Id.* at 17–18.
54. *Id.* at 18.
55. *Id.* at 19.

Applicable Law under the GDPR

The GDPR, unlike the Directive, specifically refers to biometric data, due to the widespread development of biometric technologies following the adoption of the Directive.

A definition of "biometric data" is added in Article 4 (11) of the GDPR: "(11) 'biometric data' means any data relating to the physical, physiological or behavioural characteristics of an individual which allow their unique identification, such as facial images, or dactyloscopic data."[56]

In addition, a definition of "genetic data" has been added in Article 4 (10) of the GDPR: "(10) 'genetic data' means all data, of whatever type, concerning the characteristics of an individual which are inherited or acquired during early prenatal development."

Genetic data, which may be obtained from DNA, is considered a special category of personal data that is generally prohibited under Article 9(1) of the GDPR, unless an exception from Article 9(2) applies (e.g., this would include cases where the data subject consents to the processing under Article 9(2)(a) "except where Union law or Member State law provide that the prohibition referred to in paragraph 1 may not be lifted by the data subject").

Processing operations involving biometric data and genetic data are considered to pose specific risks to the rights and freedoms of data subjects under Article 33 (2)(d) of the GDPR, and as such, trigger the requirement of the carrying out of a data protection impact assessment by a controller or a processor acting on its behalf under its Article 33(1).

The GDPR does not specifically discuss GPS or geolocation technologies, but it does recognize that location data might not necessarily be considered personal data in all instances.[57] However, it also acknowledges that reference to location data may be used to identify a data subject.[58]

III. CLOUD COMPUTING

Generally, technology is marked by rapid development, and cloud computing has been no exception to this rule.[59] In the initial phase, growth within the cloud-computing world largely remained unchecked with respect to privacy and data protection concerns. Now, organizations and individuals are increasingly aware of privacy implications associated with the use of cloud technology. Cloud-computing applications

---

56. Proposal for Regulation of the European Parliament and of the Council on the Protection of Individuals with regard to the Processing of Personal Data and on the Free Movement of such Data (General Data Protection Regulation) COM (2012) 11 final (Jan. 25, 2012) [hereinafter GDPR], art. 4(11), at 42.
57. GDPR, recital 24, at 21.
58. GDPR, art. 4(1), at 41.
59. A 2012 study made on behalf of the Commission said that "[m]ore than half of EU businesses and consumers already use some kind of cloud services." IDC, *Quantitative Estimates of the Demand for Cloud Computing in Europe and the Likely Barriers to Uptake* (SMART 2011/0045) (D4—Final Report), at 17, July 13, 2012, *available at* http://ec.europa.eu/digital-agenda/en/news/quantitative-estimates-demand-cloud-computing-europe-and-likely-barriers-take-final-report. The same study also concluded that "the market for public cloud services is growing strongly in Europe." *Id*. at 30.

include services like those of Dropbox's document storage services and Apple's iCloud, MOOCs from Khan Academy, Snapchat, as well as those of the world's largest cloud-computing company, Amazon Web Services (AWS).[60] This section will present a brief introduction to cloud computing, followed by a discussion of the European data protection and privacy law environment for cloud computing.

A. Brief Introduction to Cloud Technology

Cloud computing is the concept in which applications and data are stored on a provider or third-party server via the Internet, rendering data outside the physical control of the end user or customer. This infrastructure enables applications to run and data to be stored, transferred, and accessed on a framework of remote servers. Cloud computing has been summarized in more plain language as a situation in which, "instead of having the software and the data stored locally on a user's own computer, they can all be stored on Internet servers, or 'in the clouds,' and accessed as a service on the Internet."[61]

1. Definitions
a. Working Party

The Working Party describes cloud computing as "a set of technologies and service models that focus on the Internet-based use and delivery of IT applications, processing capability, storage, and memory space."[62]

b. NIST

The most widely cited definition of cloud computing is that of the U.S. National Institute of Standards and Technology (NIST), a standards and guideline-developing agency of the U.S. Department of Commerce:

> Cloud computing is a model for enabling ubiquitous, convenient, on-demand network access to a shared pool of configurable computing resources (e.g., networks, servers, storage, applications, and services) that can be rapidly provisioned and released with minimal management effort or service provider interaction.[63]

---

60.   See Quentin Hardy, *The Era of Cloud Computing*, N.Y. TIMES, June 11, 2014, *available at* http://nyti .ms/1pJhLjp, for a discussion of many of the current uses made of cloud computing.
61.   *See* Paul Lanois, *Caught in the Clouds: The Web 2.0, Cloud Computing, and Privacy?*, 9(2) Nw. J. TECH. & INTELL. PROP. 29 (2010–2011). Lanois also provides several examples of cloud computing services.
62.   Working Party, *Opinion 05/2012 on the Cloud Computing* (July 1, 2012) (WP 196), at 4, http:// ec.europa.eu/justice/data-protection/article-29/documentation/opinion-recommendation/files/2012/ wp196_en.pdf.
63.   Peter Mell & Timothy Grance, Nat'l Inst. of Standards and Tech., *The NIST Definition of Cloud Computing*, NIST Spec. Publ. 800-145, Sept. 2011, 2, http://csrc.nist.gov/publications/nistpubs/800-145/ SP800-145.pdf. This definition is known as the "final version." *See* NIST, Press Release, Final Version of NIST Cloud Computing Definition Published, Oct. 25, 2011, *available at* http://www.nist.gov/itl/csd/ cloud-102511.cfm.

2. NIST "Service Models"

NIST further qualifies the cloud-computing model by specifying five "essential characteristics" that are inherently linked to cloud computing: on-demand self-service, broad network access, resource pooling, rapid elasticity, and measured service.[64] There are three commonly accepted service models, presented next.

a. Software as a Service (SaaS)

This is also termed "software on demand," where the customer accesses software over the Internet or over a PC or LAN. Here, the customer has no control over the middleware, operating system (OS), or hardware and exercises limited control over a specific application or software (e.g., mail). Here, the cloud provider exercises a large degree of control over the cloud environment. SaaS can be either on demand, via subscription, or based on the pay-as-you-go model.

b. Platform as a Service (PaaS)

Here the customer is able to exercise limited control and programmability over an application and middleware but again has no control over the OS or hardware, which is still controlled by the cloud provider. This model allows for companies to purchase specific platforms, without having to purchase the expensive hardware (and software) associated with such platforms.

c. Infrastructure as a Service (IaaS)

The customer is able to exercise total control over the application, middleware, and OS, and the cloud provider maintains administrative control over the hypervisor and hardware. IaaS allows for clients to have a computing infrastructure, running multiple platforms, software, and so on without purchasing the hardware.[65]

3. NIST "Deployment Models"

Furthermore, there are four "deployment models,"[66] presented next.

a. Public Cloud

A *public cloud* is one based on the standard cloud model, in which a service provider makes resources, such as applications and storage, available to the general public over the Internet.

b. Private (or Corporate) Cloud

A *private (or corporate) cloud* is a proprietary computing architecture, which is protected by a firewall and provides hosted services to a limited number of customers.

c. Hybrid Cloud

A *hybrid cloud* is one where an organization provides and manages some resources in-house and has other resources provided by external suppliers; that is, it is a mix of public and private clouds.

---

64. Michael R. Nelson, *Briefing Paper for the ICCP Technology Foresight Forum: Cloud Computing and Public Policy—14 October 2009*, OECD Committee for Information, Computer and Communications Policy, DSTI/ICCP(2009)17, Sept. 29, 2009, at 2–3, http://www.oecd.org/dataoecd/39/47/43933771.pdf.
65. Mell & Grance, *supra* note 63, at 1–2.
66. *Id.* at 2–3.

d. Community Cloud

In a *community cloud*, several companies have similar requirements and share the infrastructure in order to capitalize on the benefits of cloud computing.

For our purposes, we will look only at the distinction between private and public clouds in the deployment models; moreover, it should be noted that the Working Party has also defined these terms.[67] This private/public cloud distinction is important in terms of the security of data, including that of personal data stored in the cloud. Additionally, it is important with respect to the level of control exercised by the data controller over the data, as compared to the level of control exercised by the cloud service provider.

B. EU Data Protection Law Applied to Cloud Computing

As we have seen, the provisions of the Directive are to be applied to the processing of personal data when using cloud-computing technologies. In 2012, the Working Party issued its long-awaited opinion on cloud computing—WP 196.[68] There, it analyzed relevant concerns related to the use of this form of technology. Here, we will look at the main issues including (a) who is responsible for the processing, (b) main data protection requirements between customers and cloud providers, and (c) the issues related to cross-border data transfers and application of foreign law. We will take each of these issues in the same order.

1. Responsibilities and Control—Who Is the Controller?

As discussed in Chapter 2 Section III, the controller is the party that generally bears the responsibilities for compliance with the Directive and is, similarly, liable for violations of the same. In cloud computing, due to often-complex processing scenarios, it is sometimes difficult to determine who the controller is. In its guidance, the Working Party assumes the general case to be that there is a "controller-processor relationship, with the customer qualifying as controller and the cloud provider qualifying as processor."[69] If an entity is a client of a cloud service provider and determines the "ultimate purpose of the processing," then it is likely to be the controller of the related personal data processing, with responsibility for such processing. Earlier, we cautioned that when a cloud provider processes data for its own purposes in addition to processing personal data on behalf of its client, it may be considered a "joint controller" with shared responsibility for compliance with data protection law provisions.

---

67. WP 196, *Annex*, *supra* note 62, at 25. Typically private clouds are used by companies with a need for great computing power (and that may be seeking cost savings), and public clouds for services such as Google apps available to the public are often used by smaller organizations.

68. *See* WP 196, *supra* note 62.

69. *Id.* at 4.

One author has observed that there is a sliding scale involved in the Working Party's analysis of the controller/processor dilemma for cloud service providers:

At one end of the spectrum, a service provider that provides only basic services is a data processor. At the other end, a service provider that is "in control," *e.g.*, has autonomy, retains the power to draft and change its contracts and policies, or provides added value for the processing of the data, should be deemed a "data controller," and should share with the customer the liability and risks associated with the processing of personal data.[70]

According to that author, one test that might be a criterion for determining joint controller status is "the expertise of the parties."[71] When looking at the different deployment models, this can help us better understand the roles, for example:

a. SaaS service providers will act as processors for the bulk of personal information processed within the software, as the customer generally controls the input and objectives for processing. However, to the extent that a service provider would like to use contact details or registration information of customers (e.g., their employees) for its own objectives, it will qualify as a controller for this type of data. This could be the case for marketing additional products or services, or to improve the software capabilities, and so on.
b. Furthermore, one can imagine that in certain PaaS and IaaS scenarios, where providers are making decisions with respect to the means of processing, this could trigger their designation as controllers.

As a reminder, the allocation and qualification as a controller is a functional concept. Therefore, it is always important to reflect on the circumstances at hand and also assess the risks involved in the processing and the cloud relationship. Controllers must ensure control vis-à-vis third parties and processors through appropriate technical and organizational measures and contractual protections.

Compliance with EU/EEA data protection law, including, where appropriate, electronic communications law, is the responsibility of the controller. As such, controllers must select a cloud provider (processors) that will likewise ensure this compliance when handling personal data.

The ITU-T, the Telecommunication Standardization Sector of the International Telecommunication Union (ITU), the United Nations specialized agency for

---

70. *See* Françoise Gilbert, *Cloud Service Providers as Joint-Data Controllers*, 15 (2) J. INTERNET L. 3, 12 (2011).
71. *Id.* at 9.

information and communication technologies, has set out the following questions that should be addressed so as to determine data privacy and security risks:

- Who are the stakeholders involved in the operation?
- What are their roles and responsibilities?
- Where is the data kept?
- How is the data replicated?
- What are the relevant legal rules for data processing?
- How will the service provider meet the expected level of security and privacy?[72]

Prior to entering into the cloud-computing relationship, the controller should identify the relevant risks of the relationship and seek to minimize such risks. The Working Party, while cautioning that risks related to outsourcing should also be taken into account,[73] has enumerated several risks:

- Lack of availability of data due to vendor lock-in (lack of interoperability);
- Lack of data integrity resulting from resource sharing;
- Foreign law enforcement risk on confidentiality;
- Lack of ability to intervene with respect to the data due to the "complexity and dynamics of the outsourcing chain," which may affect the ability to respond to requests to exercise data subject rights;
- Risk of linking data from different controllers due to a lack of isolation;
- Lack of knowledge of subcontracting;
- The application of various national laws because of the geographical dispersion of processing and resulting difficulties in case of disputes; and
- Possible cross-border transfer of personal data to jurisdictions not providing an adequate level of data protection.[74]

The European Union Agency for Network and Information Security (ENISA) has also issued a report on risks and related security concerns.[75]

The International Working Group on Data Protection in Telecommunications (IWGDPT, or Berlin Group), whose membership includes DPA representatives "and other bodies of national public administrations, international organisations and

---

72. ITU, *Privacy in Cloud Computing*, ITU-T Tech. Watch Rep. 5 (Mar. 2012), http://www.itu.int/dms_pub/itu-t/oth/23/01/T23010000160001PDFE.pdf.

73. *See* WP 196, *supra* note 62, at 5.

74. *Id.* at 5–6.

75. *See* European Union Agency for Network and Information Security (ENISA), *Cloud Computing: Benefits, Risks and Recommendations for Information Security*, Mar. 2009, *available at* http://www.enisa.europa.eu/activities/risk-management/files/deliverables/cloud-computing-risk-assessment.

scientists from all over the world,"[76] cautions that there is a lack of transparency concerning "cloud service provider processes, procedures and practices" including regarding subcontracting and that this "makes it difficult to conduct a proper risk assessment."[77] These same sentiments are reflected in WP 196 and by various DPAs, including the CNIL.[78] The Berlin Group made general recommendations regarding cloud computing, carrying out privacy impact and risk assessments and pushing cloud providers to offer greater transparency "in particular regarding information on potential data breaches and more balanced contractual clauses to promote data portability and data control by cloud users."[79] It also set out guidance on best practices regarding controller risk assessments. This highlights that risk assessments should be done throughout the lifetime of the processing relationship and should also extend to any subcontractors involved in processing.[80]

2. Compliance with Data Protection Principles: Ensuring Compliance through Cloud Contracts

Earlier on, in Chapter 1 Section II, we cautioned that roles and responsibilities need to be clearly set out in the contract between the cloud provider and its client; this will also help when determining who will be considered the controller under the Directive. Generally, cloud providers as processors do not have the same level of responsibility. They may process the personal data only upon the controller's instructions and need to be bound by contractual agreements.

a. Perceived Imbalance in Contractual Power

One of the main concerns related to these contractual agreements is the perceived imbalance of power between clients and cloud providers. When dealing with larger cloud providers, many companies—especially SMEs—are in a position where they must simply approve standard service-level and related agreements for cloud services. The Working Party made the following warning:

> [t]he imbalance in the contractual power of a small data controller with respect to big service providers should not be considered as a justification for the controller

---

76. *See* http://www.datenschutz-berlin.de/content/europa-international/international-working-group-on-data-protection-in-telecommunications-iwgdpt.

77. *See* International Working Group on Data Protection in Telecommunications, *Working Paper on Cloud Computing—Privacy and Data Protection Issues*, at 2, Apr. 24, 2012, *available at* http://www.datenschutz-berlin.de/attachments/873/Sopot_Memorandum_Cloud_Computing.pdf?1335513083.

78. *See generally* WP 196, *supra* note 62, at 8–9 and CNIL, *Recommendations for Companies Planning to Use Cloud Computing Services* and *Appendix: Models of Contractual Clauses*, at 5–7, June 25, 2012, http://www.cnil.fr/fileadmin/documents/en/Recommendations_for_companies_planning_to_use_Cloud_computing_services.pdf. The CNIL emphasizes that the effort to minimize potential risks should begin with the good choice of a service provider. It recommends that a service provider "offering sufficient guarantees" be selected, and that a series of steps be undertaken in making one's choice: (1) determine the service provider's legal qualification, and (2) assess the level of protection given by the service provider for the data being processed.

79. *Working Paper on Cloud Computing, supra* note 77, at 3.

80. *Id.* at 5.

to accept clauses and terms of contracts which are not in compliance with data protection law.[81]

Thus, the overall responsibility of the controller for compliance with data protection rules must be kept in mind.

b. Content of the Cloud Contract

The cloud service contract should clearly allocate responsibility for data protection compliance, include standardized data protection safeguards, technical and organizational measures, and provisions regarding cross-border data flows, in addition to "additional mechanisms that can prove suitable for facilitating due diligence and accountability (such as independent third-party audits and certifications of a provider's services.)."[82] Specifically, the Working Party recommended that the following items be included in the contractual agreement:

- The client's instructions to the provider, detailing subject matter and time frame;
- Security measures and a requirement to inform the client in case of a data breach;
- Access only for authorized persons and a requirement that the service provider and its employees be bound by confidentiality provisions (which should survive the termination of the agreement);
- The obligation to cooperate with the controller, including monitoring processing and helping data subjects exercise their rights;
- The right to log and audit processing operations; and
- The duty to notify the controller in case of third-party (such as law enforcement) access requests.[83]

Most importantly, the Working Party notes that service agreements should include information on where the data will be processed and by whom. Where subprocessors are contemplated, the contract must "ensure effective control over and allocate clear responsibility for processing activities."[84]

c. Special Contractual Protections on Subcontracting

The Working Party suggests relying on the C-to-P Model Contracts or using a similar approach in service or processing agreements with service providers. The contracts binding the subcontractors should set out the relevant "obligations and responsibilities deriving from data protection legislation," impose the same obligations on the

---

81. Working Party, *Opinion 1/2010 on the Concepts of "Controller" and "Processor"* (WP 169) (Feb. 16, 2010), at 26, http://ec.europa.eu/justice/policies/privacy/docs/wpdocs/2010/wp169_en.pdf.
82. WP 196, *supra* note 62, at 8.
83. *Id.* at 19–21.
84. *Id.* at 9.

subprocessor as are placed on the processor, and require prior written consent of the controller to such subprocessing.[85]

In practice, this means that subprocessing may be allowed only with the controller's consent and where the subprocessor is bound by provisions similar to the ones imposed on the processors.[86] This permits controllers to know where their personal data is located and who is handling it, as well as aiding the controller in recovery for liability. Liability coverage could also be dealt with by the inclusion of a statement that the processor agrees to cover the acts (violations) by the subprocessor as if it were acting in its place or by the requirement to include third-party beneficiary rights for the controllers in the processor's service arrangements with its subprocessors.[87] With respect to the controller's consent, this may be given at the outset of the processing service together with a statement that the processor will inform the controller in case of any intended changes to the processing (e.g., location, use of other subprocessors, etc.) with a residual right to object to such use.

d. CNIL Guidance on Cloud Contracts

The CNIL has also published essential elements that should appear in contract, including issues related to information on processing, the guarantees put in place by the service provider, location and transfers, formalities with the CNIL (where appropriate), and security and confidentiality.[88] Perhaps more interestingly, however, it has also furnished models of contract clauses to be inserted into cloud service contracts. These cover a full gamut of issues that should be included in the contract.[89]

3. Data Protection Principles and Requirements Applied to Cloud Computing

a. Transparency and Purpose Limitation

The cloud client is obliged to provide the data subject with information as to the purpose of the processing and on data collected and processed concerning the data subject's identity. In addition, information as to the recipients (or categories of recipients) of the data subject's data should be provided to the data subject.[90] The controller must make certain that neither the cloud service provider nor any of its subcontractors (if permitted) diverts and uses the data for any other incompatible purpose.

The cloud client must first establish the purpose or purposes of the data processing, give the data subject notice of this, and ensure that the data is not processed for further purposes. The risk of this "must . . . be assessed as being quite high," according to the

---

85. *Id.*
86. *Id.*
87. *Id.* at 10.
88. *See* CNIL, *Recommendations for Companies Planning to Use Cloud Computing Services, supra* note 78, at 8–11.
89. *Id.* at 12–21.
90. WP 196, *supra* note 62, at 10–11. The Working Party distilled requirements contained in the Directive. *See* Directive 95/46/EC of the European Parliament and of the Council of 24 Oct. 1995 on the protection of individuals with regard to the processing of personal data and on the free movement of such data [hereinafter Directive], 1995 O.J. (L 281) 31 (Nov. 23, 1995), art. 10, at 41.

Working Party, and it recommends that this risk be lessened by including technical and organizational requirements, such as "logging and auditing of relevant processing operations" and the use of penalties for breaches of data protection law[91] (this would entail liquidated damages in a common law contract).

Article 6(1)(e) of the Directive provides that personal data must be "kept in a form which permits identification of data subjects for no longer than is necessary for the purposes for which the data were collected or for which they are further processed."[92] Following such period, the data must be erased or "truly anonymized." There may be legal restrictions that prevent erasure (the Working Party mentions tax regulations), in which case access to the data should be blocked. Each instance of the data on whatever the medium must be erased "irretrievably." The Working Party points out that log data may qualify as personal data "relating to the person who initiated the respective processing operation"[93] [citation omitted], and as such is subject to erasure requirements. In the relevant contractual arrangements, controllers must include secure erasure where "the storage media . . . be destroyed or demagnetised or the stored personal data is deleted effectively through overwriting."[94]

b. Data Security: Technical and Organizational Measures

As outlined earlier, Article 17(2) of the Directive requires a controller to "choose a processor providing sufficient guarantees in respect of the technical security measures and organizational measures governing the processing to be carried out."[95]

c. Availability and Integrity

The cloud client needs to be ensured that it will have "timely and reliable access to personal data," or availability.[96] This requirement may be impaired by malicious acts harming server performance such as Denial of Service (DoS) attacks or by "accidental loss of network connectivity," hardware and power failures, and "other infrastructure problems."[97] Cloud providers should have measures to deal with these risks including "backup internet network links, redundant storage and effective data backup mechanisms," according to the Working Party.[98]

The Working Party has also identified means of detecting alteration to personal data as "cryptographic authentication mechanisms such as message authentication codes or signatures," and if extended to IT systems, "intrusion detection/prevention systems."[99]

---

91. WP 196, *supra* note 62, at 11.
92. Directive, art. 6(1)(e), at 40.
93. WP 196, *supra* note 62, at 12.
94. *Id.* at 11–12.
95. Directive, art. 17(2), at 43.
96. WP 196, *supra* note 62, at 14.
97. *Id.*
98. *Id.*
99. *Id.* at 15.

d. Confidentiality

One key element of improving security, and therefore confidentiality, is that data (whether "at rest" or "in transit") be properly encrypted.[100] The Working Party highlights that communications between cloud parties and then between them and data centers all should be encrypted. Other means identified for ensuring confidentiality are "authorization mechanisms and strong authentication," in addition to the confidentiality requirement for service providers and their employees.[101]

e. Isolation, Intervenability, and Portability

Isolation is particularly relevant to public clouds and is related to the principle of purpose limitation. Where there is sharing of resources, such as storage, memory, and networks, there are risks of disclosure and illegitimate processing. Isolation's goal is to contribute to guaranteeing the maintenance of confidentiality and purpose limitation—thus, the proper administration of access rights and roles. Technical measures also play a role in obtaining isolation; the Working Party prescribes measures "such as the hardening of hypervisors and proper management of shared resources if virtual machines are used to share physical resources between different cloud customers."[102]

Intervenability refers to the necessity of being able to intervene with respect to the data in order to allow for data subjects to exercise their rights under Articles 12 and 14 of the Directive.[103]

Finally, portability involves being able to receive data in standard formats and "service interfaces facilitating interoperability and portability between different cloud providers" so that a client is not locked in to a specific provider and may move to another provider.[104] Guarantees regarding such portability should be verified and sought.[105]

C.   Cross-Border Transfers of Personal Data

The Working Party is of the opinion that "sole self-certification with Safe Harbor may not be deemed sufficient in the absence of robust enforcement of data protection principles in the cloud environment."[106] Evidence of compliance should be obtained. Furthermore, if the Safe Harbor and adequacy determinations for cross-border transfers of personal data are not available for all transfers involved in a cloud relationship, which is likely to be the case where so many different countries may be involved, then some other mechanism such as standard contractual clauses or processor BCRs may need to be implemented in order to allow for the relevant data flows. In such a case, the client should verify that the clauses and/or BCRs comply with relevant national

---

100.   *See, e.g., Working Paper on Cloud Computing, supra* note 77, at 4.
101.   WP 196, *supra* note 62, at 15.
102.   *Id.* at 15–16.
103.   *Id.* at 16.
104.   *Id.*
105.   *Id.*
106.   *Id.* at 17.

law (this may include requirements of traceability of data, information as to location, and the identity of subcontractors).

The Working Party also considers that the Safe Harbor principles "by themselves may also not guarantee the data exporter the necessary means to ensure that appropriate security measures have been applied by the cloud provider in the US, as may be required by national legislations" pursuant to the Directive.[107] Additional cloud-related safeguards may be required. Article 26 exemptions should generally not be relied on in the cloud context.[108]

With regard to issues with Model Clauses in certain specific cases, the Working Party offers the following advice:

> When the cloud provider acting as processor is established in the EU, the situation might be more complex since the model clauses applies [sic], in general, only to the transfer of data from a EU controller to a non EU processor (see recital 23 of the Commission decision on the model Clauses 2010/87/EU and WP 176).
>
> As regards the contractual relationship between the non EU processor and the sub-processors, a written agreement which imposes the same obligations on the subprocessor as are imposed on the processor in the Model clauses should be put in place.[109]

As we have seen, the international nature of the cloud-computing industry may involve cross-border transfers, and this may require special precautions and specific actions by the cloud-computing parties.

Applicable Law under the GDPR

First, one area of changes brought by the GDPR that affect the cloud-computing sector are those changes regarding cross-border data transfers. For these, the reader is referred to Chapter 3, Section III.

Next, the GDPR adds the concept of "joint controller" directly into the text (as we have seen, it is possible for a cloud service provider, in certain cases, to be considered a joint controller), to apply when the "purposes, conditions and means of the processing" are

---

107.   *Id.* at 18.
108.   *Id.* at 17–18.
109.   *Id.* at 19.
110.   GDPR, art. 24, at 56.

determined jointly. In such cases, the joint controllers need to divide up responsibilities in an "arrangement,"[110] which, as a practical matter, would take the form of the contract binding each of them to the other.

One of the most significant changes made by the GDPR regarding the cloud-computing context, however, is the increase in responsibility for the processor (so, in general, for cloud service providers), including that for security of personal data. This can be seen by the inclusion of processors in the Data Security Section of the GDPR, including Articles 30–32. The heart of the security obligation is contained in Article 30, which replaces and modifies Article 17 of the Directive:

Article 30

Security of processing

1. The controller and the processor shall implement appropriate technical and organisational measures to ensure a level of security appropriate to the risks represented by the processing and the nature of the personal data to be protected, having regard to the state of the art and the costs of their implementation.

2. The controller and the processor must, following an evaluation of the risks, take the measures referred to in paragraph 1 to protect personal data against accidental or unlawful destruction or accidental loss and to prevent any unlawful forms of processing, in particular any unauthorised disclosure, dissemination or access, or alteration of personal data.[111]

...

Furthermore, additional requirements are imposed upon processors (which include in most cases cloud providers) in Articles 26–29 of the GDPR.

Article 26(2) further specifies required elements of the controller-processor contract, including, inter alia, the requirements that the processor shall:

(b) employ only staff who have committed themselves to confidentiality or are under a statutory obligation of confidentiality;[112]

---

111. GDPR, art. 30(1)–(2), at 60.
112. GDPR, art. 26(6)(b), at 57.

Moreover, the processor shall:

(d) enlist another processor only with the prior permission of the controller;

(e) insofar as this is possible given the nature of the processing, create in agreement with the controller the necessary technical and organizational requirements for the fulfilment of the controller's obligation to respond to requests for exercising the data subject's rights laid down in Chapter III;

(f) assist the controller in ensuring compliance with the obligations pursuant to Articles 30 to 34;

(g) hand over all results to the controller after the end of the processing and not process the personal data otherwise;

(h) make available to the controller and the supervisory authority all information necessary to control compliance with the obligations laid down in this Article.[113]

We can see that, in a general manner, the additional rights accorded to data subjects under the GDPR (e.g., the right to erasure and to be forgotten,[114] and the right to data portability[115]) impose a requirement that controllers not only have the cooperation of processors such as cloud providers (which now becomes a processor requirement under Article 26(2)) and subprocessors (if any) in order to support the controller in complying with any exercise request regarding these rights by the data subject, but also that it be technically and organizationally possible to reply with this request. This is particularly relevant where, in a cloud relationship, there may be processing occurring in several locations and numerous subprocessors. Moreover, new documentation requirements are provided in Article 28,[116] which would help to create audit trails, as well as a requirement in Article 29 that both controllers and processors (which, again, would usually include cloud providers) cooperate with supervisory authorities.[117]

Furthermore, the new data breach notification provisions contained in the GDPR[118] will require close coordination between cloud clients and cloud providers in the event of the occurrence of a data breach.

Finally, the GDPR places other potential requirements on both controllers and processors, which in concrete terms may apply to cloud providers. They include potentially having to conduct a data protection impact assessment,[119] obtaining prior authorization of and consulting with a supervisory authority before engaging in processing,[120] or having to designate a data protection officer.[121]

---

113. GDPR, art. 26(2)(d)–(h), at 57–58.
114. GDPR, art. 17, at 51–53.
115. GDPR, art. 18, at 53.
116. GDPR, art. 28, at 58–59.
117. GDPR, art. 29, at 59.
118. GDPR, arts. 31–32, at 60–62.
119. GDPR, art. 33, at 62–63.
120. GDPR, art. 34, at 63–64.
121. GDPR, art. 35, at 65–66.

"Big Data" and "The Internet of Things," the titles of the next two sections, are the last of the new technologies that this chapter will examine.

IV. BIG DATA

First this section will look at the definition of big data, distinguishing it from open data, and will detail certain privacy concerns and one way to deal with them: anonymization. Then this section will provide certain Working Party and UK ICO guidance on anonymization, before mentioning the prospect of international cooperation.

A. Definition of Big Data

Two authors of a highly cited work caution that there is no "rigorous definition of big data," although they think of the concept now as referring to "things one can do at a large scale that cannot be done at a smaller one, to extract new insights or create new forms of value, in ways that change markets, organizations, the relationship between citizens and governments, and more."[122] "Big data" has been defined by the Working Party as a term referring to

> [t]he exponential growth both in the availability and in the automated use of information: it refers to gigantic digital datasets held by corporations, governments and other large organisations, which are then extensively analysed (hence the name: analytics) using computer algorithms. Big data can be used to identify more general trends and correlations but it can also be processed in order to directly affect individuals.[123]

This concept of big data is often closely tied to open data, which is identified by the Working Party as follows:

> Open data projects take accessibility of information processed by public bodies to a whole new level. Such projects often involve (i) making entire databases available (ii) in standardised electronic format (iii) to any applicant without any screening process (iv) free of charge and (v) for any commercial or non-commercial purposes under an open license. This new form of accessibility is the main purpose of open data, but it is not without risks if applied indiscriminately and without appropriate safeguards.[124]

---

122. *See* Viktor Mayer-Schönberger & Kenneth Cukier, Big Data: A Revolution That Will Transform How We Live, Work and Think 6 (2013).
123. Working Party, *Opinion 03/2013 on Purpose Limitation* (WP 203) (Apr. 2, 2013), at 35, http://ec.europa.eu/justice/data-protection/article-29/documentation/opinion-recommendation/files/2013/wp203_en.pdf.
124. *Id.* at 35.

As this book is concerned with big data (which deals with *private* industry use of massive amounts of data), and not with open data (which deals with data processed by *public* bodies), it will focus on the former. Readers who are interested in open data may consult WP 203 and other sources listed in the footnotes.[125]

B. Big Data and Privacy Law Concerns

Similar to cloud computing discussed in Chapter 7 Section III, big data is more of a way of doing business, a new process, rather than a new invention in and of itself. It has numerous applications and may result in great economic opportunities; nevertheless, it raises data privacy concerns. As Neelie Kroes, then vice president of the European Commission responsible for the digital agenda, commented:

> Let me be clear. Nothing we do should be at the expense of fundamental rights. Mastering big data means mastering privacy too.
>
> …
>
> For data that does concern people, we need firm and modern data protection rules that safeguard this fundamental right.
>
> And we need digital tools to help people take control of their data, so that they know they can be confident to trust this technology.
>
> Then we have a virtuous circle, where technological progress, our legal framework, and our fundamental rights mutually support each other.
>
> Privacy is essential. But it cannot be an excuse to avoid this topic.[126]

The Working Party recently pointed out that big data "raises important social, legal and ethical questions."[127] It acknowledges that "big data processing operations do not

---

125.   *See e.g., id.* at 48–50; *see generally* Working Party, *Opinion 06/2013 on Open Data and Public Sector Information (PSI) Reuse* (WP 207) (June 5, 2013), http://ec.europa.eu/justice/data-protection/article-29/documentation/opinion-recommendation/files/2013/wp207_en.pdf; *see also,* HM Government (UK), *Open Data White Paper: Unleashing the Potential* (June 2012), https://www.gov.uk/government/uploads/system/uploads/attachment_data/file/78946/CM8353_acc.pdf; *see* CNIL, *Compte Rendu: Séminaire "Open Data, quels enjeux pour la protection des données personnelles?"* [Minutes: "Open Data: Personal Data Protection Issues" Seminar] [Fr.], http://www.cnil.fr/fileadmin/documents/approfondir/dossier/OpenData/CR_Workshop_Open_Data_9_juillet_2013.pdf.

126.   Speech, Eur Comm'n, *Big Data for Europe*, SPEECH/13/893 (Nov. 7, 2013), *available at* http://europa.eu/rapid/press-release_SPEECH-13-893_en.htm.

127.   Working Party, *Statement on Statement [sic] of the WP29 on the Impact of the Development of Big Data on the Protection of Individuals with Regard to the Processing of Their Personal Data in the EU* (WP 221) (Sept. 16, 2014), at 2, http://ec.europa.eu/justice/data-protection/article-29/documentation/opinion-recommendation/files/2014/wp221_en.pdf. Regarding ethical questions raised by big data, two authors have suggested that the gap between law and rapidly advancing technologies should be filled in part by cultivating "ethical sensibilities around information technologies," through, inter alia, "privacy and information professionalism," using professionals such as "[c]hief privacy officers, chief security officers, privacy lawyers, and data security consultants," to further norms and protections. *See* Neil M. Richards & Jonathan H. King, *Big Data Ethics*, 49 Wake Forest L. Rev. 393, 429 (2014).

always involve personal data," but when they do, "they require particular care."[128] Furthermore, big data often relies in essence on the anonymization of personal data in order to allow its processing, as discussed next.

C. Anonymization of Data

Recital 26 of the Directive makes it clear that for "data rendered anonymous in such a way that the data subject is no longer identifiable," the Directive does not apply. The Working Party, while highlighting that "[o]nce a dataset is truly anonymised and individuals are no longer identifiable, European data protection law no longer applies,"[129] has cautioned that, for this to be true, the data has to be made anonymous "in such a way that the data subject is no longer identifiable."[130] In other words, the anonymization must be "irreversible."[131]

Professor Paul Ohm claims that "EU lawmakers have . . . relied upon the power of anonymization to avoid difficult balancing questions," and that they "have imagined that they could strike a balance through the power of technology," allowing data administrators to share anonymized data so as to permit innovation and free expression, "so long as data subjects were no longer 'directly or indirectly' identifiable," he said, referring to the Directive's definition of "personal data."[132] He contends that EU and U.S. legislation alike embrace "the assumption that anonymization protects privacy, most often by extending safe harbors from penalty to those who anonymize their data," and that this legislation must be reexamined.[133]

D. Working Party Guidance on Anonymization of Data

As part of its recent reexamination of anonymization in the context of existing legislation, the Working Party suggests that personal data should generally be anonymized "by default." It considers anonymization itself to be a "further processing" of personal data, and thus subject to the purpose limitation principle discussed in Chapter 1 Section III. Anonymization is considered to be "compatible with the original purposes of the processing" only to the extent that the "process is such as to reliably

---

128. WP 221, *supra* note 127, at 3.
129. Working Party, *Opinion 05/2014 on Anonymisation Techniques* (Apr. 10, 2014) (WP 216), at 5, http://ec.europa.eu/justice/policies/privacy/docs/wpdocs/2014/wp216_en.pdf.
130. Directive, recital 26, at 33.
131. WP 216, *supra* note 129, at 5.
132. Paul Ohm, *Broken Promises of Privacy, Responding to the Surprising Failure of Anonymization*, 57 UCLA L. REV. 1701, 1738 (2010).
133. *Id.* at 1740. Ohm also posits that "easy reidentification" of anonymized data through the advances in reidentification science "makes laws like the [Directive] overbroad—in fact, essentially boundless" because of the way the Directive's definition of "personal data" is phrased. He continues, "As reidentification science advances, it expands the EU Directive like an ideal gas to fit the shape of its container. A law that was meant to have limits is rendered limitless, disrupting the careful legislative balance between privacy and information and extending data-handling requirements to all data in all situations." *Id.* at 1741.

produce anonymised information" in the sense described in Opinion 05/2014 (WP 216).[134] In this regard, the Working Party stated:

> An effective anonymisation solution prevents all parties from singling out an individual in a dataset, from linking two records with a dataset (or between two separate datasets) and from inferring any information in such dataset. Generally speaking, therefore, removing directly identifying elements in itself is not enough to ensure that identification of the data subject is no longer possible. It will often be necessary to take additional measures to prevent identification, once again depending on the context and purposes of the processing for which the anonymised data are intended.[135]

The Working Party highlights that, contrary to effectively anonymized data, pseudonymized data continues to be subject to the EU data protection law regime (which includes the provisions of the Directive).[136] WP 216 includes a more technical discussion of the robustness of the different anonymization technologies, typical mistakes, and recommendations, followed by a "primer" on various techniques.[137]

The Working Party has also written a letter to the White House's Counselor to the President John Podesta on June 11, 2014, welcoming the U.S. report on big data. In the letter, the Working Party "notes" the report's support of greater international interoperability standards to permit the exchanges of data. This indicates the possible development of interoperability of data on a global scale—albeit this will not come overnight, nor is it likely anytime in the next few years.[138]

E. UK ICO Guidance on Anonymization of Data

The UK ICO has also published a code of practice for anonymization, in which it repeats the key points that data protection law "does not apply to data rendered anonymous in such a way that the data subject is no longer identifiable. Fewer legal restrictions apply to anonymised data."[139]

---

134. WP 216, *supra* note 129, at 7.
135. *Id.* at 9.
136. *Id.* at 10.
137. *Id.* at 11–37.
138. Working Party, Letter to Mr. John Podesta, Counselor to the President, U.S.A, June 11, 2014, http://ec.europa.eu/justice/data-protection/article-29/documentation/other-document/files/2014/20140611_letter_to_podesta.pdf; *see also* Executive Office of the President, *Big Data: Seizing Opportunities, Preserving Values*, May 1, 2014, http://www.whitehouse.gov/sites/default/files/docs/big_data_privacy_report_may_1_2014.pdf.
139. UK ICO, *Anonymisation: Managing Data Protection Risk Code of Practice*, Nov. 20, 2012, at 6, http://ico.org.uk/~/media/documents/library/Data_Protection/Practical_application/anonymisation-codev2.pdf.

1. Discussion of UK Data Protection Law

Furthermore, the UK data protection law "does not require anonymisation to be completely risk free—you must be able to mitigate the risk of identification until it is remote."[140] As the UK ICO points out, UK law regarding anonymization "is framed in terms of identification or the likelihood of identification" while the Directive refers to "likely reasonably" as the test, although the UK ICO minimizes the importance of this distinction, after remarking that "in some cases the UK courts have used the 'likely reasonably' test."[141]

One such case cited by the UK ICO is *R (on the application of the Department of Health) v Information Commissioner*, which involves an appeal under the UK Freedom of Information Act 2000 by the UK Department of Health against an Information Tribunal order for a disclosure of late-term abortion statistics and the definition of personal data in the context of anonymization (the Information Tribunal had reasoned that the statistics were personal data). The court found that the Department of Health's anonymization of data into statistics rendered the concerned individuals nonidentifiable and that therefore the relevant data was not personal.[142]

2. Guidance on Whether Data Can Be Anonymized

In determining whether or not data can be anonymized, the UK ICO has detailed the following factors to be taken into account:

- The likelihood of reidentification being attempted;
- The likelihood that reidentification would be successful;
- The anonymisation techniques that are available to use; and
- The quality of the data after anonymisation has taken place and whether this will meet the needs of the organization using the anonymized information.

The data should then be tested for lack of reasonable likelihood of identification, given the relevant level of acceptable risk, and the entire process documented, "for example as part of a PIA."[143] The UK ICO advises that, in borderline cases, "where the consequences of re-identification could be significant eg because they would leave an individual open to damage, distress or financial loss," the following steps should be taken:

---

140. *Id.*
141. *Id.* at 12. "However, the practical problems that arise are much the same whether the test is of 'likelihood' of identification or 'reasonable likelihood' of it."
142. *See id.* at 14–15, for a discussion of that case. In order to review the case itself, *see* [2011] EWHC 1430 (Admin), *available at* http://www.bilii.org/ew/cases/EWHC/Admin/2011/1430.html. For a discussion of certain UK cases related to anonymization, including a criticism of the result in *R (on the application of the Department of Health) v Information Commissioner, see* Francis Aldhouse, *Anonymisation of Personal Data—A Missed Opportunity for the European Commission*, 30 Computer L. & Sec. Rev. 403, 407–13 ("Unfortunately, this conclusion takes no heed of the special techniques available to information technologies to facilitate the reidentification of anonymized data." *Id.* at 413.).
143. UK ICO, *Anonymisation, supra* note 139, at 17.

- seek data subjects' consent for the disclosure of the data, explaining its possible consequences;
- adopt a more rigorous form of risk analysis and anonymisation.[144]

Regarding qualitative data, the UK ICO points out that several methods exist for anonymisation, such as redacting names from documents, blurring faces in videos, disguising or recording over audio, and changing place names, dates, and other details in reports. More generally, in determining whether reidentification is likely, the UK ICO uses the "motivated intruder" test—"considering whether an 'intruder' would be able to achieve re-identification *if* motivated to attempt this."[145]

3. Guidance Concerning Governance

In addition, the UK ICO has identified key points regarding governance:

- Organizations anonymizing personal data need an effective and comprehensive governance structure.
- The UK ICO will ask about an organization's governance if it receives a complaint or is carrying out an audit.
- An organization should have senior-level oversight of its governance arrangements.[146]

This highlights the need for planning and involvement of senior management if anonymization is relied upon to allow big data use.

F. Need for International Cooperation

Finally, the Working Party underscores that big data is an area for future international cooperation between regulators, both "in order to ensure the EU data protection rules are best applied in respect of" its development and "to provide unified guidance and operational answers on then implementation of data protection rules to global players, as well as to implement joint enforcement of these rules" and to reassure data subjects.[147] The need for "harmonization, or even standardization, in data protection standards,"[148] which has been identified, may then be addressed.

---

144. *Id.* at 20.
145. *Id.* at 22.
146. *Id.* at 39.
147. WP 221, *supra* note 127, at 3.
148. *See* Christopher Kuner, Fred H. Cate, Christopher Millard, & Dan Jerker B. Svantesson, *Editorial: The Challenge of "Big Data" for Data Protection*, 2(2) Int'l Data Privacy L. 47, 48 (2012). The coauthors comment:

> Big data also ratchet up the importance of harmonization, or even standardization, in data protection standards. As personal data are universally collected and shared across sectoral and national boundaries, inconsistent data protection laws pose increasing threats to individuals, institutions, and society.

Applicable Law under the GDPR

In the recitals to the GDPR, the Commission underscored the already existing concept that the "principles of data protection should not apply to data rendered anonymous in such a way that the data subject is no longer identifiable."[149] The definition of "data subject" in the GDPR now subsumes much of the Directive's definition of "personal data" and gives additional examples of this beyond an identification number, to include specifically "location data" and an "online identifier."[150] As a consequence, it is certainly no less broad than the precedent definition and, if anonymization proves ineffective, would in most cases result in the application of the GDPR.

In such circumstances, the expanded information requirements to the data subject[151] and the purpose limitation requirements of the GDPR[152] may be difficult to meet, possibly requiring new data subject consent, as indicated in the UK ICO guidance presented earlier. In addition, the exercise of data subject rights, such as the new rights to data portability,[153] the right to be forgotten, and the right to erasure,[154] may prove problematical.

Furthermore, the new section of the GDPR on measures based on profiling must be kept in mind, especially if reidentification of anonymized data is possible:

[t]he right not to be subject to a measure which produces legal effects concerning this natural person or significantly affects this natural person, and which is based solely on automated processing intended to evaluate certain personal aspects relating to this natural person or to analyse or predict in particular the natural person's performance at work, economic situation, location, health, personal preferences, reliability or behaviour.[155]

This section allows for some profiling in connection with a contract, or authorized by law, or on consent of the data subject,[156] but in those cases, information to be provided to the data subject must include notice of the processing for profiling and of the "envisaged effects" on the data subject.[157]

Where data is reidentified to a data subject, then the big data processors would assume the responsibilities imposed upon a processor under the GDPR (unless considered a joint controller, in which case the responsibilities of a controller would apply). See the GDPR part of Chapter 3 Section IV. for the processor responsibilities.

Finally, the GDPR cross-border transfer derogations have been criticized in a big data context, as they allow for the following derogation, where there has been no adequacy

---

149.   GDPR, recital 23, at 21.
150.   GDPR, art. 4(1), at 41.
151.   GDPR, art. 14, at 48–50.
152.   GDPR, art. 5(b), at 43. The relevant text is unchanged from the beginning of the Directive, art. 6(1)(b), at 40.
153.   GDPR, art. 18, at 53.
154.   GDPR, art. 17, at 51–53.
155.   GDPR, art. 20(1), at 54.
156.   GDPR, art. 20(2), at 54.
157.   GDPR, art. 20(4), at 54.

> decision regarding a Third Country under Article 41 or appropriate safeguards under Article 42:
>
>> [t]he transfer is necessary for the purposes of the legitimate interests pursued by the controller or the processor, which cannot be qualified as frequent or massive, and where the controller or processor has assessed all the circumstances surrounding the data transfer operation or the set of data transfer operations and based on this assessment adduced appropriate safeguards with respect to the protection of personal data, where necessary.[158]
>
> The criticism goes that "[w]hile the use of the term 'massive' hints at an appreciation of the challenge of big data, no attempt is made to define the concept or even to put it in a relative context," signaling that "practical risk implications" may not be understood.[159]

V. THE INTERNET OF THINGS

In issuing its Opinion 8/2014 covering the Internet of Things (WP 223),[160] the Working Party has learned from past mistakes and understands that timing is key. Recently issued opinions have been published shortly after the creation and development of innovations and new technologies that affect privacy and data protection. By timely issuing its guidance, the Working Party is able to contribute and shape the application of the data protection framework to the use of new technologies in the European Union.

The "Internet of Things" is the development of technology and sensors "embedded in common everyday devices" that are then linked to individuals in order to process data.[161] The personal data processing relies on a number of activities from different stakeholders, including developers of apps and social media platforms, manufacturers of devices, and aggregators. WP 223 covering this subject was set against the recent backdrop of Google Glass, Fitbit, Nike's Fuel Band, and Android and Apple watches.[162] WP 223 focuses on three developments within the Internet of Things: wearable computing, the quantified self, and domestic automation or "domotics":

---

158. GDPR, art. 44(1)(h), at 73 (emphasis added). Please note the additional provisions of GDPR art. 44(3)–(4) and (6)–(7), at 74, relative to this derogation.

159. *Editorial: The Challenge of "Big Data" for Data Protection, supra* note 148, at 48.

160. Working Party, *Opinion 8/2014 on the on Recent Developments on the Internet of Things* (WP 223) (Sept. 16, 2014), http://ec.europa.eu/justice/data-protection/article-29/documentation/opinion-recommendation/files/2014/wp223_en.pdf.

161. *Id.* at 4.

162. *See generally id.*

- Wearable computing are normal everyday items, including items like Google Glass and the Android or Apple watches, which have other capabilities. These can be sensors, microphones, cameras, etc.
- The quantified self refers to devices that help individuals to track information regarding them, in order to quantify certain activities. This includes being able to monitor sleep patterns and athletic performance or tracking movements.
- Finally, domotics are devices within homes or offices that can be controlled remotely over the Internet. This includes smart devices, fire alarms, refrigerators, ovens, thermostats, and so on.[163]

WP 223 highlights the related privacy challenges, including lack of control and information asymmetry; the "quality" of a user's consent; possible inferences from the data, including repurposing for different purposes other than for which the information was collected; the possibility that these technologies create and analyze behavior patterns and profiling; the lack of anonymity when using services; and, finally, the security risks.[164] Without delving into all of the Working Party's practical applications, WP 223 recommended the following takeaways involving the Internet of Things:

1. Performance of privacy impact assessments—referencing its Opinion WP 180.
2. Deletion of raw data as soon as the necessary information for the processing has been extracted, including deletion on the same device.
3. Application of the principles of privacy by design and privacy by default to all items in the Internet of Things.
4. Empowerment of users, so that data subjects are in control of their information.[165]
5. Provision of notice and permitting users to refuse or request (provide consent) in right places and times.[166]

---

163. *Id.* at 4–6.
164. *Id.* at 6–9.
165. *Id.* at 21.
166. *Id.* at 22.

8

What Is on the Horizon?

We are close to the end of our discussion of European privacy and data protection law, but before we arrive at our concluding points at the end of this chapter, we will first cover what is on the horizon, including the current play on EU data protection law reform and the General Data Protection Regulation (GDPR).

It has been over three and one-half years since the European Commission proposed the GDPR, as discussed in the preface of this book, and in each section we have pointed out, where relevant, the corresponding provisions of the Commission's original proposal for such legislation. Such a time period is not surprising, given the lobbying that has occurred regarding the GDPR, which when adopted will affect one of the world's most important economic sectors—information technology.[1] Former Commission Vice-President and Justice Commissioner Viviane Reding compared the adoption process for the GDPR to that of the Directive, saying that the latter "took five years to negotiate."[2] In addition, we have seen other past examples of prolonged adoption processes for EU legislation, such as the chemicals regulation REACH, which took approximately three years to adopt after the Commission published its proposal.[3]

This chapter will look at the current and future legislative process regarding the GDPR, certain key amendments made to the GDPR in the European Parliament, and finally the right to be forgotten, which follows an important European court decision.

I. CURRENT AND FUTURE LEGISLATIVE PROCESS

On March 12, 2014, the European Parliament voted overwhelmingly in plenary session (621 votes for, 10 against, and 22 abstentions)[4] for a version of the proposed GDPR, as amended by its LIBE (Civil Liberties, Justice, and Home Affairs) committee (the LIBE

---

1. For a short discussion of the lobbying on the GDPR, *see* W. Gregory Voss, *Looking at European Union Data Protection Law Reform through a Different Prism: The Proposed EU General Data Protection Regulation Two Years Later* 17(9) J. Internet L. 1, 19 (2014).

2. *See* Press Release, Commission, *Data Protection Day 2014: Full Speed on EU Data Protection Reform*, MEMO/14/60 (Jan. 27, 2014), *available at* http://europa.eu/rapid/press-release_MEMO-14-60_en.htm.

3. *See* Commission, *History of the Adoption Process for the New Chemicals Legislation, available at* http://ec.europa.eu/environment/chemicals/reach/background/index_en.htm (last visited on Feb. 28, 2015).

4. *See* Press Release, Commission, *Progress on EU Data Protection Reform Now Irreversible Following European Parliament Vote*, MEMO/14/186, Mar. 12, 2013, *available at* http://europa.eu/rapid/press-release_MEMO-14-186_en.htm.

Draft) on October 21, 2013.[5] In order to be finally adopted through the codecision process with the Council, the GDPR must be voted in the same form in both the European Parliament and the Council. Keep in mind that the GDPR is an organic instrument, as there is room for further amendment both by the Council and the European Parliament.

Select Steps in the Progress Made on the GDPR

Date (or Range of Dates)	Progress Made on GDPR
May 19, 2009	Stakeholder Conference[6]
July 9, 2009—December 31, 2009	Public Consultation on the Data Protection Legal Framework[7]
July 1, 2010	Stakeholder Consultation[8]
November 4, 2010–January 15, 2011	Commission Data Protection Comprehensive Approach Consultation[9]
January 25, 2012	Proposal of the GDPR by the Commission[10]
January 10, 2013	Presentation of Amendments to the GDPR by the Rapporteur Jan Philipp Albrecht (LIBE)[11]
October 21, 2013	European Parliament LIBE Committee Vote on LIBE Draft of the GDPR[12]
March 12, 2014	European Parliament Vote in Plenary in Favor of the LIBE Draft of the GDPR[13]

---

5. *See* Press Release, Commission, *LIBE Committee Vote Backs New EU Data Protection Rules*, MEMO/13/923, Oct. 22, 2013, *available at* http://europa.eu/rapid/press-release_MEMO-13-923_en.htm. *See* Eur. Parliament, Committee on Civil Liberties, Justice and Home Affairs, *Report on the proposal for a regulation of the European Parliament and of the Council on the protection of individuals with regard to the processing of personal data and on the free movement of such data (General Data Protection Regulation)*, A7-0402/2013, Nov. 21, 2013, http://www.europarl.europa.eu/document/activities/cont/201403/20140306 ATT80606/20140306ATT80606EN.pdf.

6. *See* http://ec.europa.eu/justice/newsroom/data-protection/events/090519_en.htm.

7. *See* http://ec.europa.eu/justice/newsroom/data-protection/opinion/090709_en.htm.

8. *See* http://ec.europa.eu/justice/newsroom/data-protection/events/100701_en.htm.

9. *See* http://ec.europa.eu/justice/newsroom/data-protection/opinion/101104_en.htm.

10. *See* Proposal for Regulation of the European Parliament and of the Council on the Protection of Individuals with regard to the Processing of Personal Data and on the Free Movement of such Data (General Data Protection Regulation) COM (2012) 11 final (Jan. 25, 2012).

11. Press Release, Commission, *Commission Welcomes European Parliament Rapporteurs' Support for Strong EU Data Protection Rules*, MEMO/13/4, Jan. 10, 2013, *available at* http://europa.eu/rapid/press-release_MEMO-13-4_en.htm.

12. *See LIBE Committee Vote Backs New EU Data Protection Rules, supra* note 1.

13. *See* Press Release, Eur. Parliament, *MEPs tighten up rules to protect personal data in the digital era*, Mar. 12, 2014, *available at* http://www.europarl.europa.eu/news/en/news-room/content/20140307IPR38204/ html/MEPs-tighten-up-rules-to-protect-personal-data-in-the-digital-era.

| June 15, 2015 | Council finalizes a common position on all points of the proposed GDPR.[14] |
| June 24, 2015 | Beginning of trilogue discussions among Council, European Parliament and European Commission.[15] |

Although today it is uncertain whether or not the GDPR will be adopted by trilogue with the Council, the European Parliament's vote of the GDPR as amended by the LIBE Draft was described by Viviane Reding as progress that was then "irreversible," and it certainly was an important step in the legislative process for the proposed GDPR.[16] The LIBE committee of the European Parliament had been appointed as the committee with responsibility for the GDPR. Other parliamentary committees were involved in the review and reporting on the GDPR (IMCO—Internal Market and Consumer Protection, ITRE—Industry, Research and Energy, ECON—Economic and Monetary Affairs, JURI—Legal Affairs, and EMPL—Employment and Social Affairs).

However, the European Parliament and the Commission are not the only EU institutions involved in the data protection reform process. The Council, through its working parties, also reviewed the proposed GDPR, although the Council had yet to establish common positions on many issues raised by the GDPR.[17] The Council finally adopted a common position on all points of the GDPR on June 15, 2015.[18] On June 24, 2015, the Council, Commission and European Parliament began trilogue discussions on the GDPR.[19] An agreement between the European Parliament and the Council on the text of the GDPR in two successive readings is required for it

---

14. Press Release, Eur. Comm'n, Commission Proposal on New Data Protection Rules to Boost EU Digital Single Market Supported by Justice Ministers (June 15, 2015), http://europa.eu/rapid/press-release_IP-15-5176_en.htm.

15. Press Release, Eur. Parl., Data Protection: Parliament's Negotiators Welcome Council Negotiating Brief (June 15, 2015), available at http://www.europarl.europa.eu/sides/getDoc.do?pubRef=-//EP//NONSGML+IM-PRESS+20150615IPR66464+0+DOC+PDF+V0//EN&language=EN.

16. See *Progress on EU Data Protection Reform Now Irreversible Following European Parliament Vote*, *supra* note 4. For a discussion of the consequences of a vote in plenary session of the European Parliament and of future prospects, *see* Voss, *Looking at European Union Data Protection Law Reform through a Different Prism, supra* note 1. Please note that the aforementioned article was written before the European Parliament vote on the LIBE Draft.

17. For an earlier description of the legislative process, *see* W. Gregory Voss, *Preparing for the Proposed EU General Data Protection Regulation: With or without Amendments*, 22 Bus. L. Today (Nov. 2012); *see also*, W. Gregory Voss, *One Year and Loads of Data Later, Where Are We? An Update on the Proposed European Union General Data Protection Regulation*, 16(10) J. Internet L. 1 (2013).

18. See Commission Proposal on New Data Protection Rules to Boost EU Digital Single Market Supported by Justice Ministers , *supra* note 14."

19. *See* Data Protection: Parliament's Negotiators Welcome Council Negotiating Brief *supra* note 15.

to become binding and directly applicable in Member States.[20] The GDPR's entry into force would occur 20 days after publication in the Official Journal of the European Union; however, in the GDPR as proposed by the Commission, it would apply (become effective) only two years after such date.[21]

II. KEY AMENDMENTS TO THE GDPR IN THE EUROPEAN PARLIAMENT

It is not certain that the amendments to the GDPR contained in the LIBE Draft will be included in the final text of the GDPR. However, a select few are noted below.[22]

A. Territorial Scope

The LIBE Draft extends the territorial scope of the GDPR to the processing of personal data in connection with the offering of goods or services to data subjects in the European Union, by both a controller "or processor" where they are not established in the European Union, "irrespective of whether a payment of the data subject is required."[23] This extends the scope of the GDPR to the offering to data subjects in the European Union of free online services and products (such as cloud storage and online office automation tools financed by advertising) from service providers from outside of the European Union.

B. Right to Be Forgotten and Right to Erasure

The LIBE Draft changes the "right to be forgotten and right to erasure" to a "right to erasure,"[24] in the process modifying the responsibilities of controllers with respect to third-party publications of personal data. Nonetheless, it remains to be seen how a recent ECJ decision, discussed in Section III, will affect future GDPR developments in this regard.

C. Designation of the Data Protection Officer

Under the LIBE Draft, the requirement of the designation of a DPO would change from being based on the number of employees (250, according to the GDPR) to a more risk-based approach where "the processing is carried out by a legal person and relates to more than 5000 data subjects in any consecutive 12-month period," or, inter alia, where "the core activities of the controller or the processor consist of processing special categories of data . . . , location data or data on children or employees in large

---

20. For details of the "ordinary legislative procedure" (formerly known as the "co-decision procedure"), which is the procedure that applies to the adoption of the GDPR, see Treaty on the Functioning of the European Union (TFEU), art. 294, at 173–75.
21. GDPR, art. 91, at 99.
22. For a discussion of a few other amendments contained in the LIBE Draft, see Voss, *Looking at European Union Data Protection Law Reform through a Different Prism, supra* note 1, at 15–18.
23. LIBE Draft amend. 97, art. 3 (2), at 62.
24. *Id.* amend. 112, art. 17, at 86–89.

scale filing systems."[25] This amendment aims to deal with a concern that the GDPR provision on DPOs would unfairly burden SMEs.

D. Administrative Sanctions

The LIBE Draft provides a higher maximum level of administrative sanctions: up to €100 million or "up to 5% of the annual worldwide turnover in case of an enterprise, whichever is higher."[26] Thus, there would be an even greater incitation to comply with data protection law under the GDPR as amended by the LIBE Draft.

E. Points of Divergence between the European Parliament and the Council

Since the adoption of the Council's common position, mentioned above, the European Parliament's rapporteur and lead negotiator for the GDPR, Jan Philipp Albrecht, "stressed that several important issues still needed to be worked out with the Council, such as the need for consumers to give consent for the use of their data, the duties of data controllers and what fines should be imposed on companies that break the rules."[27] Thus work needs to be done before the GDPR is finalized.

III. THE RIGHT TO BE FORGOTTEN

The "right to be forgotten," which we have seen has been changed to a "right to erasure" in the LIBE Draft, was applied by the ECJ in *Google Spain SL and Google Inc. v. AEPD and González*.[28] In its opinion, the ECJ clarified several points regarding the Directive's territorial scope and definitions.[29]

This right has resulted in search engines putting forms on their websites for the exercise of the right to be forgotten, and Google organized "The Advisory Council to Google on the Right to Be Forgotten" hearings throughout Europe—in Madrid, Rome, Paris, Warsaw, Berlin, London, and Brussels,[30] following which it issued a

---

25. *Id*. amend. 132, art. 35 (1), (b) and (d).

26. *Id*. amend. 188, art. 79 (2a) (c), at 169–70.

27. Press Release, Eur. Parl., Albrecht on Data Protection Reform: People Will Be Better Informed (June 17, 2015), http://www.europarl.europa.eu/pdfs/news/public/story/20150616STO66729/20150616 STO66729_en.pdf.

28. Case C-131/12, Google Spain SL, Google Inc. v. Agencia Española de Protección de Datos (AEPD), Mario Costeja González (May 13, 2014), *available at* http://eur-lex.europa.eu/legal-content/EN/TXT/ HTML/?uri=CELEX:62012CJ0131&rid=14.

29. *See generally* W. Gregory Voss, *The Right to Be Forgotten in the European Union: Enforcement in the Court of Justice and Amendment to the Proposed General Data Protection Regulation*, 18(1) J. INTERNET L. 3, 6 (2014).

One of this book's coauthors commented there on that case in the following words:

The related rulings have shown that search engines are involved in processing separate from that of the original web publishers whose content they index, and that the use of distinct European subsidiaries for local advertising work will not necessarily shield non-EU processing from being considered as in the context of the activities of the European subsidiary and thus subject to the European data protection law, including the requirement for a legitimate basis for processing of personal data and the provision of data subject rights such as the right to object to such processing.

30. *See* https://www.google.com/advisorycouncil/ (last visited on Feb. 28, 2015).

report setting out criteria for assessing and adjudicating delisting requests.[31] However, one may wonder whether this exercise was aimed merely to help Google carry out a legal obligation or also to influence the debate on the issue in Europe.[32]

IV. CONCLUSION

Are we entering a new era of corporate advocacy in the field of privacy and data protection, and will lobbying further delay the adoption of European legislation to replace the Directive? Will the result be a better GDPR both for companies and for data subjects? Although the horizon is somewhat unclear, the answers to these questions will be telling, and the road ahead interesting.

As we have seen, EU data protection and privacy law is not always what it appears to be. The rules were drafted based on already-dated notions of computing. We have also seen how today businesses, organizations, and individuals struggle to put the law into practice: balancing on one hand the legal protections and on the other the practical realities related to rapidly evolving technology and its increasingly present role in our day-to-day lives. All the while, we will have noticed the increasing importance of personal data in today's economy and, therefore, the heightened concern regarding changes in data protection law.

For many reasons described earlier, data protection law reform seems necessary, given the changes in technologies and the use of personal data since the adoption of the Directive. Once reform comes, it will have an impact beyond Europe, just as the Directive did, as, for example, "in a globalizing economy, European regulation casts a net wider than Europe [citations omitted]. In a globalizing economy, European law also constrains U.S. domestic privacy policies and practices [citations omitted]."[33]

Does the future of data privacy law lie in agreements on global interoperability, so as to permit the global, regulated exchange of information? Will countries include specific legal protections for data in bilateral, regional, or multilateral treaties and agreements? Will these be sector-specific? Will we see a broader inclusion? All of this remains unclear. What we do know is that protections of personal data and privacy are here to stay and will continue to protect individuals' personal information moving forward, regardless of the technological means.

---

31.   The Advisory Council to Google on the Right to be Forgotten, *Report on the Right to Be Forgotten*, Feb. 6, 2015, *available at* https://drive.google.com/a/google.com/file/d/0B1UgZshetMd4cEI3SjlvV0hNbDA/view?pli=1.

32.   For a taste of the issues discussed following the Google Spain ruling, *see* Press Release, Working Party, *97th Plenary—16th —17th September 2014—follow-up to the ruling of the Court of Justice of the EU*, Sept. 18, 2014,http://ec.europa.eu/justice/data-protection/article-29/press-material/press-release/art29_press_material/20140918_wp29_press_release_97th_plenary_cjeu_google_judgment__17sept_adopted.pdf.

33.   *See* Gregory Shaffer, *Globalization and Social Protection: The Impact of EU and International Rules in the Ratcheting Up of U.S. Privacy Standards*, 25 YALE J. INT'L L. 1, 4 (2000).

Appendixes

Appendix A

Notification/Registration on DPA Websites

Jurisdiction	Website	Registry
Austria	http://www.dsb.gv.at/	http://www.dsb.gv.at/site/6298/default.aspx
Belgium	http://www.privacycommission.be/	French: https://eloket.privacycommission.be/elg/searchPR.htm?eraseResults=true&siteLanguage=fr Dutch: https://eloket.privacycommission.be/elg/searchPR.htm?eraseResults=true&siteLanguage=nl
Bulgaria	https://www.cpdp.bg/	https://212.122.176.6:8081/CPDP_ERALD/pages/publicRegisters/confirmed-PublicRegisterCaptcha.faces
Croatia	http://www.azop.hr/	https://registar.azop.hr/
Cyprus	http://www.dataprotection.gov.cy/	No online register
Czech Republic	http://www.uoou.cz	http://www.uoou.cz/uoou.aspx?menu=29&submenu=30&loc=503
Denmark	http://www.datatilsynet.dk/	https://anmeld.datatilsynet.dk/frontend/fortegnelse/default2.asp
Estonia	http://www.aki.ee	http://www.aki.ee/et/delikaatsed-isikuandmed/diat-register
Finland	http://www.tietosuoja.fi	No online register
France	http://www.cnil.fr/	http://www.cnil.fr/vos-obligations/declarer-a-la-cnil/"
Germany	Federal DPA: http://www.bfdi.bund.de Federal District DPA: Baden-Württemberg: http://www.baden-wuerttemberg.datenschutz.de Bayern: http://www.datenschutz-bayern.de Berlin: http://www.datenschutz-berlin.de Brandenburg: http://www.lda.brandenburg.de Bremen: http://www.datenschutz-bremen.de/ Hamburg: http://www.datenschutz-hamburg.de Hessen: http://www.datenschutz.hessen.de Mecklenburg-Vorpommern: http://www.lfd.m-v.de Niedersachsen: http://www.lfd.niedersachsen.de	

	Nordrhein-Westfalen: http://www.ldi.nrw.de	
	Rheinland-Pfalz: http://www.datenschutz.rlp.de	
	Saarland: http://www.datenschutz.saarland.de	
	Sachsen: http://www.datenschutz.sachsen.de	
	Sachsen-Anhalt: http://www.datenschutz.sachsen-anhalt.de	
	Schleswig-Holstein: http://www.datenschutzzentrum.de	
	Thüringen: https://www.tlfdi.de/tlfdi/	
Greece	http://www.dpa.gr	No online register. Information on notifications: http://www.dpa.gr/portal/page?_pageid=33,24852&_dad=portal&_schema=PORTAL
Hungary	http://www.naih.hu/	No online register. Information on notifications: http://www.naih.hu/bejelentkezes.html
Iceland	http://www.personuvernd.is	http://www.personuvernd.is/bitar/misc/hugvitForms/leit.jsp
Ireland	http://www.dataprotection.ie	http://www.dataprotection.ie/ViewDoc.asp?fn=/documents/register/default.asp&CatID=27&m=g
Italy	http://www.garanteprivacy.it/	https://web.garanteprivacy.it/rgt/NotificaEsplora.php
Latvia	http://www.dvi.gov.lv	http://www.dvi.gov.lv/lv/personas-datu-apstrades-un-specialistu-registracijas-kartiba/personas-datu-apstrades-registrs/?doing_wp_cron=1415560442.3252539634704589843750
Liechtenstein	http://www.llv.li/#/1758/datenschutzstelle	http://www.llv.li/#/20/230/anmeldung-fur-das-register-der-datensammlungen-gemass-datenschutzgesetz-dsg-dsv-furbehorden-und-private
Lithuania	https://www.ada.lt/	https://www.ada.lt/go.php/Duomenu-valdytoju-paieska369
Luxembourg	http://www.cnpd.public.lu	http://www.cnpd.public.lu/fr/registre/application/index.html
Malta	http://idpc.gov.mt/	http://idpc.gov.mt/public/dcregister.aspx
The Netherlands	http://www.cbpweb.nl	https://www.collegebeschermingpersoonsgegevens.nl/asp/ORSearch.asp
Norway	http://datatilsynet.no/	http://melding.datatilsynet.no/melding/report_search.pl
Poland	http://www.giodo.gov.pl/	http://egiodo.giodo.gov.pl/search_basic.dhtml
Portugal	http://www.cnpd.pt/	http://www.cnpd.pt/bin/registo/registo.htm
Romania	www.dataprotection.ro	http://www.dataprotection.ro/notificare/cautari.do

Slovakia	http://www.dataprotection.gov.sk	https://dataprotection.gov.sk/uoou/sk/content/osobitna-registracia-informacnych-systemov
Slovenia	https://www.ip-rs.si	http://www.ip-rs.si/?id=159
Spain	https://www.agpd.es/	http://www.agpd.es/portalwebAGPD/ficheros_inscritos/titularidad_privada/index-idesidphp.php
Sweden	http://www.datainspektionen.se/	No online register
Switzerland	http://www.edoeb.admin.ch	https://www.datareg.admin.ch
UK	https://ico.org.uk/	https://ico.org.uk/for-organisations/register/

Appendix B

A Quick-Reference Subject Matter Guide to Certain Article 29 Working Party Opinions and Working Documents[1]

Subject Matter	Article 29 Working Party Document Number
Accountability	WP 173
Adequacy of Level of Protection (non-EU Countries)	WP 4, WP 15, WP 22, WP 24, WP 39, WP 40, WP 63, WP 78, WP 79, WP 82, WP 85, WP 87, WP 88, WP 95, WP 103, WP 141, WP 142, WP 165, WP 166, WP 177, WP 182, WP 198, WP 212, WP 214, WP 219
Anonymity/ Anonymization	WP 6, WP 216
Applicable Law	WP 179
Apps	WP 202
Behavioral Advertising	WP 171, WP 188
Big Data	WP 216, WP 221
Binding Corporate Rules (BCRs)	WP 74, WP 102, WP 107, WP 108, WP 133, WP 153, WP 154, WP 155, WP 204, WP 212
Biometrics	WP 80, WP 96, WP 112, WP 193
Blacklists	WP 65
Children	WP 147, WP 160
Cloud Computing	WP 196
Codes of Conduct (including FEDMA)	WP 13, WP 77, WP 174
Consent	WP 187
Controller	WP 169, WP 217
Cookie Consent	WP 194, WP 208
Credit—Credit Histories and Consumer Credit	WP 61, WP 164
Cross-Border Data Transfers	WP 4, WP 9, WP 12, WP 19, WP 21, WP 23, WP 27, WP 31, WP 32, WP 38, WP 47, WP 49, WP 62, WP 66, WP 74, WP 78, WP 84, WP 85, WP 87, WP 88, WP 95, WP 97, WP 102, WP 103, WP 108, WP 114, WP 121, WP 122, WP 124, WP 132, WP 133, WP 138, WP 151, WP 153, WP 154, WP 155, WP 161, WP 176, WP 178, WP 195, WP 195a, WP 204

1. References are to Article 29 Working Party Documentation Numbers Beginning in "WP." The corresponding documents are *available at* http://ec.europa.eu/justice/data-protection/article-29/documentation/opinion-recommendation/index_en.htm.

Safe Harbor (U.S.–EU)	WP 19, WP 21, WP 23, WP 27, WP 31, WP 32, WP 62
Search Engines	WP 148
Smart Borders	WP 206
Smart Grid, Smart Metering	WP 183, WP 205, WP 209
Social Networking	WP 163
Spam	WP 90
Standard Contractual Clauses	WP 9, WP 38, WP 47, WP 84, WP 161, WP 176, WP 214
SWIFT	WP 128
Territoriality	WP 56
Traffic Data for Billing	WP 69
Unique Identifiers	WP 58
Video Surveillance	WP 67, WP 89
Whistle-Blowing Hotlines	WP 117
Whois Directories/Reverse Directories	WP 33, WP 76

Appendix C

Glossary of Terms and Abbreviations Used

ACB: anticorruption and antibribery.

Adequacy: a proper level of protection of personal data of EU residents offered by the data protection laws of a Third Country.

Adequacy determination: a determination by the Commission and/or the Council, as the case may be, of the adequacy of a Third Country's data protection laws, thus allowing cross-border transfers of personal data to such Third Country. See Chapter 3 Section III.A.

Ad hoc data transfer agreements: agreements between an entity and an EU Member State, whereby the entity provides adequate safeguards with respect to the protection of personal data and privacy in order to obtain Member State prior authorization of a transfer or set of transfers of personal data to a Third Country that does not benefit from an adequacy determination. See Chapter 3 Section III.B.4.

AML: anti-money laundering/counterterrorist financing.

AML Directive: Directive 2005/60/EC of the European Parliament and of the Council of 26 October 2005 on the prevention of the use of the financial system for the purpose of money laundering and terrorist financing. See Chapter 5, note 34.

Anonymization: rendering data anonymous in such a way that the data subject is no longer identifiable, so that the data are no longer considered personal data and the Directive no longer applies. See Chapter 7 Section IV.C.

Article 26(1) Exemptions: derogations contained in Article 26(1) of the Directive (and in Article 44 of the GDPR) from the principle that a determination of the adequacy of data protection of a Third Country is necessary in order to allow cross-border transfers of data to that country. See Chapter 3, Section III.C.

BCRs: binding corporate rules.

Behavioral advertising: advertising that is based on the observation of the individuals' behavior over time, in order to study its characteristics through the individuals' actions, so as to develop a specific profile for each of the individuals and then provide them with advertising tailored to them. See Chapter 6 Section II.D.; see also WP 171.

Berlin Group: the International Working Group on Data Protection in Telecommunications. Also known as IWGDPT.

Big data: deals with private industry use of massive amounts of data for various purposes including predictive ones based on correlations observed in the data. See Chapter 7 Section IV.A.

Binding corporate rules: internal data protection and privacy rules set out by multinational companies to facilitate intra-group transfers of personal data. See Chapter 3 Section III.B.2.

Biometrics: technologies using biometric data, which Article 4(11) of the GDPR defines as "any data relating to the physical, physiological or behavioural characteristics of an individual which allow their unique identification, such as facial images, or dactyloscopic data."

BYOD (bring your own device): employees' use of their own devices (such as smartphones, laptops and tablets) at the workplace.

CAN-SPAM Act of 2003: U.S. Controlling the Assault of Non-Solicited Pornography and Marketing Act of 2003.

CAP: UK Committee of Advertising Practice.

CDD: customer due diligence.

Charter: Charter of Fundamental Rights of the European Union.

Cloud client: cloud-computing services customer.

Cloud computing: system where applications and data are stored on a provider or third-party server accessible via the Internet, rendering data outside the physical control of the end user or customer. See Chapter 7 Section III.A.

Cloud provider: cloud-computing services provider.

CNIL: France's DPA, the "Commission nationale de l'informatique et des libertés."

Codes of conduct: generally industry or trade association codes providing self-regulation rules regarding the handling of personal data. See Chapter 3 Section III.B.3.

Commission: the European Commission.

Controller: the natural or legal person, public authority, agency, or any other body that alone or jointly with others determines the purposes and means of the processing of personal data (Directive, Article 2(d)); See Chapter 1 Section II.E.

Convention 108: the Council of Europe's Convention for the Protection of Individuals with regard to Automatic Processing of Personal Data.

Cookie Directive: Directive 2009/136/EC of the European Parliament and of the Council of Nov. 25, 2009, amending Directive 2002/22/EC on universal service and users' rights relating to electronic communications networks and services, the e-Privacy Directive, and Regulation (EC) No. 2006/2004 on cooperation between national authorities responsible for the enforcement of consumer protection laws.

Cookies: small files downloaded to a computer or terminal device such as a smartphone or tablet when the user accesses certain websites. These are used for recognizing a returning user's device or computer, as they are sent back to the originating website on each subsequent visit. See Chapter 6 Section II.A.

Council: the Council of the European Union.

Council of Europe: a human rights organization consisting of 47 member states (which includes all 28 of the current EU Member States).

Council of the European Union: the institution that deals with broad issues in the European Union, often working through national Member State ministers from the ministries relevant to the issue at hand. The Council has law-making powers, generally upon proposal of the Commission and in coordination with the Parliament.

C-to-C Model Contract: Model Contract for controller-to-controller transfers.

C-to-P Model Contract: Model Contract for controller-to-processor transfers. Also called "C2P Model Contract."

Data processing agreement: a contract with specific provisions on the protection of confidentiality and security of processing to be concluded in writing (or equivalent) between a controller and a processor, which may be in the form of a separate document from the related service agreement between the same parties. A similar concept is that of a "security document" between controller and processor under Spanish law (see Chapter 3 Section IV.A.2).

Data protection: the protection, from a legal, organizational, and security perspective, of data—usually referring specifically to the personal data of individuals (or data subjects).

Data protection impact assessment: Article 33(1) of the GDPR refers to data protection impact assessments as an "assessment of the impact of the envisaged processing operations on the protection of personal data." See Chapter 3 Section II.E.; see also "privacy impact assessment."

Data retention period: a period of time following data collection during which personal data may be kept prior to its deletion, erasure, anonymization, or destruction.

Data subject: a natural person (or "individual") to whom personal data relates—the individual who is identified or is identifiable by personal data.

Directive: Directive 95/46/EC; the European Union "Data Protection Directive."

Direct marketing: marketing directly to the customer or potential customer; in the electronic context, this usually means through e-mail, but could also include, inter alia, SMS or MMS marketing. See "e-Marketing"; see also Chapter 6 Section I.

Dodd Frank: Dodd Frank Wall Street Reform and Consumer Protection Act.

DoS attacks: denial of service attacks on servers.

DPA /DPAs: Member State data protection authority/authorities, for example, the UK ICO, or France's CNIL. For information about interaction with DPAs, see Chapter 3 Section I.

DPIA: data protection impact assessment; see PIA.

DPO: data protection officer; see Chapter 3 Section I.C.

EASA: European Advertising Standards Alliance.

ECHR: European Convention on Human Rights, adopted by the member states to the Council of Europe.

ECJ: Court of Justice of the European Union, the highest court of the European Union.

EEA: European Economic Area formed among the nations that are parties to the Agreement creating the European Economic Area, comprised of the 27 Member States (Croatia, the 28th Member State, is in the process of having its application to the Area ratified) together with Iceland, Lichtenstein, and Norway.

Electronic mail: "any text, voice, sound or image message sent over a public communications network which can be stored in the network or in the recipient's terminal equipment until it is collected by the recipient." See Article 2(h) of the e-Privacy Directive.

e-Marketing: direct marketing by electronic communications, including e-mail, fax, automated, calling and electronic messages, such as MMS and SMS.

ENISA: European Union Agency for Network and Information Security.

e-Privacy Directive: Directive 2002/58/EC of the European Parliament and of the Council of July 12, 2002, Concerning the Processing of Personal Data and the Protection of Privacy in the Electronic Communications Sector, as amended by the Cookie Directive.

Establishment: refers to a place where a controller conducts the "effective and real exercise of activities," where the controller has "human and technical resources necessary" in order to achieve certain services through "stable arrangements." This term is used in determining whether the Directive is applicable. See Chapter 2 Section I.

EU: the European Union.

European Parliament: Parliament of the European Union.

European Union: an economic and political partnership of 28 European Member States (as of this writing), with a single market and various institutions, the principal ones of which are the Commission, the Council, the European Parliament, and the ECJ. Its primary law includes the TFEU and the TEU, and its secondary law includes, inter alia, regulations and directives.

Existing customer exception: an exception to the "opt-in" rule for e-marketing to the e-mail of an existing customer of a company, for that company's own products and services that are similar to those already purchased, so long as the customers are clearly and distinctly given the opportunity to opt out without charge, both at the time of collection of their e-mail address and at the time of each communication.

Facial recognition: technology using a digital image containing an individual's face in order to identify an individual.

FATF: Financial Action Task Force (on Money Laundering).

FCPA: U.S. Foreign Corrupt Practices Act.

FEDMA: Federation of European Direct and Interactive Marketing.

Filing system (or **"personal data filing system"**): any structured set of personal data that are accessible according to specific criteria, whether centralized, decentralized, or dispersed on a functional or geographic basis (Directive, Article 2(c)); see Chapter 1 Section II.D.

Finality: a data protection principle; see "purpose limitation."

FTC: U.S. Federal Trade Commission.

GDPR, or **General Data Protection Regulation**: Proposal for Regulation of the European Parliament and of the Council on the Protection of Individuals with regard to the Processing of Personal Data and on the Free Movement of such Data. The GDPR, if and when finally adopted, will repeal the Directive.

Geolocation: technology involving the geographical locating of individuals or objects.

GPS: global positioning system; one form of geolocation technology using a satellite-based navigation system providing, inter alia, location data.

GRECO: Council of Europe Group of States against Corruption.

Hotline(s): Whistle-blowing hotline(s) to take reports of misconduct within companies and to handle compliance issues and complaints.

Household use exemption: an exemption from the scope of the Directive applies under its Article 3(2) to the processing of personal data "by a natural person in the course of a purely personal or household activity"; see Chapter 2.

HR: human resources.

IAB: Internet Advertising Bureau.

ICO: see UK ICO.

Icon: a small image used as an information notice.

Implicated person: an individual named in any relevant hotline report.

Information society service: "any service normally provided for remuneration, at a distance, by electronic means and at the individual request of a recipient of services." See Chapter 6 note 26.

Informed consent: consent given by a data subject to the processing of his or her personal data, after the data subject has been given all necessary information and notice at the moment his or her consent is requested. See Chapter 3 Section II.C.1.

Internet of Things: the development of technology and sensors "embedded in common everyday devices," which are then linked to individuals in order to process data, and may be connected to the Internet.

Intervenability: the ability to intervene with respect to the data in order to allow for data subject exercise of their rights.

IP: intellectual property.

Isolation: when data are stored in a public cloud environment, this involves the proper administration of access rights and roles to isolate one cloud client's data from those of other cloud clients, so as to help guarantee confidentiality and purpose limitation by limiting risks of disclosure and illegitimate processing.

ISP: Internet service provider; an entity that provides access to the Internet.

ITU: International Telecommunications Union.

IWGDPT: see Berlin Group.

JavaScript: a computer programming language used to create small programs on websites (e.g., a code to open a new window when an object is clicked on), usually for interactivity for the user but also potentially for tracking purposes (such as those used in web traffic analytics programs).

Joint controller or **joint data controller:** an additional controller with respect to the same personal data where, in addition to processing the data for the original controller, an entity or individual also processes the data for its own purposes. See Chapter 2 Section III. Note that the GDPR adds a definition of joint controller that refers to the purposes, conditions, and means of the processing being determined jointly, with responsibilities usually divided up by contract.

JV: joint venture.

KYC: know your customer; a form of due diligence.

Legitimate bases (or **legitimate basis**): Criteria (or a criterion) for which data may be legitimately (legally) processed; see Directive Article 7; and see also Chapter 2 Section IV.

Legitimate interest: a lawful, real, and present interest (used to provide a legal basis for processing) that is sufficiently specific to allow the balancing test to be carried out against the interests and fundamental rights of the data subject. See Chapter 2 Section IV.

LIBE Committee: Committee on Civil Liberties, Justice and Home Affairs of the European Parliament. This Committee was the lead committee in the European Parliament review and discussion of the GDPR.

LIBE Draft: LIBE Committee Report on the GDPR voted by the LIBE Committee on October 21, 2013, serving as the basis for the legislative resolution passed overwhelmingly by the European Parliament sitting in plenary session in first reading on March 12, 2014.

Location data: "any data processed in an electronic communications network or by an electronic communications service, indicating the geographic position of the terminal equipment of a user of a publicly available electronic communications service." *See* Article 2(c) of the e-Privacy Directive, as amended. The terminal equipment concerned could be a smartphone or a connected tablet, for example. These data are considered personal data.

LOPD: the Spanish data protection law.

Member States: the various European Union Member States.

MMS: multimedia messaging service.

Model Contracts: Commission-approved standard contractual clauses or model contracts used in order to allow cross-border data transfers. See Chapter 3 Section III.B.1.

Modernization Text: a 2012 revision of the Convention 108.

Mutual Legal Assistance: Cooperation between nations, often formalized through agreements, for gathering and exchanging information, often as evidence, for criminal investigations and procedures.

NIST (National Institute of Standards and Technologies): organization that provided the most widely used definition of cloud computing.

OECD: Organisation for Economic Co-operation and Development.

OECD Guidelines: guidelines meant to help harmonize national legislation on privacy and data flows, with the aim of protecting the privacy of individuals while at the same time taking into account the possibilities that varying restrictions and national legislation could restrain the free flow of personal data and disrupt economic activity.

Open data: deals with data processed by public bodies being made accessible to the public. See Chapter 7 Section IV.A.

Opt-in: means that prior consent of the relevant recipients is generally required (or exercised) in the European Union in order to receive commercial communications, such as electronic mail for the purposes of direct marketing.

Opt-out: means that prior consent is not required in order to receive commercial communications; however a recipient of such communications must be provided a means to object to or oppose receiving future such communications.

Ordinary legislative procedure: set out in Article 294 of the TFEU.

Passenger name record: records of each passenger's travel requirements contained in air carriers' reservation systems including information necessary for reservations processing and control by the airlines.

PEPs: politically exposed persons.

Personal data: any information related to an identified or identifiable natural person (Directive Article 2(a)); see Chapter 1 Section II.A.

PIA: privacy impact assessment; also referred to as data protection impact assessment (DPIA).

PIPEDA: Canadian Personal Information Protection and Electronic Documents Act.

PNR: passenger name record.

Pop-up screen: a new window that opens on a webpage, for example, to display information, to allow a web user to indicate (or refuse) consent (such as to the placing of cookies on the user's terminal), or to display an advertisement.

Portability: the ability to receive data in standard formats and interfaces allowing interoperability and the possibility to easily move data between different providers (including cloud providers, in the case of cloud computing). The GDPR contains a new data subject right to portability.

Privacy by design: embedding privacy proactively into the technology itself. See WP 193.

Privacy impact assessment: An assessment of both privacy and security risks for personal data involved in the processing of such data. Such assessments may involve recommendations for eliminating or mitigating risks. See Chapter 3 Section II.E.; see also "data protection impact assessment."

Privacy policy: an entity's policy with respect to protection of personal data and rights to privacy, usually committing to respect key privacy principles. See Chapter 3 Section II.B.

Private cloud: a proprietary computing architecture protected by a firewall, providing hosted services to a small number of customers.

Processing: an operation or set of operations performed upon personal data; see Chapter 1 Section II.C.

Processor: a natural or legal person, public authority, agency, or any other body that processes personal data on behalf of the controller (Directive Article 2(e)); see Chapter 1 Section II.E.

Proportionality: a principle by which personal data used in connection with processing must be proportional, which is to say, adequate, relevant, and not excessive. See Chapter 1 Section III.B.4.

Public cloud: cloud system whereby the provider makes applications and/or storage available to the general public over the Internet.

Purpose limitation: privacy principle that involves limiting how an individual's data may be collected and used. Collection must be for specific, explicitly defined and legitimate purposes, and processing must not be incompatible with the relevant purposes. This principle is also referred to as the "finality" principle. See Chapter 1 Section III.A.

Reidentification: processing anonymized data so that it is possible to identify data subjects, or that they are so identified, and in doing so the data becomes personal data again, subject to the Directive.

Revised OECD Guidelines: these revised guidelines lay out core principles forming the basis of modern global data protection legislation.

RFID: radio-frequency identification. This technology involves the use of tags containing electronically stored data accessible through electromagnetic or radio-frequency transmissions. The tags, which are attached to objects, are used for identification and/or tracking.

Right to be forgotten: this has been described as a right for a data subject who no longer wants his or her personal data to be processed or stored by a data controller, where there is no legitimate reason for keeping it, to have his or her data removed from their system. Obsolescence of the data is one grounds for their removal; however a balancing test weighing, on the one hand the data subject's fundamental right against, on the other hand, the right to free speech, may be required. The GDPR contains a right to be forgotten, while the LIBE Draft reduces this to a "right to erasure" of the data.

SaaS: software as a service.

Safe Harbor: An agreement negotiated between the Commission and the U.S. Department of Commerce whereby U.S. companies who self-certify under privacy principles negotiated in this context and bind themselves to provide certain protections to personal data and certain data subject rights, subject to potential prosecution by the U.S. Federal Trade Commission for noncompliance. Signing on to the Safe Harbor allows companies to transfer personal data from the European Union to the United States. See Chapter 3 Section III.A.4.

Sensitive data: see "special categories of data."

SMEs: small and medium-sized enterprises.

SMS: short message service.

SNS (social network services): "online communications platforms which enable individuals to join or create networks of like-minded users." See Chapter 4 note 76.

SOX: Sarbanes Oxley Act.

Spam: unsolicited communications; generally, commercial communications for which the recipient has not opted in.

Special categories of data: or "special categories of personal data," means personal data that reveals racial or ethnic origin, political opinions, religious or philosophical beliefs, trade-union membership, and data concerning health or sex life. Member State national law may expand this category. Under the Directive the processing of such data is generally prohibited. In common speech, this kind of data is also referred to as "sensitive data." See Chapter 4 Section III.

STR: suspicious transaction reporting.

Subprocessor: an entity or individual that processes data at the request of a processor. It will be subject to similar obligations to the processor, and subject to the controller's instructions. See Chapter 2 Section III.

TEU: Treaty on European Union.

TFEU: Treaty on the Functioning of the European Union, as the Treaty of Rome reorganized after the ratification of the Treaty of Lisbon is called.

Third Country: each of the non-EEA countries and territories; see Chapter 3 Section III.A.

Transparency: this data privacy principle involves requirements for providing notice and information to a data subject regarding personal data concerning him or her and its collection and processing. Such information is necessary, inter alia, for the exercise of data subject rights under the Directive. See Chapter 1 Section III.

TTIP: Transatlantic Trade and Investment Partnership Agreement currently being negotiated between the United States and European Union.

UK ICO: the UK's DPA, the United Kingdom Information Commissioner's Office (also referred to as ICO).

Unambiguous consent: a clear expression of the data subject's intent to allow processing, involving some affirmative action taken by the data subject. See Chapter 2 Section IV.A.

Value-added service: "any service which requires the processing of traffic data or location data other than traffic data beyond what is necessary for the transmission of a communication or the billing thereof." See Article 9(3) of the e-Privacy Directive.

Video surveillance: the monitoring of individuals and/or premises through the use of video camera technology, often involving the collection, and most often recording, of personal data.

Vital interest: with respect to a data subject, refers to cases of medical emergency where personal data is directly necessary for the data subject's medical treatment (including essential diagnosis), and is the basis for one of the Article 26(1) exemptions.

VPN: virtual private network. A method using identifiers, passwords, encryption technologies, and specific programs installed on computers or other terminals used to communicate with other so-configured computers, terminals, or servers in a secured fashion over the Internet, as if there were a private connection between them.

Website filtering: also known as "web filtering," means the use of software to block access to certain websites and/or content on the Internet.

WiFi: local area wireless technology allowing devices to connect to the Internet.

Working Party: the European Union's Article 29 Data Protection Working Party, an independent advisory panel that gives guidance on EU privacy and data protection laws.

Works council: "a body or committee formed by an employer among workers within his organization for the discussion of problems of industrial relations." These works councils exist in many EU countries and are called for by relevant national labor laws. See Chapter 3 note 46; see also Chapter 3 Section II.D.2.

WP: abbreviation for "Working Party," used followed by a number to identify documentation such as opinions, working documents, and recommendations issued by the Working Party.

Bibliography

I. BOOKS AND ARTICLES (IN ENGLISH)

Francis Aldhouse, *Anonymisation of personal data—A missed opportunity for the European Commission*, 30 Comp. L. & Sec. Rev. 403

American Bar Association, *The 2014 Information Privacy Law Sourcebook*, Vol. 3 (2014)

Robert Bond, *The EU E-Privacy Directive and Consent to Cookies*, 68 Bus. Law. 215 (2012)

Dave Chaffey & Fiona Ellis-Chadwick, *Digital Marketing, Strategy, Implementation and Practice* (5th ed.) (2012)

Roger Clarke, *A History of Privacy Impact Assessments*, Feb. 6, 2004

D.C. Dowling, Jr., *Sarbanes-Oxley Whistleblower Hotlines across Europe: Directions through the Maze*, 42 Int'l Law. 1 (2008)

Carmen Draghici, *The Human Rights Act in the Shadow of the European Convention: Are Copyist's Errors Allowed?*, Eur. Hum. Rts. L. Rev. 2014, 2, 154–169 (2014).

Françoise Gilbert, *Proposed EU Data Protection Regulation: The Good, the Bad, and the Unknown*, 15(10) J. Internet L. 1 (2012), *Cloud Service Providers as Joint-Data Controllers*, 15(2) J. Internet L. 3 (2011)

P. Gilly, compiled by, *10 Things You Need to Know about the Interaction between Works Councils and Data Privacy*, (2010)

Quentin Hardy, *The Era of Cloud Computing*, N.Y. Times (June 11, 2014)

Markus Heyder, *The APEC Cross Border Privacy Rules—Now That We've Built It, Will They Come?*, privacyassociation.org, Sep. 4, 2014

Michael Higgins, *High Tech, Low Privacy*, 85 A.B.A. J. 52, May 1999

Douwe Korff, *Data Protection Laws in the European Union* (2005)

Christopher Kuner, Fred H. Cate, Christopher Millard, and Dan Jerker B. Svantesson, *Editorial: The Challenge of 'Big Data' for Data Protection*, 2(2) Int'l Data Privacy L. 47 (2012)

Paul Lanois, *Caught in the Clouds: The Web 2.0, Cloud Computing, and Privacy?*, 9(2) Nw. J. Tech. & Intell. Prop. 29, Nov. 2010.

Lawrence Lessig, *Code and Other Laws of Cyberspace* (1999)

Viktor Mayer-Schönberger and Kenneth Cukier, *Big Data: A Revolution that Will Transform How We Live, Work and Think* (2013)

Justin Mitchell, *Making Photo Tagging Easier*, Dec. 15, 2010

Paul Ohm, *Broken Promises of Privacy, Responding to the Surprising Failure of Anonymization*, 57 UCLA L. Rev. 1701 (2010)

Nadezhda Purtova, *Property Rights in Personal Data: A European Perspective* (2012)

Neil M. Richards and Jonathan H. King, *Big Data Ethics*, 49 Wake Forest L. Rev. 393 (2014)

Marc Rotenberg & David Jacobs, *Updating the Law of Information Privacy: The New Framework of the European Union*, 36 Harv. J.L. & Pub. Pol'y 605 (2013)

Paul Allan Schott, *Reference Guide to Anti-Money Laundering and Combating the Financing of Terrorism and Supplement on Special Recommendation IX* (2d ed. International Bank for Reconstruction and Development, The International Monetary Fund and the World Bank 2006)

Paul M. Schwartz, *The EU-U.S. Privacy Collision: A Turn to Institutions and Procedures*, 126 Harv. L. Rev. 1966 (2013)

Gregory Shaffer, *Globalization and Social Protection: The Impact of EU and International Rules in the Ratcheting Up of U.S. Privacy Standards*, 25 Yale J. Int'l L. 1 (2000)

Graham Smith, *Internet Law and Regulation* (4th ed.) (2007)

Jacob M. Victor, *The EU General Data Protection Regulation: Toward a Property Regime for Protecting Data Privacy*, 125 Yale L.J. 513 (2013)

W. Gregory Voss, *European Union Data Privacy Law Developments*, 70 Bus. Law. 253 (2014), *The Right to Be Forgotten in the European Union: Enforcement in the Court of Justice and Amendment to the Proposed General Data Protection Regulation*, 18(1) J. Internet Law 3 (2014), *Looking at European Union Data Protection Law Reform through a Different Prism: The Proposed EU General Data Protection Regulation Two Years Later* 17(9) J. Internet L. 1 (2014); *One Year and Loads of Data Later, Where Are We? An Update on the Proposed European Union General Data Protection Regulation*, 16(10) J. Internet L. 1 (2013); *Preparing for the Proposed EU General Data Protection Regulation: With or Without Amendments*, 22 Bus. L. Today (Nov. 2012); *Survey of Recent European Union Privacy Developments*, 68 Bus. Law. 205 (2012)

W. Gregory Voss, Katherine H. Woodcock, Cecil Saehoon Chung, Kyoung Yeon Kim, Jai Lee and Doil Son, *Privacy, E-Commerce, and Data Security*, 49 ABA/SIL YIR 97 (2015)

W. Gregory Voss, Katherine Woodcock, Rob Corbet, Chris Bollard, Jennifer L. Mozwecz, and João Luís Traça, *Privacy, E-Commerce, and Data Security*, 48 ABA/SIL YIR 103 (2014)

W. Gregory Voss, Katherine Woodcock, Rob Corbet, Jan Dhont, Bruce A. McDonald, Demetrios Eleftheriou, Emily Hay, Cecil Saehoon Chung, & Jae Hyun Park, *Privacy, E-Commerce and Data Security*, 47 ABA/SIL YIR 99 (2013)

W. Gregory Voss, Katherine Woodcock, David Dumont, Nicholas Wells, Jonathan I. Ezor, João Luís Traça, Bernardo Embry & Fatima Khan, *Privacy, E-Commerce and Data Security*, 46 INT'L LAW. 97 (2012)

James Q. Whitman, *The Two Western Cultures of Privacy: Dignity versus Liberty*, 113 YALE L. J. 1151 (2004)

Miriam H. Wugmeister & Christine Lyon, eds., *Global Employee Privacy and Data Security Law* (Bloomberg BNA, 2d ed., 2011)

II. BOOKS AND ARTICLES (IN OTHER LANGUAGES)

A. French

Alain Bensoussan, *Informatique et libertés* (2008)

Céline Castets-Renard and Gregory Voss, *Le "droit à l'oubli numérique" en Europe et en Californie* [*The "Digital Right to Be Forgotten" in Europe and in California*], REVUE LAMY DROIT DE L'IMMATÉRIEL (No. 100), (Jan. 2014) 51

Guillaume Desgens-Pasanau, Fabrice Naftalski, and Sophie Revol, *Informatique et Libertés : Enjeux, risques, solutions et outils de gestion* (2013)

Jessica Eynard, *Les Données personnelles : Quelle définition pour un régime de protection efficace?* (2013)

Gérard Haas and Yaël Cohen-Hadria, *Guide juridique Informatique et Libertés : Collecte, traitement et sécurité des données dans l'univers numérique : ce que vous devez savoir* (2012)

Nathalie Martial-Braz, sous la direction de, *La Proposition de Règlement Européen Relatif aux Données à Caractère Personnel : Propositions du Réseau Trans Europe Experts* (2014)

Isabelle Pingel, sous la direction de, *De Rome à Lisbonne: Commentaire Article par Article des Traités UE et CE* (Dalloz, Paris, 2d ed., 2010)

Alex Türk, *La Vie privée en péril : Des citoyens sous contrôle* (2011)

B. Spanish

Elfrén Santos Pascual and Iciar López-Vidriero Tejedor, *Protección de Datos Personales: Manual práctico para empresas* (2005)

III. CASES

A. European Court of Human Rights

Airey v. Ireland, ser. A, no. 32, Application no. 6289/73, Oct. 9, 1979

Wemhoff v. Germany, Application no. 2122/64, June 27, 1968

B. European Union (Court of Justice of the European Union (ECJ))

Case C-101/01, Bodil Lindqvist, Nov. 6, 2003

Joined Cases C-317/04 and C-318/04, European Parliament v Council of the European Union, May 30, 2006

Case C-524/06, Heinz Huber v Bundesrepublik Deutschland, Dec. 16, 2008

Case C-131/12, Google Spain SL, Google Inc. v. Agencia Española de Protección de Datos (AEPD), Mario Costeja González, May 13, 2014

Case C-212/13, František Ryneš v. Úřad pro ochranu osobních údajů, Dec. 11, 2014

Case C-362/14, Maximillian Schrems v. Data Protection Commissioner, Oct. 6, 2015

C. France

Cour de cassation [Cass.] [supreme court for judicial matters] soc., Oct. 2, 2001, Bull. civ. V, No. 291, p. 233 (Fr.)

Cour de cassation [Cass.] [supreme court for judicial matters] 1ᵉ civ., Apr. 10, 2013, Bull. civ. I, No. 11-19.530 (Fr.)

Société Google Inc., Ordonnance du 7 février 2014 [Ordinance dated Feb. 7, 2014], Conseil d'Etat [Council of State], No. 374595

Cour de cassation [Cass.] [supreme court for judicial matters] com., Feb. 10, 2015, No. 13-14.779 FS-PB.

D. United Kingdom

R (on the application of the Department of Health) v Information Commissioner [2011] EWHC 1430 (Admin)

IV. STATUTES, REGULATIONS, AND DECISIONS

A. European Union

Council Directive 95/46/EC on the Protection of Individuals with regard to the Processing of Personal Data and on the Free Movement of such Data (the Directive)

Directive 97/66/EC of the European Parliament and of the Council of 15 December 1997 Concerning the Processing of Personal Data and the Protection of Privacy in the Telecommunications Sector

Directive 98/48/EC of the European Parliament and of the Council of 20 July 1998, amending Directive 98/34/EC of the European Parliament and of the Council of

22 June 1998 Laying Down a Procedure for the Provision of Information in the Field of Technical Standards and Regulations

Directive 2000/31/EC of the European Parliament and of the Council of 8 June 2000 on Certain Legal Aspects of Information Society Services, in Particular Electronic Commerce, in the Internal Market (Directive on Electronic Commerce)

Commission Decision 520/2000/EC of July 26, 2000 Pursuant to Directive 95/46/EC of the European Parliament and of the Council on the Adequacy of the Protection Provided by the Safe Harbour Privacy Principles and Related Frequently Asked Questions Issued by the U.S. Department of Commerce

Directive 2002/14/EC of the European Parliament and of the Council of 11 March 2002 Establishing a General Framework for Informing and Consulting Employees in the European Community—Joint Declaration of the European Parliament, the Council, and the Commission on Employee Representation

Directive 2002/21/EC of the European Parliament and of the Council of 7 March 2002 on a Common Regulatory Framework for Electronic Communications Networks and Services (Framework Directive)

Directive 2002/58/EC of the European Parliament and of the Council of July 12, 2002 Concerning the Processing of Personal Data and the Protection of Privacy in the Electronic Communications Sector (Directive on privacy and electronic communications), as amended by Directive 2009/136/EC of the European Parliament and of the Council

Commission Decision on the Adequate Protection of Personal Data in Argentina, June 30, 2003

Directive 2005/60/EC of the European Parliament and of the Council of 26 October 2005 on the prevention of the use of the financial system for the purpose of money laundering and terrorist financing, Nov. 25, 2005

Council Decision 2008/651/CFSP/JHA on the Signing, on behalf of the European Union, of an Agreement between the European Union and Australia on the Processing and Transfer of European Union-sourced Passenger Name Record (PNR) Data by Air Carriers to the Australian Customs Service, Jun. 30, 2008

Framework Decision on the protection of personal data processed in the framework of police and judicial cooperation in criminal matters, 2008/977/JHW, Nov. 27, 2008

Directive 2009/136/EC of the European Parliament and of the Council amending Directive 2002/22/EC on universal service and users' rights relating to electronic communications networks and services, Directive 2002/58/EC concerning the processing of personal data and the protection of privacy in the electronic communications sector and Regulation (EC) No. 2006/2004 on cooperation between national authorities responsible for the enforcement of consumer protection laws, Nov. 25, 2009

Commission Decision of Feb. 5, 2010 on Standard Contractual Clauses for the Transfer of Personal Data to Processors Established in Third Countries under Directive 95/46/EC of the European Parliament and of the Council

Commission Decision 2011/61/EU on the Adequate Protection of Personal Data by the State of Israel with Regard to Automated Processing of Personal Data, Jan. 31, 2011

Commission Decision of June 6, 2011 Establishing an EU Anti-Corruption Reporting Mechanism for Periodic Assessment, June 6, 2011

Commission Decision on the Adequate Protection of Personal Data by New Zealand, Dec. 19, 2012

B. Belgium

Loi relative au statut du régulateur des secteurs des postes et des télécommunications belges [Belgian Telecom Act] of Jan. 17, 2003

Loi relative aux communications électroniques [Act on Electronic Communication] of June 13, 2005

C. France

Code Pénal [Criminal Code] (art. 226-15)

Code du Travail [Labor Code] (arts. L. 1221-9 ; L. 1222-4 ; L ; and 2323-13)

Loi 78-17 du 6 janvier 1978 relative à l'informatique, aux fichiers et aux libertés [Law 78-17 of Jan. 6, 1978 on Information Technology, Data Files, and Civil Liberties] [the French Data Protection Act]

Loi n° 91-646 du 10 juillet 1991 relative au secret des correspondances émises par la voie des télécommunications

Ordonnance n° 2011-1012 du 24 août 2011 relative aux communications électroniques [Ordinance No. 2011-1012 on Electronic Communications]

D. Germany

Bundesdatenschutzgesetz [BDSG] [German Federal Data Protection Act], Jan. 14, 2003, as amended by art. 1 of the Act of Aug. 14, 2009

E. Hungary

Hungarian Act CXII of 2011 on the Right of Informational Self-Determination and on Freedom of Information

F. Netherlands

Wet algemene bepaling burgerservicenummer [Dutch General Law on the Citizen Service Number] [Neth.], Staatsblad van he Koninkrijk der Nederlanden [Stb.] 443 (Oct. 30, 2007)

G. Poland

Polish Act of 29 Aug. 1997 on the Protection of Personal Data, as amended

H. Slovakia

Slovak Act No. 122/2013 Coll. on Protection of Personal Data and on Changing and Amending of other acts, resulting from amendments and additions executed by the Act. No. 84/2014 Coll.

I. Spain

Real Decreto 1720/2007, de 21 de diciembre, por el que se aprueba el Reglamento de desarrollo de la Ley Orgánica 15/1999, de 13 de diciembre, de protección de datos de carácter personal [Royal Decree 1720/2007, of Dec. 21, 2007 which Approves the Regulation Implementing Organic Law 15/1999, of Dec. 13, 1999, on the Protection of Personal Data]

J. United Kingdom

Bribery Act 2010 (c. 23)

Data Protection Act 1998 (c. 29)

The Privacy and Electronic Communications (EC Directive) Regulations 2003

The Privacy and Electronic Communications (EC Directive) (Amendment) Regulations 2011

K. Non-EU Nations
1. Canada

The Personal Information Protection and Electronic Documents Act (PIPEDA)
2. United States

Federal Trade Commission Act of 1914 (sec. 5) 15 U.S.C §§ 41-58, as amended, 15 U.S.C. § 45 (Federal Trade Commission: Unfair methods of competition unlawful; prevention by Commission)

U.S. Foreign Corrupt Practices Act of 1977, 15 U.S.C.A. §§ 78dd-1 (2010) (Prohibited foreign trade practices by issuers)

Currency and Foreign Transactions Reporting Act of 1970, Pub. L. No. 91-508, 84 Stat. 1118 (1970) (codified at 31 U.S.C. §§ 321, 5311-5314, 5316-5322 (1988 & Supp. V 1993))

Pub. L. No. 99-570, 100 Stat. 3207 (1986)(codified at 18 U.S.C. §§ 1956–57 (1988)).

Sarbanes-Oxley Act of 2002, Pub. L. No. 107-204, 116 Stat. 745, July 30, 2002

CAN-SPAM (Controlling the Assault of Non-Solicited Pornography and Marketing) Act of 2003, Pub. L. No. 108-187, 117 Stat. 2699 (2003) (codified at 15 U.S.C. §§ 7701–7713 and 18 U.S.C. § 1037)

Dodd-Frank Wall Street Reform and Consumer Protection Act, Pub. L. No. 111-203, 124 Stat. 1376, 12 USC § 5301 et seq., July 21, 2010

V. WORKING DOCUMENTS, OPINIONS, REPORTS, COMMUNICATIONS, AND CORRESPONDENCE OF NATIONAL AND SUPRANATIONAL BODIES

A. Article 29 Data Protection Working Party (WP29) (WP Document Numbers Correspond to Those Indicated in the Quick Reference Guide)

WP 12: Working Document Transfers of Personal Data to Third Countries: Applying Articles 25 and 26 of the EU Data Protection Directive, Jul. 24, 1998

WP 13: Future Work on Codes of Conduct: Working Document on the Procedure for the Consideration by the Working Party of Community Codes of Conduct, Sep. 10, 1998

WP 16: Working Document: Processing of Personal Data on the Internet, Feb. 23, 1999

WP 37: Working Document Privacy on the Internet—An Integrated EU Approach to On-line Data Protection, Nov. 21, 2000

WP 48: Opinion 8/2001 on the Processing of Personal Data in the Employment Context, Sep. 13, 2001

WP 55: Document on Surveillance and Monitoring of Electronic Communications in the Workplace, May 29, 2002

WP 56: Working Document on Determining the International Application of EU Data Protection Law to Personal Data Processing on the Internet by Non-EU Based Web Sites, May 30, 2002

WP 66: Opinion on Transmission of Passenger Manifest Information and Other Data from Airlines to the United States, Oct. 24, 2002

WP 67: Working Document on the Processing of Personal Data by means of Video Surveillance, Nov. 25, 2002

WP 74: Working Document: Transfers of Personal Data to Third Countries: Applying Article 26(2) of the EU Data Protection Directive to Binding Corporate Resolutions for International Data Transfers, Jun. 3, 2003

WP 77: Opinion 3/2003 on the European Code of Conduct of FEDMA for the Use of Personal Data in Direct Marketing, Jun. 13, 2003

WP 78: Opinion 4/2003 on the Level of Protection Ensured in the US for the Transfer of Passengers' Data, Jun. 13, 2003

WP 80: Working Document on Biometrics, Aug. 1, 2003

WP 89: Opinion 4/2004 on the Processing of Personal Data by Means of Video Surveillance, Feb. 11, 2004

WP 90: Opinion 5/2004 on unsolicited communications for marketing purposes under Article 13 of Directive 2002/58/EC, Feb. 27, 2004

WP 114: Working document on a common interpretation of Article 26(1) of Directive 95/46/EC of 24 Oct. 1995, Nov. 25, 2005

WP 115: Opinion on the Use of Location Data with a View to Providing Value-Added Services, Nov. 25, 2005

WP 117: Opinion 1/2006 on the Application of EU Data Protection Rules to Internal Whistleblowing Schemes in the Fields of Accounting, Internal Accounting Controls, Auditing Matters, Fight against Bribery, Banking and Financial Crime, Feb. 1, 2006

WP 128: Opinion 10/2006 on the processing of personal data by the Society for Worldwide Interbank Financial Telecommunication (SWIFT), Nov. 22, 2006

WP 136: Opinion 4/2007 on the Concept of Personal Data, Jun. 20, 2007

WP 148: Opinion 1/2008 on Data Protection Issues Related to Search Engines, Apr. 4, 2008

WP 163: Opinion 5/2009 on Online Social Networking, WP 163, Jun. 12, 2009

WP 169: Opinion 1/2010 on the Concepts of "Controller" and "Processor," Feb. 16, 2010

WP 171: Opinion 2/2010 on Online Behavioural Advertising, Jun. 22, 2010

WP 174: Opinion 4/2010 on the European Code of Conduct of FEDMA for the Use of Personal Data in Direct Marketing, Jul. 13, 2010

WP 179: Opinion 8/2010 on Applicable Law, Dec. 16, 2010

WP 180: Opinion 9/2011 on the Revised Industry Proposal for a Privacy and Data Protection Impact Assessment Framework for RFID Applications, Feb. 11, 2011

WP 185: Opinion 13/2011 on Geolocation Services on Smart Mobile Devices, May 16, 2011

WP 186: Opinion 14/2011 on data protection issues related to the prevention of money laundering and terrorist financing and its Annex, Jun. 13, 2011

WP 187: Opinion 15/2011 on the Definition of Consent, Jul. 13, 2011

WP 188: Opinion 16/2011 on EASA/IAB Best Practice Recommendation on Online Behavioural Advertising, Dec. 8, 2011

WP 192: Opinion 02/2012 on Facial Recognition in Online and Mobile Services, Mar. 22, 2012

WP 193: Opinion 3/2012 on the Developments in Biometric Technologies, Apr. 27, 2012

WP 194: Opinion 04/2012 on Cookie Consent Exemption, Jun. 7, 2012

WP 195: Working Document 02/2012 Setting up a Table with the Elements and Principles to be Found in Processor Binding Corporate Rules, Jun. 6, 2012

WP 196: Opinion 05/2012 on the Cloud Computing, Jul. 1, 2012

WP 203: Opinion 03/2013 on Purpose Limitation, Apr. 2, 2013

WP 207: Opinion 06/2013 on Open Data and Public Sector Information ("PSI") Reuse, June 5, 2013

WP 208: Working Document 02/2013 Providing Guidance on Obtaining Consent for Cookies, Oct. 2, 2013

WP 214: Working Document on 01/2012 on Draft Ad Hoc Contractual Clauses "EU Data Processor to Non-EU Sub-Processor," Mar. 21, 2014

WP 216: Opinion 05/2014 on Anonymisation Techniques, Apr.10, 2014

WP 217: Opinion 06/2014 on the Notion of Legitimate Interests of the Data Controller under Article 7 of Directive 95/46/EC, Apr. 9, 2014

WP 221: Statement on Statement [sic] of the WP29 on the impact of the development of big data on the protection of individuals with regard to the processing of their personal data in the EU, Sep. 16, 2014

WP 223: Opinion 8/2014 on the [sic] on Recent Developments on the Internet of Things, Sep. 16, 2014

Advice Paper on Special Categories of Data ("Sensitive Data"), Apr. 20, 2011

Letter to Mr. Ethiopis Tafara, Director, Office of International Affairs, Securities and Exchange Commission, Jul. 3, 2006

Letter to the OBA Industry—IAB Europe and EASA, Aug. 3, 2011

Letter to the OBA Industry—IAB Europe and EASA, Dec. 08, 2011

Letter to Mr. Larry Page of Google and Appendix: Google Privacy Policy: Main Findings and Recommendations, Oct. 16, 2012

Letter to Mr. John Podesta, Counselor to the President, U.S.A., Jun. 11, 2014

Press Release, The Article 29 Working Party Approves the Community Code of Conduct: The European Code of Conduct of FEDMA for the Use of Personal Data in Direct Marketing, Jun. 13, 2003

Press Release, 97th Plenary—16th—17th September 2014—follow-up to the ruling of the Court of Justice of the EU, Sep. 18, 2014

B. Council of Europe

Consultative Committee of the Convention for the Protection of Individuals with regard to Automatic Processing, Final document on the modernisation of Convention 108, TPD(2012)04 rev2, Oct. 16, 2012

C. Council of the European Union (Notice)

The Stockholm Programme—An Open and Secure Europe Serving and Protecting Citizens, May 4, 2010

D. European Commission (Reports, Communications, Press Releases, and Proposed Legislation)

Ad-Hoc Query on a Certificate of Good Conduct when Migrants Apply for a Residence Permit, Apr. 13, 2012

Commission Explanatory Memorandum to the Amended Proposal, Oct. 15. 1992, COM(92)422 final

Commission Staff Working Document on the Implementation of the Commission Decisions on Standard Contractual Clauses for the Transfer of Personal Data to Third Countries (2001/497/EC and 2002/16/EC) SEC(2006)95, Jan. 20, 2006

Communication, A Comprehensive Approach on Personal Data Protection in the European Union, Nov. 4, 2010, COM(2010)609 final

Communication from the Commission to the European Parliament and the Council on the Functioning of the Safe Harbour from the Perspective of EU Citizens and Companies Established in the EU, COM(2013) 847, Nov. 27, 2013

History of the adoption process for the new chemicals legislation

IDC, Quantitative Estimates of the Demand for Cloud Computing in Europe and the Likely Barriers to Uptake, July 13, 2012

Douwe Korff, EC Study on Implementation of Data Processing Directive: Comparative Summary of National Laws, Sept. 2002

Press Release, Commission Proposal on New Data Protection Rules to Boost EU Digital Single Market Supported by Justice Ministers, IP-15-5176, June 15, 2015

Press Release, Commission Welcomes European Parliament Rapporteurs' Support for Strong EU Data Protection Rules, MEMO/13/4, Jan. 10, 2013

Press Release, Data Protection Day 2014: Full Speed on EU Data Protection Reform, MEMO/14/60, Jan. 27, 2014

Press Release, European Commission Calls on the U.S. to Restore Trust in the EU-U.S. Data Flows, IP/13/1166, Nov. 27, 2013

Press Release, LIBE Committee Vote Backs New EU Data Protection Rules, MEMO/13/923, Oct. 22, 2013

Press Release, Progress on EU Data Protection Reform Now Irreversible Following European Parliament Vote, MEMO/14/186, Mar. 12, 2013

Proposal for a [PNR Directive], 2011, COM(2011)32 final

Proposal for a Directive of the European Parliament and of the Council on the Protection of Individuals with Regard to the Processing of Personal Data by Competent Authorities for the Purposes of Prevention, Investigation, Detection or Prosecution of Criminal Offenses or the Execution of Criminal Penalties, and the Free Movement of Such Data, COM (2012) 10 final, Jan. 25, 2012

Proposal for a Regulation of the European Parliament and of the Council on the Protection of Individuals with Regard to the Processing of Personal Data an on the

Free Movement of Such Data (General Data Protection Regulation), Jan. 25, 2012, COM(2012)11 final

Report from the Commission to the European Parliament and the Council on the application of Directive 2005/60/EC on the prevention of the use of the financial system for the purpose of money laundering and terrorist financing, Apr. 11, 2012

Speech, Big Data for Europe, SPEECH/13/893, Nov. 7, 2013

E. European Parliament (Report, Press Release)

Committee on Civil Liberties, Justice and Home Affairs, Report on the proposal for a regulation of the European Parliament and of the Council on the protection of individuals with regard to the processing of personal data and on the free movement of such data (General Data Protection Regulation), A7-0402/2013, Nov. 21, 2013

Press Release, MEPs tighten up rules to protect personal data in the digital era, Mar. 12, 2014

Press Release, Data Protection: Parliament's Negotiators Welcome Council Negotiating Brief, June 15, 2015

Press Release, Albrecht on Data Protection Reform: People Will Be Better Informed, June 17, 2015

F. European Union Agency for Fundamental Rights

Access to Data Protection Remedies in EU Member States, 2013

Summary: Access to Data Protection Remedies in EU Member States, 2013

G. European Union Agency for Fundamental Rights and the Council of Europe– European Court of Human Rights

Handbook on European Data Protection Law, 2014

H. European Union Agency for Network and Information Security (ENISA)

Cloud Computing: Benefits, risks and recommendations for information security, Mar. 2009

I. Financial Action Task Force (on Money Laundering) (FATF)

International Standards on Combating Money Laundering and the Financing of Terrorism & Proliferation: The FATF Recommendations, Feb. 16, 2012

J. International Telecommunication Union (a United Nations Agency)

Privacy in Cloud Computing, ITU-T TECH. WATCH REP., Mar. 2012

K. International Working Group on Data Protection in Telecommunications (IWGDPT, or Berlin Group)

Working Paper on Cloud Computing—Privacy and data protection issues, Apr. 24, 2012

L. Organisation for Economic Co-operation and Development (OECD)

Michael R. Nelson, Briefing Paper for the ICCP Technology Foresight Forum: Cloud Computing and Public Policy — 14 October 2009, OECD Committee for Information, Computer and Communications Policy, Sept. 29, 2009

OECD Guidelines Governing the Protection of Privacy and Transborder Flows of Personal Data, Sep. 23, 1980

OECD Guidelines, as amended on July 11, 2013

Hon. Michael Kirby, "Remarks on the 30th anniversary of the OECD Privacy Guidelines," in OECD, Thirty Years after the OECD Privacy Guidelines, 2011

M. Member State and EEA National Data Protection Agencies and Other Government Agencies
1. Belgium (Commission de la protection de la vie privée (CPVP)—Belgian Privacy Commission)

Control and Recommendation Procedure Initiated with Respect to the Company SWIFT SCR (Belgian Privacy Commissioner's Decision), Dec. 8, 2008

Protection of Personal Data in Belgium, Apr. 23, 2012

Recommandation n° 08/2012 du 2 mai 2012 d'initiative relative au contrôle de l'employeur quant à l'utilisation des outils de communication électronique sur le lieu de travail [Recommendation no. 08/2010 of May 2, 2012 on Cybersurveillance in the Workplace]

2. France (CNIL)

Ce que le "Paquet Télécom" change pour les cookies [What the Telecoms Package Changes for Cookies], Oct. 26, 2011

CNIL Orders Google to Comply with the French Data Protection Act, within Three Months, June 20, 2013

Compte Rendu: Séminaire "Open Data, quels enjeux pour la protection des données personnelles?," July 9, 2013

Decision No. 2005-110 McDonald's France and CNIL, May 26, 2005

Decision No. 2005-111 Compagnie européenne d'accumulateurs and CNIL, May 26, 2005

Deliberation No. 2013-420 of the Sanctions Committee of CNIL imposing a financial penalty against Google Inc., Jan. 3, 2014

Google: Failure to Comply before Deadline Set in the Enforcement Notice, Sept. 27, 2013

Google Privacy Policy: Six European Data Protection Authorities to Launch Coordinated and Simultaneous Enforcement Actions, Apr. 2, 2013

Google Privacy Policy: State of Play of the Enforcement Actions Taken by European Data Protection Authorities, July 23, 2013

Guide: Security of Personal Data, 2010 edition (2010)

Guideline document adopted by the "Commission nationale de l'informatique et des libertés" (CNIL) on 10 November 2005 for the implementation of whistleblowing systems in compliance with the French Data Protection Act of 6 January 1978, as amended in August 2004, relating to information technology, data filing systems and liberties, Nov. 11, 2005

Methodology for Privacy Risk Management: How to Implement the Data Protection Act, June 2012 (English translation)

Recommendations for companies planning to use Cloud computing services and Appendix: Models of contractual clauses, June 25, 2012

Resolution No. 81-094 of 21 July 1981 on the adoption of a recommendation relative to general measures for computer system security, July 21, 1981

22nd Annual Report for 2001, Extracts of Chapter 3 "Current Debates": A Century of Biometrics, July 2002

Article, Workers being globalised in spite of themselves! (http://www.cnil.fr/english/topics/human-resources/workers-being-globalised-in-spite-of-themselves/)

3. Norway (Datatilsynet)

Draft agreement—data processor agreement pursuant to the Personal Data Act

4. Poland (Generalny Inspektor Ochrony Danych Osobowych, or GIODO)

Czy pracodawca ma prawo za pomocą specjalnego urządzenia skanować linie papilarne pracowników w celu rejestracji godzin ich przyjścia i wyjścia z zakładu pracy? [Does the employer have the right to use a special device to scan the fingerprints of employees to register their hours coming in and going out of the workplace?], Feb. 12, 2010

5. Spain (Agencia Española de Protección de Datos)

Guía de Seguridad de Datos [Data Security Guide], 2010

6. United Kingdom Government

HM Government, Open Data White Paper: Unleashing the Potential (June 2012)

Ministry of Justice, The Bribery Act 2010: Guidance about Procedures Which Relevant Commercial Organizations Can Put into Place to Prevent Persons Associated with Them from Bribing (Section 9 of the Bribery Act 2010), Feb. 11, 2012

7. United Kingdom (Information Commissioner's Office)

Anonymisation: managing data protection risk code of practice, Nov. 20, 2012

Bring your own device (BYOD), Mar. 7, 2013

Conducting Privacy Impact Assessments Code of Practice, Feb. 25, 2014

Data Controllers and Data Processors: What the Difference Is and What the Governance Implications Are, June 5, 2014

Guidance on the Rules on Use of Cookies and Similar Technologies, May 2012

Outsourcing: A Guide for Small and Medium-Sized Businesses, Feb. 28, 2012

N. Other Nations' Administrative Agencies
1. Switzerland (Swiss Federal Data Protection and Information Commissioner)

Etat de la protection des données dans le monde, July 30, 2012

2. United States

Commission Staff Working Document SEC(2006)95

Executive Office of the President, Big Data: Seizing Opportunities, Preserving Values, May 1, 2014

FTC, GeoCities, Docket No C-3849 (Final Order Feb. 12, 1999)

Peter Mell and Timothy Grance, Nat'l Inst. of Standards and Tech. [NIST], The NIST Definition of Cloud Computing, NIST Spec. Publ. 800-145, Sept. 2011

NIST, Press Release, Final Version of NIST Cloud Computing Definition Published, Oct. 25, 2011

VI. TREATY, CONVENTION, AND OTHER MATERIALS

Additional Protocol to Convention 108 regarding Supervisory Authorities and Transborder Data Flows (ETS No. 181)

Charter of Fundamental Rights of the European Union, Dec. 7, 2000

Consolidated Version of the Treaty on the Functioning of the European Union (TFEU), May 9, 2008

Consolidated Version of the Treaty on European Union (TEU), Oct. 26, 2012

Convention for the Protection of Individuals with regard to Automatic Processing of Personal Data, Jan. 28, 1981, ETS No. 108 (Convention 108)

Council of Europe, Criminal Law Convention on Corruption, Jan. 27, 1999

Convention on Combating Bribery of Foreign Public Officials in International Business Transactions, OECD, Dec. 17, 1997

Inter-American Convention against Corruption, adopted Mar. 29, 1996

European Convention on Human Rights

United Nations Convention against Corruption, Dec. 14, 2005

United Nations Convention against Transnational Organized Crime and the Protocols thereto, Sept. 23, 2003

VII. CODES OF CONDUCT

EASA, Best Practice Recommendation on Online Behavioural Advertising, Setting Out a European Advertising Industry-Wide Self-Regulatory Standard and Compliance Mechanism for Consumer Controls in Online Behavioural Advertising, Apr. 13, 2011

FEDMA, European Code of Practice for the Use of Personal Data in Direct Marketing Electronic Communications Annex, Jun. 2010

UK Committee of Advertising Practice (CAP), Appendix 3 Online Behavioural Advertising to the CAP Code, Nov. 21, 2012

Index